GW00362939

STRUCTURE AND SCALE IN
THE ROMAN ECONOMY

STRUCTURE AND SCALE IN THE ROMAN ECONOMY

RICHARD DUNCAN-JONES

Fellow of Gonville and Caius College, Cambridge

CAMBRIDGE
UNIVERSITY PRESS

Published by the Press Syndicate of the University of Cambridge
The Pitt Building, Trumpington Street, Cambridge CB2 1RP
40 West 20th Street, New York, NY 10011-4211, USA
10 Stamford Road, Oakleigh, Melbourne 3166, Australia

© Cambridge University Press 1990

First published 1990
Reprinted 1992, 1994

Printed in Great Britain by
Antony Rowe Ltd, Chippenham, Wiltshire

British Library cataloguing in publication data

Duncan-Jones, Richard
  Structure and scale in the Roman economy.
  1. Ancient Rome. Economic conditions. BC 31–AD 476
  I. Title
  330.937'06

Library of Congress cataloguing in publication data

Duncan-Jones, Richard.
  Structure and scale in the Roman economy / Richard Duncan-Jones.
    p. cm.
  Bibliography.
  ISBN 0–521–35477–3
  1. Rome – Economic conditions. I. Title.
HC39.D886 1900
330.937 – dc20   89–7345 CIP

ISBN 0 521 35477 3

SE

TO JULIA

CONTENTS

FIGURES

TABLES

PREFACE

This book, a sequel to *The Economy of the Roman Empire: Quantitative Studies*, carries the discussion into further areas of the Roman economy. Some related discussions of numismatic and metrological problems have been separately published as articles, and are referred to in the text where necessary.

Eight of the thirteen chapters are new. The remaining five, which are versions of studies first published as articles, have been reworked for the purposes of the book (chapters 5, 7, 8, 9 and 11: the corresponding earlier publications are listed in the Bibliography under the years (1977), (1979A), (1980A); (1978); (1976A); (1976B); and (1985).

I should like to express a continuing debt to the teaching of the late Professor A.H.M. Jones, notwithstanding the fact that two of the chapters below seek to modify certain conclusions in Jones's pioneering survey of the Later Roman Empire. I should also like to thank Dr J.D. Thomas and Dr J.H. Pryor for expert help of different kinds with the first chapter; Dr J.R. Rea for kindly allowing me to use in the same chapter an important Oxyrhynchus papyrus in advance of publication; Professor A.J. Graham for helpful comments on a draft of chapters 2, 3 and 12; Mr H.R. Hurst for bibliographical help and advice with chapter 2; Professors E. Lo Cascio, L. Camilli and G. Clemente both for their kindness in inviting me to speak in 1988 at the Universities of L'Aquila and Firenze and at the Istituto Universitario Orientale in Naples, and for their comments on the draft of the fourth chapter that I read there; Professor E.A. Wrigley for salutary comments on a draft of chapter 6; Dr R.S. Schofield and Dr C.M. Hills for answering technical questions also raised by this chapter; Professor J.F. Oates for providing summaries from a long unpublished Yale papyrus referred to in chapter 8; Dr D.E.L. Johnston for his advice about legal sources used in chapter 10; and Dr S.P. Brock for kindly explicating one of the Syriac texts used in chapter 13.

I also want to thank those who helped me with the earlier versions of chapters first published as articles: Dr A.D. Barbour, Dr A.W.F. Edwards, Professor M.I. Finley and Miss V.F. Stewart (chapter 5); Professor S.S. Frere, Dr A.K. Bowman, Dr P. Brennan, Professor M.H. Crawford, Professor J.F. Gilliam,

Professor A.J. Graham and Professor F.G.B. Millar (chapter 7); and Mr M.J. Farrell and Dr A.D. Barbour (chapter 8).

All responsibility for the views expressed, and for shortcomings, rests with the author.

R.P.D.-J.

ABBREVIATIONS

Titles of journals are normally abbreviated as in the *Année Philologique*. Standard abbreviations are used for collections of papyri and ostraca (see J.F. Oates, R.S. Bagnall, W.H. Willis, K.A. Worp *Checklist of editions of Greek papyri and ostraka*[3] (*BASP* Supplement 4, 1985), or E.G. Turner *Greek papyri* (Oxford 1968))

AE	*Année épigraphique*
BMCRE	H. Mattingly and others *Coins of the Roman Empire in the British Museum*
CAM	R.P. Duncan-Jones, 'The choenix, the artaba and the modius', *ZPE* (1976) 43–52
ChLA	*Chartae Latinae Antiquiores*
CIL	*Corpus Inscriptionum Latinarum*
CJ	*Codex Justinianus*
CTh	*Codex Theodosianus*
D.	*Digesta Iustiniani*
ERE[2]	R.P. Duncan-Jones *The Economy of the Roman Empire: quantitative studies*[2] (1982)
ESAR	T. Frank (ed.) *An Economic Survey of Ancient Rome* (1933–40)
FIRA	*Fontes Iuris Romani Anteiustiniani*[2] ed. S. Riccobono (1940–3)
HA	*Historia Augusta*
HS	Sesterces
IG	*Inscriptiones Graecae*
IGRR	*Inscriptiones Graecae ad res Romanas pertinentes* (1901–27)
ILAf	R. Cagnat, A. Merlin, L. Chatelain *Inscriptions latines d'Afrique* (1923)
ILAlg	S. Gsell, H-G. Pflaum *Inscriptions latines de l'Algérie* (1922–)
ILS	H. Dessau *Inscriptiones Latinae Selectae* (1892–1916)
ILTun	A. Merlin *Inscriptions latines de la Tunisie* (1944)
IRT	J.M. Reynolds, J.B. Ward Perkins *Inscriptions of Roman Tripolitania* (1952)

MSR   F. Hultsch (ed.) *Metrologicorum Scriptorum Reliquiae* (1864–6)
ND   *Notitia Dignitatum*
NIust   *Iustiniani Novellae*
NMaj   *Majoriani Novellae*
NVal   *Valentiniani Novellae*
OGIS   W. Dittenberger *Orientis Graeci Inscriptiones* (1903)
RE   Pauly–Wissowa–Kroll *Real-Encyclopädie der klassischen Altertumswissenschaft* (1894–)
RIC   H. Mattingly, A.E. Sydenham and others *Roman Imperial Coinage* (1923–)
SP   A.S. Hunt, C.C. Edgar *Select Papyri* (1932)
Syll³   W. Dittenberger *Sylloge Inscriptionum Graecarum* (1915–24)
TAE   P. Garnsey, K. Hopkins, C.R. Whittaker (edd.) *Trade in the ancient economy* (1983)
TAM   *Tituli Asiae Minoris*

Introduction

This book explores central areas of the Roman economy, and ways in which they connect and interact.

In a vast and unwieldy domain like the Roman empire, the speed of communication by sea and the number of shipping movements were obviously important for the processes of government as well as for the economy. What we know of message-speeds is usually disjointed. But more systematic results can be gained from Egyptian documents, which provide thousands of precisely dated co-ordinates identifying the emperor in power. When the emperor changes, the co-ordinates can show how soon this essential fact became known in one of Rome's eastern provinces, and how long the news took to spread inside the province. The results in the period when the evidence is fullest mainly suggest dependence on commercial shipping, with news getting through faster the more closely its date happened to coincide with two main shipping movements in the year. Seasonal differences are very striking in the pattern from the Flavians onwards, and the arrival of news apparently depended on a limited number of shipping-links. The transit-times of government decrees sent to Africa under the later Empire again suggest two main shipping movements during the year (chapter 1).

This has some relevance to inter-regional trade. Can substantial trade flows be inferred by arguing that government taxation drew money out of provinces with large tax bills to an extent which only increase in trade could have corrected? Coin-finds in different parts of the empire, although cited in support of this model, do not show homogeneous characteristics when their composition is studied in any detail (chapter 2). And a re-examination of the format of Roman provincial taxation produces only limited support for the assumption that direct taxes in the provinces were generally levied in money (chapter 12). It remains uncertain whether imperial taxes can have changed the underlying character of Mediterranean trade, and whether they created a positive commercial stimulus. The find-patterns of Roman lamps identified by brand-name (drawing on the survey by Harris (1980A) show groupings within regions and separations between regions which, as far as they go, argue for a pattern of local trading zones rather than a single national market (chapter 3).

Although evidence in the first chapter suggests slower contact by sea by the Late Empire, presumably because of fewer shipping-links, systematic evidence for economic change within the period of the Principate is difficult to run to earth. Dated series of town monuments show provincial responses to change of emperor and to changes in imperial policy more readily than responses to economic change. But denser information from papyri and coins suggests responses to discrete economic events, one of them the plague under Marcus Aurelius, reflected here in ways which are not immediately demographic (chapter 4).

The second part of the book is directly concerned with demography. The large samples of ages at death provided by Roman tombstones show numerical distortions which can readily be measured. The distortions vary in systematic ways which have direct social interest. But the degree of distortion tends to be so high as to suggest that many individuals had little effective grasp of their own age (chapter 5). This largely undermines any attempt to measure Roman life-expectancy from tombstone-ages. But Roman demographic evidence is not limited to age-reporting by the individual. One of the exceptions is the complete list of the town council of Canusium in southern Italy in the early third century. The ages of town councillors on tombstones show much less numerical distortion than most of the tombstone age-evidence. Analysis of the totals for office-holders in the Canusium list provides some pointers to life-expectancy within the local aristocracy in a south Italian town (chapter 6). A further chapter, concerned in a broader sense with manpower, derives totals for army units which provide indications of the size and make-up of the Diocletianic army, and seriously modify previous conclusions (chapter 7).

The third part of the book concentrates on the agrarian economy, first examining one of the central dossiers of commodity prices, the Egyptian prices for wheat. These show recognisable seasonal and regional variation, and a slow long-term upward movement, which accelerates very sharply at the end of the third century. They thus reflect another axis of change within the economy of the Principate (chapter 8). The companion chapter considers private landownership, and examines the violent economic contrasts that are implied in lists of Roman landowners and their properties.

The focus in the fourth section is the cities where landowners often lived, and the impact which office-holding and compulsory local spending had on owners of property (chapters 10 and 11). The shape of the surviving evidence tends to suggest a mounting crisis, with increases in the friction of Roman urban institutions on the propertied class. But although some inherent difficulties can be identified, chronological skewness in the surviving juristic evidence is so great that any cumulative change or deterioration in this area during the Principate remains difficult to establish.

The tax burden represented by local offices and liturgies, though often serious enough in itself, was only part of the fiscal liabilities of the owner of property. The final part of the book is concerned with state taxes and the format of taxation. The complex of indirect taxes evidently held considerable importance as a source of government revenue in cash, as in some later pre-industrial empires. But collection of direct taxes in kind continued on a large scale (chapter 12).

The mainstay of assessment for land-taxation in many provinces under the Late Empire was the *iugum* or plough-unit. A fuller examination of the evidence implies that the *iugum* was also being used early in the Principate, and establishes its size at something close to a standardised measure (chapter 13). The results argue against seeing major discrepancies between the tax-rates of different provinces in the Late Empire. They also have important demographic implications, because the redefined *iugum* brings the ratio of manpower to land-area in tax-lists of the Late Empire close to ratios of the Principate, instead of being much lower as previous works have argued.

PART I

TIME AND DISTANCE

I

Communication-speed and contact by sea in the Roman empire

1 Change of emperor: a worm's eye view

'The good genius of the world and source of all good things, Nero, has been declared Caesar. Therefore ought we all wearing garlands and with sacrifices of oxen to give thanks to all the gods' (*POxy* 1021, 17 November AD 54).

Egypt has left far more documentary evidence than any other Roman province. One way in which its extraordinary wealth of data can throw light on communication-speed is by showing how long it took Egyptians to learn that one emperor had been replaced by another. The results can be compared with later Roman evidence for the travelling-time of Edicts (section 2), and with evidence for voyage-times from the Renaissance period (section 3).[1]

1.1 Introduction

The emperor typically lived and died in central Italy. This meant that Egypt was not well placed for hearing of any change at an early stage. Nevertheless journeys to Alexandria of 6 and 7 days from Sicily and 9 days from Puteoli were recorded, though only as exceptional events.[2] Typical delays in Egyptian awareness of change of emperor turn out to have been much longer, suggesting that even urgent news in practice travelled slowly to provinces overseas.

The most direct route from Rome to the Egyptian interior involved one journey by sea and another by river. Occasionally the two stages can be separated. Galba's accession was known in Alexandria by 6 July, within 27 days of Nero's

---

[1] Egyptian examples of delay in hearing of imperial deaths were noted as long ago as 1899 by Wilcken, though there were not enough to show the underlying patterns. (*W.O.* 1.899; see also Préaux and Châlon cited below, with E. Van't Dack, *ANRW* 2.1 (1974) 833). The evidence for the first citation of new emperors does not seem to have been studied systematically for any long period during which accession-dates are independently known. For the period AD 54–211, the enormous list of imperial titles identified by regnal year in Bureth (1964) has been used as a starting-point; but a search of documents published since the early 1960s changed a substantial number of the co-ordinates extracted from Bureth's references. The recent checklist of first and last 'sightings' of emperors in Egyptian evidence in the period 217–285 (Rathbone (1986)) has been utilised for the period 217 to 222. The survey is based on evidence dated by year, month and day.

[2] Pliny *NH* 19.3.

death on 9 June AD 68. The news had reached parts of the Thebaid within 14 days, but was still unknown in other parts on 8 August, 33 days later.[3]

By contrast, news of Pertinax's accession was not officially announced in Alexandria until 6 March, more than two months after Commodus's assassination in Rome on the night of 31 December 192. But in the Thebaid hundreds of miles south, dating by Pertinax is nevertheless found on 7 March, only a day later. Thus news had evidently reached Egypt before 6 March, and the official announcement in Alexandria was late.[4]

As just seen, news of Galba took 2 to 4 weeks to travel south inside Egypt. But governor's edicts sent from Alexandria could take as much as 54 or even 84 days to be promulgated in the south. The time allowed for the northbound journey from the Thebaid in a contemporary legal source was 50 days.[5]

From what we can see, news of a change of emperor generally travelled inside Egypt faster than this. But variations in internal transmission-time like those in the case of Galba (see also 1.4 below) mean that datings from the interior cannot be translated into datings at Alexandria by a standard discount of so many days. Nevertheless, almost all available evidence refers to the date of receipt in the interior, and it will show slower passage of news than 'quayside' information from Alexandria would show if it had survived.

However, the present dossier always uses the 'best case', the one in which delay is shortest, which reduces the effect of local variation in transmission-times. It is likely that the very large variations in transit-time that are still seen in this evidence primarily show variation in the time that news took to reach Egypt by sea (see also 2.1 below).

1.2 Preliminary approach

Table 1 shows that on median average, dating by a given emperor did not last more than 52 days after his death. Dating by a new emperor started on median

---

[3] *OGIS* 669; *OBod* 604; *W.O.* 1399 (Châlon (1964) 92).

[4] *BGU* 646; Préaux (1952) 574; *OBod* 1047, 1079. News of Pertinax had reached Tarraco before 11 February, but the distance was much less and could have been covered overland by this date (*CIL* II 4125).

[5] Châlon (1964) 92; Gnomon of the Idios Logos, 100 (*BGU* 5.1210). Because they are so extreme, these cases may reflect bureaucratic or scribal delay rather than slow passage of news. Diodorus gives 10 days as a fast sailing-time down the Nile from Alexandria as far as Ethiopia, which if true would mean an even shorter time for the distance from Alexandria to the Thebaid (3.34.7). By contrast, in the twelfth century El-Edrisi gave the travelling-time from Misr (Cairo) to Syene as 25 days, with a further 6 days from Alexandria to Misr (*Déscription de l'Afrique et de l'Espagne*, trans. R. Dozy, M.J. de Geoje (1866) 59, 180; it is not entirely clear that these figures refer to travel by river; in one case (p.25), El-Edrisi shows the time by land over a given route as 6 days, but the time by river as only 4). For the very wide discrepancy between the best sailing-times and the time that it normally took messages to arrive, see section 4. For inland shipping contracts in Egypt, see Sijpestein–Worp (1976).

Table 1. *'Last appearance' and 'first appearance' in Egypt (AD 54–222)*
(measured in days from death of emperor)

	Median	Mean	Maximum	Minimum	Standard deviation
Last dating by old ruler	52	69.1	265	4	60.1
First dating by new ruler	62	62.7	134	17	35.3

Source: Tables 9 and 10.

average 62 days after the death of his predecessor. These termini are based on aggregation and analysis of hundreds of documents from the first and last years of fifteen reigns, but they cannot always show the true outer limits, because documentation necessarily remains localised and incomplete. Further documentation can be expected to make last datings later and first datings earlier. But we can estimate a mean 'cognition-time' from a given sample of substantial size, like the present one, by averaging the co-ordinates for last and first 'sightings'. The resulting figure is 57 days. But that still does not allow for seasonal differences, which show a more complex situation (section 1.3).

1.3 Seasonal differences
As far as the available data show, the Egyptian reign-termini embody two communication-patterns. One pattern, seen in the majority of cases, is subject to extreme seasonal variation, which apparently reflected the rhythm of commercial contact between Rome and Egypt. The second pattern, mainly confined to a short period, shows faster times, with little modulation by the seasons. This second pattern implies the despatch of important news by the fastest available means, regardless of seasonal constraints; but it is obviously difficult to detect except where fast communication-speeds directly conflict with the seasonal configuration

The evidence from the time of the Flavians onwards shows heavy seasonality in communication-times. The conspicuous cases of 'counter-seasonal' fast timings are almost all earlier. They are set out in Table 2.

The examples in Table 2 all show fast transmission of news at times of year when the remaining evidence shows news of a change of emperor as travelling slowly. The powerful contrast (seen in figs. 1 and 2) probably implies that these fast timings, two of which belong to a period of civil war, were achieved by

Table 2. *'Counter-seasonal' fast timings*

New ruler	First news in Egypt (in days from death of predecessor)	Date of death of predecessor (AD)	Provenance	Source
Nero	35 days	13.10.54	Oxyrhynchus	*POxy* 1021
Galba	27 days	9.6.68	Alexandria	*OGIS* 669
Otho	26 days	15.1.69	Memphis	*SB* 11044
Trajan	31 days	25.1.98	Edfu	*OE* 430

sending off fast transport, presumably galleys, to inform the provinces of the new ruler with the shortest possible delay.[6]

The remaining evidence (fig. 1) offers a coherent picture of variation within the year if read in seasonal terms. There are possible dangers in interpreting the evidence in seasonal terms when it may also be subject to variation from year to year. Nevertheless, the most important elements in the Mediterranean weather pattern as they affected sailing were relatively stable,[7] and this makes it realistic to interpret contact-times over a given route as reflecting inherent seasonal changes if they show a coherent pattern. But, as can be seen from figure 1, the speed-

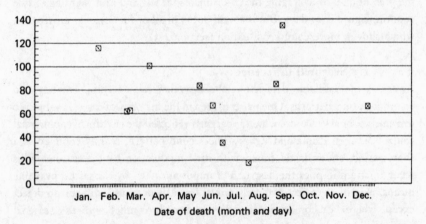

Figure 1. Time-lapse in days between emperor's death and first Egyptian evidence of his successor (examples showing seasonality)

[6] Despite what might be expected about summer sailings, the short passage-time of 27 days for news of Galba from 9 June is counter-seasonal in terms of this evidence, because its calendar-date falls between much longer times for Elagabalus (83 days from 8 June), and for Titus (66 days from 24 June; see Table 10).

Galleys were sent on urgent missions such as Nero's hunt for African treasure (Tac. *Ann.* 16.2). For Roman naval craft, see Reddé (1986) 11–141. Reddé points out (451) that under Diocletian there were sailors who worked for the *cursus publicus* (*PBeatty Panop* 2.275).

[7] See Pryor (1988) Table I and chapter 1.

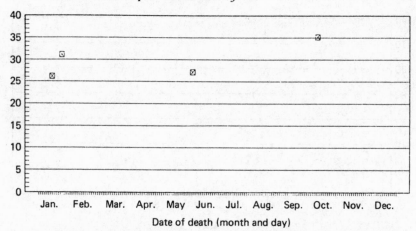

Figure 2. Time-lapse in days between emperor's death and first Egyptian evidence of his successor (counter-seasonal evidence)

constrictions are not limited to periods of adverse weather conditions. That probably suggests that the number of available sailing-links was limited (see 1.6 below).

Although the data cover a period of many years, their seasonal oscillations show noticeable cohesion. Their pattern contains two main peaks divided by a central trough (fig. 1). They suggest that news of a change of emperor reached Egypt soonest if the change fell in March, late June, July or August. When the change occurred in autumn, winter, or late spring/early summer, news apparently took much longer to get through. The speed appears to vary seasonally by a factor of as much as 7; but the shortest time belongs to a shorter route (17 days for the transmission of news from Selinus in Cilicia, where Trajan died).

Wide differences in transmission-time may also reflect long-term change. In fig. 3, time-lapse between death and first attestation of a new ruler is plotted by year. There is again a noticeable pattern, with 'slow' times in the late first century and at the start of the third, separated by faster times during the second century. These differences might appear plausible as a specific reflection of settled conditions and efficient organisation under the Antonines.

But the dates on which these deaths occurred show that second-century emperors tended to die outside the winter season when news travelled more slowly (see Table 10). This makes it risky to associate fast passage of news with greater efficiency in the second century. Strong seasonal variation in passage-times is an inherent characteristic of Mediterranean travel in the pre-modern period virtually wherever evidence is available, and it is likely to be the dominant factor here.

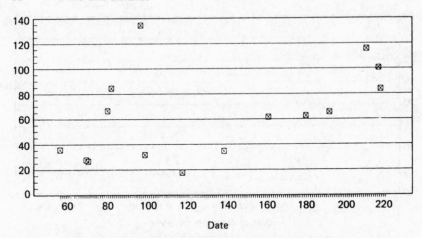

Figure 3. Time-lapse in days between death of emperor and first Egyptian evidence of his successor (plotted by year)

The one distinction which probably can be drawn is between the fast transmission of news at periods of relative uncertainty (fig. 2), and transmission through 'normal channels' at other times, with results that varied enormously, but were generally much slower (fig. 1).

The evidence for persistence of dating by the old emperor also shows marked seasonality (Table 10). It is very striking that news reached different places in Egypt at different times (section 1.4 below). One town might go on dating by the old emperor for weeks or months after another town had begun to date by his successor. Local divergences were at their worst when the emperor died in the winter. When that occurred, dating by his predecessor could easily persist in some parts of Egypt for a very long time after the date when the first news of his successor was being acted on elsewhere in the province.

To take the most dramatic cases, Septimius Severus, who died on 4 February, was still the source of dating in one Oxyrhynchus papyrus 265 days later, 150 days after the first trace in Egypt of Caracalla as sole emperor. Commodus, murdered at the end of December, was still being recognised in an Egyptian document 154 days later, at least 89 days after news of Pertinax was first known. In a third case, Nerva, who died on 25 January, was still the source of dating in one papyrus 90 days later, at least 59 days after Trajan's first emergence in Egyptian documents (Tables 9 and 10). This secondary seasonality, demonstrating the non-arrival of news, mainly reflects breakdown in the machinery of transmission within the province, apparently because of contacts being initiated at an unfavourable time of year.

When death fell near the middle of the year, anomalies were fewer and much less serious. In this evidence as a whole, big regional anomalies are the exception rather than the rule; and the averages in Table 1 show attestation of the old emperor as ceasing 10 days before the first attestation of his successor emerges in the documents.

The Nile flood took place in late summer, and at its height, usually in September, it probably impeded internal communication.[8] This may have affected internal transmission of news about change of emperor, but no seasonal effects associated with it are readily identifiable in the present dated evidence.

1.4 Regional variation within Egypt

Though the 'sea' component cannot normally be separated from the 'land' component in these journey-times, we can identify the zones of Egypt from which the documents come.

Table 3. *Arrival of news analysed by zone within Egypt**

Date of change of emperor (AD)	Zone of last dating by old ruler (A)	Zone of first dating by new ruler (B)	Difference in days between A and B	Geograph-ical sequence
October 54	South	Centre	− 11	Normal
June 68	South	North	− 33	Normal
January 69	South	Centre	+ 22	Normal
June 79	South	Centre	+ 28	Normal
September 81	South	Centre	+ 31	Normal
September 96	Centre	South	+ 35	Reverse
January 98	Centre	South	− 59	Reverse
August 117	South	North	− 15	Normal
July 138	Centre	South	− 17	Reverse
March 161	Centre	Centre	+ 16	—
March 180	South	South	− 12	—
December 192	Centre	North	− 89	Normal
January 211	Centre	Centre	− 150	—
April 217	South	Centre	+ 12	Normal
June 218	South	Centre	+ 35	Normal

**Zones:* North = Alexandria and the Delta
Centre = Arsinoite, Heptanomia and Oxyrhynchite
South = Thebaid and regions further south

Source: Tables 9 and 10.

Table 3 shows the local sequence in 15 cases in which change of emperor is documented in Egypt by both 'first' and 'last' co-ordinates. In 9 of these 15 cases, the geographical sequence is normal, remembering that news arrived first in the

[8] For seasonality of the Nile flood, cf. Bonneau (1964) 24.

north: last mention of the old emperor comes from a region further south, and first mention of his successor comes from a region further north. In three of the remaining cases, the sequence is reversed, with the south apparently knowing of change before the centre or north (AD 96, 98 and 138). And in the last three cases, both co-ordinates come from the same region, and therefore show no primary geographical sequence (AD 161, 180 and 211).

The 9 normal cases fall into two sub-groups, one in which first mention of the new emperor comes after the last mention of his predecessor, and another in which the two co-ordinates overlap. In AD 69, news of Otho had reached the central zone 22 days after the last extant mention of Galba, which comes from the south. In AD 79, 81, 217 and 218 the sequence was essentially the same, with time-lapses of 28, 31, 12 and 35 days between last record of the old emperor (always in the south) and first record of his successor (always in the central zone). Though news apparently reaches the centre before the south, there is no clear implication in these five figures about how fast news travelled between the two zones.

The second sub-group, where the co-ordinates overlap, starts in AD 54. News of Nero had reached the central zone 11 days before the last extant dating by Claudius in the south. There were similar discrepancies, though now between southern and northern zones, in AD 68 (33 days) and AD 117 (15 days). On the face of it, these three examples suggest times for passage of news to the south from the centre (11 days) or from the north (33 and 15 days).[9] But the co-ordinates are only termini by default, and they do not define the date on which news first arrived, or the latest date by which news had not arrived. The last figure in the group, from AD 192, shows Commodus still being acknowledged in the Fayum 89 days after news of Pertinax had reached Alexandria. This is one of a group of anomalies apparently associated with change of emperor in winter (see 1.3).

The three 'abnormal' cases where the south appears to hear news before the centre (AD 96, 98, 138) also divide into two. In one case the new emperor is attested in the south 35 days after his predecessor is last heard of in the centre (AD 96/7). In the other two cases, the south has already heard of the new emperor as much as 59 and 17 days *before* his predecessor is last attested in the centre (AD 98 and 138). The discrepancy of 59 days in AD 98 belongs to winter (see 1.3). The shorter discrepancy of 17 days in AD 138 is probably fortuitous.

More often than not, analysis by zone shows regions nearer to the coast receiving news sooner than regions further away. The exceptions seem mainly to be due to accidents of survival. But there is serious time-lag in the persistence of 'old' dating in some cases in the central zone (see 1.3). This may argue poor communication in neighbourhoods which lay any distance from the Nile.

---

[9] A minimum difference of 10 days transit-time between the Thebaid and the Arsinoite is assumed by Rathbone (1986) 103.

1.5 The communication-times related to place of death

Table 4. *Last appearances in Egyptian documents shown by place of death of emperor*

Emperor	Place of death	Month of death	Year	Time-lag (days after death)	Zone of Egypt
Galba	Italy	January	69	4	?
Otho	Italy	April	69	12	South
Elagabalus	Italy	March	222	26	Centre
Vespasian	Italy	June	79	38	South
A. Pius	Italy	March	161	45	Centre
Claudius	Italy	October	54	46	South
Hadrian	Italy	July	138	51	Centre
Titus	Italy	September	81	53	South
Pertinax	Italy	March	193	58	South
Nero	Italy	June	68	60	South
Nerva	Italy	January	98	90*	Centre
Domitian	Italy	September	96	99	Centre
Commodus	Italy	December	192	154*	Centre
Trajan	Cilicia	August	117	32*	South
Macrinus	Syria	June	218	48	South
M. Aurelius	Pannonia	March	180	74	South
Caracalla	Syria	April	217	88	South
Septimius	Britain	February	211	265*	Centre

*Later than earliest Egyptian dating by successor

Summary

Place of death	Median delay	Mean	Maximum	Minimum	Number	South median (n)	Centre median (n)
Italy	51	56.6	154	4	13	49.5 (6)	70.5 (6)
Outside Italy	74	101.4	265	32	5	61.0 (4)	265.0 (1)

Source: Tables 9 and 10.

The averages in Table 4 consistently show dating by emperors who died outside Italy as persisting longer than dating by emperors who died in Italy. But deaths in the small non-Italian sample mainly fall at times of year when the seasonal pattern suggests slow passages of news in any case. The longest delay refers to a death in Britain, the province furthest from Egypt. The lowest non-Italian co-ordinate refers to Trajan's death in Cilicia, news of which possibly reached Egypt sooner than it would have done if he had died in Italy.

1.6 The interpretation of the Egyptian evidence

The Egyptian material provides a measure of the efficiency of communication between the capital and one of the provinces, but it does not directly measure the speed of the transport on which communication depended. At least two other components were involved. One was 'bureaucratic' delay, the time that it took to reach and implement a decision to notify the provinces. The other was potential delay resulting from the departure-times of shipping.

Bearing these elements in mind, two broad reconstructions are possible. In one of them, the need to secure the loyalty of the provinces means that news is transmitted with the utmost speed. In the second reconstruction, events move more slowly: it may take an appreciable time to decide to notify the provinces, and the time taken to embark despatches may be subordinate to an existing pattern of sailings.

It has already been suggested that the few examples in Table 2 belong to the 'fast' reconstruction of events, whereas most of the evidence appears subject to very wide variations in communication-time, which argue a seasonal cycle (figs. 1 and 2).

The reasons for the cycle become clear if we look at sailings between Egypt and Italy. The main transport of grain from Egypt to Italy was probably carried out by ships travelling as a fleet in late spring/early summer. The recurrent crises at Rome because the grain ships were late suggest that ships tended to travel as a group.[10] A pattern of this kind would be consistent with two main transits from west to east, one in the spring (ships that wintered in Italy sailing to Egypt in time to load up with grain), and the other in late summer (ships that wintered in Egypt going back there).[11]

This synopsis closely agrees with the fact that news from outside Egypt which originated in March and in July–August is seen to travel fast, whereas news which originated in the intervening months travels much more slowly (fig. 1). The 'seasonal' evidence for the date by which news had reached a location in Egypt (which excludes the four cases shown in Table 2) shows clear 'bunching' in two brief periods of the year, without there being enough bunching in the dates of

[10] For example, Tac. *Hist*. 4.3.8; Symmachus *Ep*. 3.55; 82. Casson (n.11).

[11] Casson (1971) 297–9. If the commandeering of all available shipping in the region of Campania by the emperor Gaius was enough to cause severe famine in Rome in AD 39 (Dio 59.17.2), that should argue that the grain-supply depended heavily on ships based in Italy. Garnsey (1988) 222–3 rejects Dio's account on the ground that (from Seneca *de brev. vit*. 18) the bridge of boats seems, despite Dio's dating, to belong to the end of Gaius's reign. But Suet. *Gaius* 19.3 likewise shows it as preceding the German campaign.

death to account for this (both sets of dates are listed in Table 10). The concentrations occur in May (3 examples between 11 and 30 May), and August (4 examples between 13 and 30 August). Between them, the two groupings account for 7 of the 11 cases in the 'seasonal' evidence. The concentrations suggest that shipping from the west tended to reach Egypt at, or shortly before, the dates in question.

Pliny's best case of 9 days for the sailing-time from Puteoli to Alexandria is very remote from the evidence assembled here. The fastest times in the Egyptian evidence occur when the new emperor belonged to a new dynasty. The news of Galba's proclamation had reached Alexandria 27 days after Nero's death, while news of Otho reached Memphis in 26 days (Table 10). If most of this time was taken by the sea crossing, voyage-time is still much more than the Pliny figure.

Though diffusion of news within Egypt was certainly subject to delays, these delays did not always depend on distance (Table 3). The great variations in communication-time between Italy and inland Egypt probably reflect seasonal fluctuation in the time taken on the sea-route, because of sailings which were intermittent, slow or interrupted. In the main sailing season the winds nevertheless favoured eastbound voyages. This is powerfully illustrated by the two-fold differences later seen between the time that pilgrims took to get back to Venice, and the time they took to reach the Holy Land (section 3 below).

When the transit from Italy to Alexandria was so slow, the voyage may not have been continuous. Since the speed per hour implied in Pliny's example of a very fast crossing to Alexandria is close to the speed for other much shorter voyages (Casson (1971), Table I), that voyage presumably was continuous. The longer times in the Egyptian evidence may well suggest that voyages were not normally direct, or that sailings were intermittent.[12]

Summaries of later commercial traffic show that on long voyages, Venetian galleys in the sixteenth century spent little more than one-third of their journey-time at sea. And a pair of Florentine galleys which left on 12 June 1445 and got back 296 days later, spent well over half their time in port. Besides six other stops, the galleys spent 54 days at Tunis, 76 at Alexandria, 2 at Rhodes, 13 at Candia, 11 at Syracuse, 26 days more at Tunis and 3 at Palermo.[13]

2 Edicts sent and edicts received

2.1 Africa

Important comparisons can be made from later Roman material, the double-dated imperial edicts from the legal Codes. Double-dated edicts sent to Africa

---

[12] For coastal navigation in the Roman period, cf. Rougé (1966) 85–6. Nothing in the present evidence supports the suggestion that Egypt would have known within 10 days of Augustus's death in Italy on 19 August (Pippidi (1945) 126–7).   [13] Mallett (1967) 281; 64–5 and 160–1.

Table 5. *Double-dated edicts sent to governors of Africa*

	Departure date	Travelling-time in days	Starting-point	Destination (if stated)	Year (AD)
A.	18 January	186	Constantinople	Carthage	360
B.	30 January	86	Treves	—	378
C.	3 February	156	Milan	—	357
D.	8 February	349	Ravenna	Carthage	414
E.	17 April	31	Sirmium	—	321
F.	13 May	134	Hadrianople	Carthage	364
G.	30 May	180	Nasonaci	—	372
H.	16 June	45	Verona	—	383
J.	19 June	208	Aquileia	Hadrumetum	391
K.	13 August	61	Arles	Theveste	316
L.	2 September	71	Dinummae	Carthage	355
M.	12 September	63	Aquileia	Tacapae	364
N.	18 October	92	Paris	Carthage	365
O.	21 October	199	Constantinople	Carthage	335
P.	26 October	143	Antioch	Carthage	363
Q.	3 November	166	Treves	Hadrumetum	314
R.	8 November	99	Treves	—	313
S.	25 November	192	Rome	Carthage	407

Source: Law Codes (see Jones (1964) 3.91–92).

span a century, from AD 313 to 414, and come from 15 different starting-points (Table 5). These make up a very wide cross-section of cities in different parts of the empire, ranging from the grandest to the most obscure.

Distance caused the freight-rates for different passages between Africa and the north and east in Diocletian's Price Edict to vary by a factor of 4 or 5.[14] Similar differences could be expected here, reflecting the different distances that edicts had to travel. But little systematic relation to distance emerges in reality. An edict from Rome could take three times as long to reach Africa as one from Aquileia in the far north of Italy (192/63 days); and four times as long as one from Verona, which was further inland and much further north than Rome (192/45 days). The time taken by edicts from Treves varied by a factor of 2 (166/86 days). Most edicts

[14] From 4 to 18 denarii per castrensis modius: see text in Crawford–Reynolds (1979) 185–6. For discussion of the value of the Edict's figures, see *ERE*² 367–9. Some estimates of the underlying distances (Hopkins (1982) 85–6) suggest that the charge per kilometre may have varied by a factor of 2 or more overall. This degree of inexactness in the framing of the tariffs is quite possible. But it is not clear that the distances can be reconstructed effectively; apart from frequent problems of reconstructing the route, co-ordinates in the Edict are often very imprecise, for example, 'Africa to Sicily', or 'Africa to Gaul' (which, for unexplained reasons, the Edict shows as being the cheaper alternative).

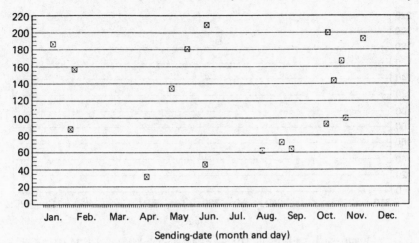

Figure 4. Time-lapse in days between sending-date and date of receipt of edicts sent to Africa, AD 313–414 (n = 17)

went to Carthage in the north (8 out of 12 certainly did), but the two sent to Tacapae and Theveste in the south arrived sooner than almost any others (in 63 and 61 days), although they had further to travel inside the province (Table 5).

If geography explains so little, the obvious alternative is the effect of the seasons. A plot of the African transit-times by date of despatch shows a strong pattern, which is more readily accounted for by seasonal change than by variation in distance (fig. 4).[15] The plot shows a clear winter peak: travelling-time is slow for edicts sent in winter and late autumn. But it appears to be slow also for edicts sent in May and June. Geographical differences aside, edicts sent to Africa (like communiqués sent to Egypt) travel fastest in spring and late summer.

There appears to be some slowing down. The three edicts despatched after 383 (lines D, J and S) account for three of the four longest journey-times. This may belong to a general change (see section 4), but the sample is too small for long-term change to be separated from seasonal variants. The overall chronological pattern shows no other strong trend (fig. 5; see n.15).

The slower transmission in part of the main sailing season obviously recalls variations in the Egyptian evidence. Close comparisons season by season are not feasible. The time elapsed is much longer (a median of 134 days, n = 17, compared with 57 days for Egypt). But the two patterns agree in showing slower transits in the winter, and faster transits during the main sailing season, with at least one serious interruption in mid-season.

Africa at this time was the major supplier of grain to Rome, with grain-sailings

---

[15] The travelling-time of almost a year in Table 5 line D differs from the average of the other times by more than three standard deviations, and has been excluded from the analyses of the African material. This unconscionably slow journey began in winter.

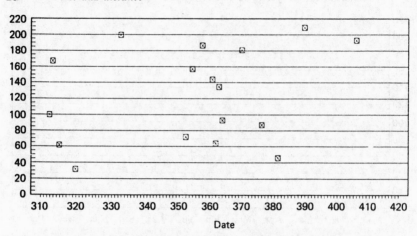

Figure 5. Time-lapse in days between sending-date and date of receipt of edicts sent to Africa, AD 313–414 (n = 17) (shown by year)

to Italy which presumably took place soon after the harvest.[16] This would tend to make north-south links more numerous, both at the beginning of the sailing-season, as vessels from the northern Mediterranean arrived in Africa to take on cargo, and at the end of the season, as vessels based in Africa went home for the winter.

Neither African nor Egyptian data fully demonstrate that there was a 'mare clausum' in the winter, even though Symmachus, Vegetius and others show that serious interruptions did take place then.[17] Set against Vegetius's termini for the closing of the seas, 11 November to 10 March, the African evidence shows three cases in which edicts sent before the start of the 'closed' season arrived before that season had ended (Table 5, lines J, M, N). Though no edict was both sent and received within Vegetius's 119 days of closure, that is hardly significant, since the median transit-time for edicts sent to Africa was more than 119 days.

Because the distances vary so much, seasonal interpretations cannot be pressed beyond a certain point. Similarities to the Egyptian pattern nevertheless suggest that seasonal variants effectively determined the speed of communication between the seats of government and Africa. The speed with which a sea-crossing could be achieved (including any time spent waiting for the next sailing) seems to have been more important in determining how long an edict took to arrive than any variation in the overall distance. The fact that none of the four edicts from the east took less than the average time to reach Africa may be significant; two took

---

[16] Cf. Rickman (1980) 129–30, 202.
[17] See notes 33–4 below. Statutes of different maritime states show that in the Middle Ages sailing during the period of closure was restricted and even subject to heavy penalties. (Ashburner (1909) cxlii–cxliii),.

considerably longer, but were sent on dates when a slow journey from any overseas starting-point was predictable from the seasonal pattern.[18]

These communication-times, with a median of 134 days (n = 17), are generally much longer than those from Egypt, where the median is some 57 days. The sailing-distances were generally shorter, which heightens the contrast even further. Bureaucratic delays might have increased by the late Empire. But some African examples actually show quite good speeds by ancient standards,[19] 31 days from Sirmium to Carthage; 61 from Arles to Theveste, a town in the extreme south a long way inland; and 63 days for the similar distance from Aquileia to Tacapae. Thus, if bureaucratic delay led to the different degrees of slowness seen in the African figures, it would have to be understood as a variable which followed the seasons in the same way as contacts by sea.

This is unconvincing. An alternative would be a decline in the efficiency or frequency of sea-communications since the second century, and some conclusion of this kind is quite likely in general (see section 4). The African evidence is not the only suggestion of slow journey-times in the late Empire. At the end of the fourth century, the period allowed for state shippers to complete a voyage and make any claims arising was as much as two years. By comparison, a specimen shipping-contract of the second century shows 200 days, about half a year, as prospective time for a trading journey which involved the long round-trip from Beirut to Brindisi and back.[20]

2.2 Egypt

Heavy modulation by the seasons is also found in fourth-century evidence for communications with Egypt. The dates of 28 edicts sent to the Prefect of Egypt, or 'Augustalis', usually from Constantinople, show a complete blank for almost one-third of the year. The evidence is mainly from the last two decades of the century. No edicts were sent between 30 July and 24 November in any of the years concerned.[21] Only four edicts belong to dates between 24 November and 4 February, but the average between 4 February and 30 July is as high as one edict every seven days. This long cessation after July is not seen in the numerous edicts to places north of the Mediterranean. It probably suggests that available sea-links were confined to a limited period of the year.

Reconstruction is naturally uncertain. But Constantinople had now become the leading overseas recipient of Egyptian corn.[22] The seasonal pattern here

---

[18] Table 5: line A, sent on 18 January, and line P, sent on 26 October.
[19] Cf. evidence below (section 4).
[20] *CTh* 13.5.21, 26; cf. Jones (1964) 2.828. *D.* 45.1.122.1 (Scaevola).
[21] The series begins in AD 354, but almost all the evidence, 25 cases out of 28, belongs to the short period AD 380–397 (*Codex Theodosianus*, Mommsen (ed.) 1, p.cxcv).
[22] *Expositio totius mundi* 36.

Table 6. *Edicts sent to the governors of Egypt and Africa*

Month	Egypt percentage	Africa percentage	Egypt (N)	Africa (N)
January	4	5	1	5
February	18	14	5	14
March	14	10	4	10
April	14	6	4	6
May	11	6	3	6
June	14	11	4	11
July	11	9	3	9
August	—	10	—	10
September	—	4	—	4
October	—	6	—	6
November	7	9	2	9
December	7	7	2	7
Total			28	97

Source: *Codex Theodosianus* Mommsen (ed.) 1 cxcii–cxcv.

seems consistent with sailings in spring and summer by grain-ships based in Constantinople, which after returning from Egypt, normally wintered at home (cf. Philo *legatio* 15).

Evidence from a nearby sector of the eastern Mediterranean reveals a very slow southward journey-time during the season when edicts were not being sent to Egypt. In AD 362 an edict sent from Antioch on 3 September took 42 days to find its way to the recipient at Tyre, a relatively short coastal journey.[23]

The gaps in the monthly pattern of edicts sent to Egypt can be seen when compared with the edicts sent to the proconsul of Africa (Table 6).

2.3 Western evidence

Two short sets of double-dated edicts from the Theodosian Code show median journey-times from Illyricum to Italy of 60 days (N = 7), and 36 days between Gaul and Italy (N = 5). These averages are of course well below the contact-times for Africa, but the Illyricum times still appear relatively slow. Contacts with Gaul were actually or potentially by land, and the tiny sample suggests no obvious seasonal element. But the Illyricum evidence shows clear seasonal variation, with shorter timings in the summer (fig. 6). Contact with Italy in this case depended on a sea-link across the Adriatic, which subjected it to seasonal differences.

[23] *CTh* 12.1.52.

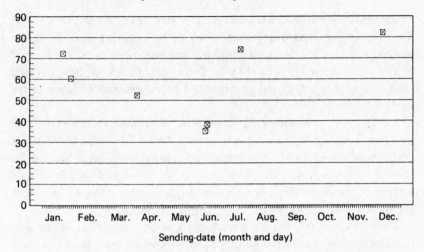

Figure 6. Time-lapse in days between sending-date and date of receipt of edicts sent to Italy from Illyricum, AD 319–359

Table 7. *Transit-time (days) in the double-dated edicts: summary*

Route	Median time	Mean	Maximum	Minimum	Standard deviation	Numbers
N. Mediterranean–Africa*	134	124	208	31	59	17
Illyricum–Italy	60	60	82	35	17	7
Gaul–Italy/Italy–Gaul	36	39	60	22	14	5

*Omitting line D, Table 5 (see n.15).

Source: see Table 5 (*CTh* 11.30.18 shows a time of 38 days from Illyricum to Italy, not 48 as in Jones (1964) 3.92).

3 Later evidence

The fullest indications of how long Mediterranean voyages took under pre-modern conditions probably come from evidence about Venetian shipping.[24] A sample of pilgrim voyages to the Holy Land in the fifteenth and sixteenth centuries under Venetian management shows a median sailing-time of 42 days from Venice to Jaffa (N = 28, mean average 44, standard deviation 11).[25] Out of

[24] For Venetian shipping and navigation, see Lane (1934); (1966). For other valuable evidence about later voyage-times, see Pryor (1988) 51–3; 73–5.

[25] Eight fifteenth-century voyages, from 1461 onwards, have been added to the sixteenth-century sample cited by Braudel (1972) 1.264–5, using the same source as Braudel (Röhricht–Meisner (1880) 481ff.). The years added are 1461, 1467, 1468, 1476, 1479, 1486, 1495 and 1498.

33 departures on known dates, 5 took place in May, 14 in June and 12 in July.[26] The dates are thus biassed towards sailings at the better times of year. Their date was partly determined by the need to fit in a long round-trip by sea and a stay of several weeks in the Holy Land before the winter. Twenty of these outward voyages took between 33 and 50 days (within one standard deviation of the median).

A sample of 15 westward voyages on the same route shows a median time of 86 days (mean average 89, standard deviation 25). Eleven fall within one standard deviation of the median.[27] The times were relatively consistent because the seasonal pattern varied so little, early summer for the outward journey and late summer or autumn for the return. On average, the voyage out took half as long as the voyage home (42/86 days).

The evidence bears out some contemporary advice. Ludolphus de Sudheim recommended the fourteenth-century pilgrim travelling from Venice or Marseilles to take food for 50 days, but food for 100 days on his voyage home, because of differences due to the prevailing winds. Tacitus, more than a thousand years earlier, cited the same prevailing winds when explaining why in the summer of 69 Vespasian in the east had more up-to-date news of Vitellius in Rome than Vitellius had of Vespasian.[28] Journey-times loosely reported by Jewish merchants based in Egypt in the Middle Ages show a similar differential: the overall speed for east-west voyages is only 1.0 knots, as against 1.65 knots for voyages from west to east, on median average (N = 5 and 12).[29]

Venetian sources of *c.* 1500, such as the diaries of Sanuto and Priuli, give a mass of further information showing the time which news took to reach Venice.[30] Some figures for contacts largely or wholly by sea have been summarised in Table 8. The mean time of 80 days taken for news to travel from the east (Damascus in this case) is not very far below the mean time for pilgrim-journeys in the same direction (89 days).

Unfortunately, these aggregates are non-comparable with the Egyptian evidence in several ways. They subsume figures from different times of year into one; Venice was further from the east than Rome (even news from Trani apparently took 12 days on average to travel up the Adriatic); the direction of the eastern contacts in Table 8 is east-west, not west-east; and ship-design had probably improved by 1500.[31] Nevertheless, the Venetian evidence demonstrates

---

[26] Nine fifteenth-century examples added to the Braudel sixteenth-century sample.

[27] Four fifteenth-century examples, from the years 1461, 1476, 1486 and 1495, have been added to the Braudel sample for the sixteenth century (see previous notes).

[28] *Archives de l'Orient Latin* 2 (1884), Documents, 330; Tac. *Hist.* 2.99.

[29] Analysis based on times and distances summarised by A.L. Udovitch, mainly using Goitein (1967) 1.325–6; these journey-times, almost always in round figures, cannot be very precise (Udovitch (1978), 503–46 at 510–11).   [30] Briefly summarised in Sardella (1948) 56–64.

[31] For ship-design, cf. Unger (1980); Kreutz (1976). For merchant-galleys, see Lane (1964) 229–33;

Table 8. *Average time-lapse for news reaching Venice c. 1500*

Link	Mean average (days)	Number
Damascus–Venice	80	56
Alexandria–Venice	65	266
Lisbon–Venice	46	35
Palermo–Venice	22	118
Trani–Venice	12	94

Source: Sardella (1948).

the inherent slowness of contacts based on Mediterranean shipping in the pre-modern period. In 1500 Venice was still a major commericial power crucially reliant on good shipping-links. Yet her receipt of news from the eastern Mediterranean remained subject to delays of two to three months, averaged over the year.

4 Conclusions

There is not enough Roman evidence about voyage-times to show categorically what speeds were typical. Under the most favourable conditions, Roman shipping could achieve average speeds of 5–6 knots over medium or long routes.[32] But such figures are quite misleading as a guide to typical communication-speed. In practice, this was heavily affected by seasonality, by the fact that sailings were intermittent and departure-dates always dependent on the weather, and by stops at intervening ports. Symmachus reveals that, as a resident in central Italy, he could expect his correspondence with friends in Spain to cease during the winter, when the seas were closed.[33] In the fourth century, Vegetius and the emperor Gratian (in 380) both describe the closure of navigation for a set period from November to March, or November to April.[34]

The literary evidence contains some useful illustrations of how long sea-based contacts could take in practice. Cicero considered three weeks a good journey-time for despatches sent from Rome to Athens in mid-October (they took six and a half weeks in another case).[35] A letter from Africa took three weeks to reach

Sacerdoti (1962); Mallett (n.13), 17.

[32] Casson (1971) Table 1, p. 283. For journey-times, cf. also Rougé (1966) 99ff.
[33] *Ep.* 4.58; 63; cf. 54. For the 'mare clausum', with further information from Symmachus, see Rougé (1952) 318–19.
[34] 4.32; *CTh* 13.9.3. See Casson (1971) 270–2. The Ides of March figures as a navigational threshold as early as the time of Augustus (*D.* 39.4.15, Alfenus).   [35] *ad fam.* 14.5; 16.21.

Cicero in Rome in March 43 BC[36]; but a letter sent by Zosimus on 21 March AD 418 was received in Carthage on 29 April, having taken five and a half weeks.[37]

According to Josephus, the last letter from the emperor Gaius to Petronius, governor of Syria, was held up at sea for three months, and only arrived 27 days after Petronius had heard by a later ship that Gaius was dead.[38] As Gaius was assassinated in midwinter (on 24 January AD 41), the news could hardly have reached Judaea much before the beginning of March. If that were so, the vessel which was 27 days behind must have docked at about the end of March, and would have begun her three-month voyage at about the end of December, probably the worst possible time in terms of sailing conditions. The letter from Petronius to which Gaius was replying had been sent at the sowing season in Judaea (November), and presumably took less than two months to make the voyage from east to west, travelling at a slightly better time of year.[39]

Another emperor's letter, though sent at a favourable time of year, was almost as slow as the one from Gaius. In AD 127 Hadrian's reply to Stratonicea, a town near the coast of south-west Turkey, left Rome on 1 March and reached its recipient 75 days later on 14 May.[40]

The Roman evidence for civil communications contains very few cases in which the complex of disabling factors fails to operate and allows news to travel at something like the optimum speed.[41] Even the best transit-times for news are normally a generous multiple of the sailing-time under optimum conditions. For example, Cicero's receipt in Rome of a letter from Africa in three weeks, approximately 21 days, though very fast when compared with other evidence for the travelling-speed of news, is a relatively high multiple of contemporary journey-times for the sea-voyage in question, ranging from two to four days.[42] The announcement of Hadrian's accession by the prefect in Alexandria only 17 days after Trajan's death at Selinus in Cilicia shows a very fast response (Table 10). Yet this again is a high multiple of the voyage-time of three days reported for the journey to Egypt from the nearby Attaleia (Plut. *Pomp.* 76.5).

If a transit-time for news of 21 days was a good result on the Africa–Ostia route, despite being a five-fold multiple (or more) of known sailing-times, that suggests that a 'fast season' figure of some 30 days from Rome to Egypt was also very favourable by contemporary standards. This is only a three-fold multiple of the best sailing-time recorded by Pliny (nine days from Puteoli to Alexandria (n.2)).

---

[36] *ad fam.* 12.25.   [37] Perler (1969) 71.   [38] *BJ* 2.203; *AJ* 18.304–9.
[39] For the season, see E. Schürer *History of the Jewish people* I (1973) 395.   [40] *FIRA* 1.80.
[41] For the literary evidence, see Friedlaender (1921–2) 1.333–42; Riepl (1913) 157–71; Casson (1971) 281–96. The use by Friedlaender and others of travelling-times in Philostratus's semi-fantastic *Life of Apollonius of Tyana* is unconvincing.   [42] Casson (1971) 283–4.

Table 9. *Emperors with known date of death (AD 54–222): latest reign-datings in Egyptian sources*

Old ruler	Date of death	Date of last attestation in Egypt	Days after death	Source	Zone**
Claudius	13.10. 54	28.11. 54	46*	*W.O* 13	South
Nero	9. 6. 68	8. 8. 68	60*	*W.O* 1326	South
Galba	15. 1. 69	19. 1. 69	4	*CPJ* 418	?
Otho	16. 4. 69	28. 4. 69	12	*W.O.* 426	South
Vespasian	24. 6. 79	1. 8. 79	38	*SB* 1926	South
Titus	13. 9. 81	5.11. 81	53	*SB* 8046	South
Domitian	18. 9. 96	26.12. 96	99	*POxy* 104	Centre
Nerva	25. 1. 98	25. 4. 98	90*	*PFay* 48	Centre
Trajan	8. 8.117	9. 9.117	32*	*IGRR* 1371	South
Hadrian	10. 7.138	30. 8.138	51*	*SB* 12138	Centre
A. Pius	11. 3.161	25. 4.161	45	*PTeb* 481	Centre
M. Aurelius	17. 3.180	30. 5.180	74*	*OLund* 8	South
Commodus	31.12.192	2. 6.193	154*	*BGU* 515	Centre
Pertinax	28. 3.193	25. 5.193	58	*OTheb* 64	South
Septimius	4. 2.211	27.10.211	265*	*POxy* 56	Centre
Caracalla	8. 4.217	5. 7.217	88	*W.O.* 991	South
Macrinus	8. 6.218	26. 7.218	48	*PRein* 142	South
Elagabalus	11. 3.222	6. 4.222	26	*POxy* 1522	Centre

*Latest attestation overlaps with the earliest documents dated by the next emperor (see Table 10).

**For the definition of zones see Table 3.

Note: Vitellius is omitted altogether, because his absence from Rome leaves it unclear whether he was in a position to notify the provinces of his accession immediately after Otho's death on 16 April 69 (the earliest Egyptian reference appears to be one from Thebes on 16 June, 61 days later, Préaux (1952) 573). And the end of Vitellius's reign, with Vespasian in Egypt and already proclaimed there in July, and Vitellius's suicide in Rome in December, does not illustrate the arrival of news in Egypt.

Communication-delays in the 'slow season' from Rome to Egypt (Table 10) were of course much greater, 80 days or more. These great seasonal differences probably reflect sailings which were fewer as well as slower. The possible fate of messages which embarked at an unfavourable time of year is clearly illustrated by the three-month journey of Gaius's last letter to the governor of Judaea in the winter of AD 41.

Thus, interpreted in the light of other Roman evidence, the Egyptian transit-times suggest not that the government was lethargic or negligent in notifying

Table 10. *Time-interval between earliest Egyptian reign-dating and death of previous emperor (AD 54–235)*

New ruler	Date of death of predecessor	Date of earliest attestation in Egypt	Days after death of predecessor	Source	Zone**
Nero	13.10. 54	17.11. 54	35*	POxy 1021	Centre
Galba	9. 6. 68	6. 7. 68	27*	OGIS 669	North
Otho	15. 1. 69	10. 2. 69	26	SB 11044	Centre
Titus	24. 6. 79	29. 8. 79	66	POxy 380	Centre
Domitian	13. 9. 81	6.12. 81	84	PLond 283	Centre
Nerva	18. 9. 96	30. 1. 97	134	OOntMus 12	South
Trajan	25. 1. 98	25. 2. 98	31*	OE 430	South
Hadrian	8. 8.117	25. 8.117	17*	POxy 3781	North
A. Pius	10. 7.138	13. 8.138	34*	SB 10329	South
M. Aurelius	11. 3.161	11. 5.161	61	PBerlLeihg 17	Centre
Commodus	17. 3.180	18. 5.180	62*	OBod 1501	South
Pertinax	31.12.192	6. 3.193	65*	BGU 646	North
Caracalla	4. 2.211	30. 5.211	115*	BGU 711	Centre
Macrinus	8. 4.217	17. 7.217	100	SB 9143	Centre
Elagabalus	8. 6.218	30. 8.218	83	StudPal xx 25	Centre

*Dating by predecessor also found after this date.

**For the definition of zones see Table 3.

Note: Vespasian and Septimius are omitted, Vespasian because he was in Egypt when proclaimed Emperor, Septimius because no 'true' accession-date is available.

Egypt of changes of ruler, but that it usually acted within the constraints of a slow communication-system made slower by seasonal delays. Contacts over the three main routes examined all show seasonality which almost certainly reflects a limited pattern of commercial sailings. The dominant patterns on all three routes (Egypt–Rome, Egypt–Constantinople, N. Mediterranean–Africa) were probably generated by the large-scale movement of grain from the southern Mediterranean to the north.

Lack of material generally prevents direct comparison between conditions in early and late Empire. Symmachus's evidence for the effects of closing the seas in winter, striking though it is, refers to a situation already familiar much earlier.[43] According to Philo, the news of Gaius's illness in the eighth month of his reign (September/October 37) soon spread everywhere because the seas were still open at that time, and the vessels that normally wintered in their home ports had not

[43] Cf. Pliny *NH* 2.122, 125.

yet gone back there.[44] When St Paul was shipwrecked on Malta in the winter, it was three months before his journey to Italy could continue. He left Malta in an Alexandrian ship which had been wintering in port, as his first vessel would have done if it had not been blown off course.[45]

However, where there are pointers to change, these tend to suggest noticeable deterioration in communication-speed. In the fourth century AD, edicts reached Africa much more slowly than news had reached Egypt earlier on, showing seasonal variation in journey-time to a degree which seems to exclude bureaucratic delay as the governing reason for slowness. By the late fourth century, edicts sent to Egypt from Asia could apparently travel only during part of the year. And edicts from Illyricum took substantially longer to reach Italy than letters from Rome had once taken to reach Athens.

At the start of the fifth century, Synesius could offer the powerful excuse for non-payment of tribute that no ships went to the capital from Cyrene.[46] The relative numbers of dated underwater wrecks from different periods seem to argue a substantial fall in the volume of shipping in the Mediterranean by the fourth century. Difficulties of interpretation surround any attempt to utilise this as a direct linear measure.[47] Nevertheless, the trend suggested in this case is hardly at variance with the other pointers in the surviving evidence.

---

[44] *Legatio* 15. Cf. Rougé (1966) 105, and n.33 above.   [45] *Acts* 27.12; 28.11.   [46] *Ep.* 147.
[47] One problem is the shortage of medieval wreck-finds; another is the fact that investigation has been very patchy, with very little work on the African littoral, for example. A further potential distortion is the fact that the chance of finding wrecks may be closely linked to whether they hold large pottery containers, which are easy to locate. For a summary of Roman wreck-totals, showing a strong peak in the first century BC and the first century AD, see Parker (1984) 108, fig.4. The 1984 fig. (which differs somewhat from the earlier version reproduced in Hopkins (1980)) is based on a sample of more than 800 classical wrecks. The third-century total is less than half that for the first century AD, and the fourth-century figure lower still.

2
Trade, taxes and money

1 Introduction

The shortage of information about the volume of ancient trade makes fresh sources of inference worth exploring. Some of the interactions between other elements of the Roman economy may have implications for trade. In one of the most arresting contributions of recent years, Keith Hopkins has argued that long-distance trade grew very considerably during the Roman Principate, under stimuli that were an incidental by-product of Roman rule.[1]

His model notes that the provinces which produced the most tax-revenue were not those which cost the most to govern. Wealthy provinces with small garrisons were probably net exporters of tax-revenue, while less wealthy provinces with large garrisons were probably net importers of tax-revenue. Each time that the tax-cycle took place, the imbalance would tend to drain money out of the tax-exporting provinces, making it more difficult for those provinces to pay their taxes in future. In the model, it is argued that the imbalance was corrected by an increase in production in the 'tax-exporting' provinces and by an increase in their exports; that in turn meant an expansion in the volume of long-distance trade within the empire.

Roman authors show some awareness of disparities like those envisaged in the model. Cicero claimed that some of Rome's provinces hardly brought in enough to pay their defence costs.[2] Strabo writing before the Claudian conquest thought he could foresee that Britain would not yield enough tribute to support the cost of one legion.[3] Appian writing a century or more after the conquest wrote that Britain was not 'rich in tribute' (*euphoros*). Appian later observed that some of Rome's possessions cost more than they provided in revenue, and Dio wrote that Mesopotamia brought in little and cost a great deal.[4]

Nevertheless there are serious obstacles to reconciling the model with wider evidence. The difficulties can be outlined briefly.

1. The pattern envisaged would result in large-scale transfer of coin between regions. The validation put forward is the existence of chronological similarities

---
[1] Hopkins (1980).   [2] *pro lege Man.* 16.   [3] 4.5.3; 2.5.3.   [4] Appian *pr.* 5; 7; Dio 75.3.3.

between coin-populations in different regions which, it is suggested, were generated by inter-regional exchange.

But further investigation suggests that local coin-populations contained distinctive *dissimilarities*; that the broad similarities referred to mainly resulted from parallel transmissions of coin from the centre, not from inter-regional exchange; and that long-distance trade did not necessarily create long-distance money-flows.

2. The prime stimulus envisaged is the government's pressure to make provincials pay direct taxes in money. But despite prevalent assumptions to the contrary, the degree to which direct taxes were levied in money under the Principate is very uncertain (chapter 12). This makes the model's starting-point uncertain also.

3. Before the Roman Principate, Mediterranean trade had already been vigorous for centuries, or even millenia. Where long-distance commercial exchange can be seen under the Principate, what it represents is not necessarily a response to new fiscal stimuli.

Nevertheless, the model raises important issues about a series of topics:
   (A) the realities and the historical context of long-distance trade;
   (B) the character and historical implications of regional coin-deposits;
   (C) the nature of taxation under the Principate;
   (D) the interaction or interrelation between these different elements.

Two parts of this discussion, touching on trade patterns and on the means of payment in Roman taxation, are long enough to form separate entities and can be found below as chapters 3 and 12.

2 Structural features

The most serious problem of studying ancient trade is the lack of quantitative indices of its volume. Lists of foreign products on sale in fifth-century Athens, or lists of dutiable goods entering the Roman empire, reflect the geographical extent of trade in special cases.[5] But they do not show whether the goods were readily obtainable in the market-place, or what quantities they were traded in.

Some features, however, in ancient Mediterranean civilisation tended to define minimum levels of trading activity.

2.1.1 Large cities which outgrew the productive capacity of their hinterland could only be maintained by transfers of essential foodstuffs from elsewhere. Where such cities existed, trade on a significant scale was likely.

[5] For Athens, Ps.-Xen. *Ath. pol.* 2.7; Dem. 35.35. For Rome, D. 39.4.16.7.

Imperial Rome is a very well known case, but the need for imports clearly existed in other large Mediterranean cities, as it did in the Middle Ages.[6]

2.1.2 Large urban centres also generated significant levels of demand for metals, timber, building-stone and slaves, which if not met locally would be met by imports.[7]

2.1.3 The existence of large cities containing a wealthy elite in its turn implied a demand for luxury goods which typically depended on imports.

2.1.4 The uneven distribution of natural resources meant that almost any city within reasonable access of the sea would sometimes attract imports. For the 'Old Oligarch', writing of the classical Greek world, there was no city which did not have to import or export; and such materials as timber, iron, copper, flax and wax might each have to come from a different place.[8] In the Roman Principate, provincial army garrisons, though not necessarily fed by long-distance, could draw in commercial imports.[9]

2.1.5 Continuous urban needs for imported foodstuffs created estab-lished patterns of voyaging. Thus in the late fourth century BC, the sea-captain Dionysodorus found it more profitable to join the regular trade between Rhodes and Egypt than to fulfil his contract to ship goods back to Athens. Two-way voyaging was almost bound to release some cargo capacity for goods other than staples. Whether or not transporting non-staples was economic in its own right, some long-distance transfer of non-staple goods was likely to continue as long as the economic and organisational capacity needed to import staples was maintained.[10]

2.1.6 Voyaging in the ancient Mediterranean was typically coastal, ships travelling as far as possible in short legs between one major port and the next. As a result, if there were long-distance trade links over a given route, this would often generate some short-distance links as well.

---

[6] Cf. Frazer (1972) 1.165. See also L. Casson *TAPhA* 85 (1954) 168–87. For import of staples to Rome, see Panella (1984). For import to another very big Italian city, see *D.* 19.2.61.1 (a cargo of grain and oil for Aquileia is held up for nine months in Cyrene; Scaevola). For urban grain-import in the Middle Ages, see Abulafia (1987) chapters 6 and 7; a thirteenth-century contract to supply Genoa with Sicilian grain is discussd in Braudel (1972) 1.579–80.

[7] For trade in marble and in slaves see Ward-Perkins (1980), Harris (1980B).

[8] Ps.-Xen. *Ath. pol.* 2.3; 2.11.

[9] For specific evidence of overseas grain-shipments, see Dio 60.24.5; the route in question (Baetica–Mauretania) is very short.

[10] Demosthenes 56; cf. Fraser (1972) 1.164. For discussion of the ratio between imported and local pottery as an index of trading activity, see Fulford (1987).

2.2 Literary evidence

Studying literary references in any depth is not practical here, but Strabo's survey deserves mention, because his work is a source of almost unique importance. Strabo had visited a large part of the Roman world, though not the whole of it, and sometimes speaks from his own experience.[11] His account stands at a junction-point. Some of the details are Roman and as late as the reign of Tiberius, while much else refers back to Hellenistic or pre-Roman conditions. Even when Strabo is up to date, the world that he describes had not yet been changed by centuries of Roman rule.[12]

When not preoccupied with other topics, Strabo (or his sources, Posidonius in particular) seems concerned to single out important centres of trade, and sometimes even to classify them in a rudimentary way. Thus Ephesus is the biggest emporium this side of the Taurus, and Cyzicus has a prodigious number of ship-sheds (more than 200); Apamea is an emporium second in Asia only to Ephesus, and receives many ships from Italy and Greece. Delos was wealthy before Mithridates partly because it stood on the route from Italy and Greece to Asia.[13]

Alexandria's favourable balance of trade can be seen by any observer from the fact that her ships leave Puteoli lighter than they came (presumably no longer weighed down by corn). Again using quayside observations, Strabo writes that the ships from southern Spain are the biggest that put into Puteoli and Ostia, and that they are almost as numerous as those that sail there from North Africa. The fleet of 120 ships that was sailing from Egypt to India the year that Strabo travelled up the Nile (25/4 BC) showed the importance of contemporary trade with the Far East.[14]

Strabo is sometimes concerned with objects of trade. In the west, Aquileia is an emporium for the tribes of the Ister, who import fish, wine in barrels and olive-oil, in exchange for slaves, cattle and hides. Britain, whose trade Strabo, writing before the Roman conquest, reported as already highly profitable to Rome, exports grain, cattle, hides, precious metals, slaves and hunting-dogs, while it imports artefacts of ivory, amber and glass.[15] Luna exports fine marble to Rome, Tibur and Gabiae marble also, and Docimea in Phrygia sends great columns and slabs of Synnadic marble. The fact that Patavium sends so many goods such as clothing to Rome shows its *euandria* and *eutechnia*.[16]

[11] 2.5.11; 13.4.14.
[12] For Strabo and the Roman world, see F. Lasserre *ANRW* 2.30.1 (1982) 867–96. For Strabo's economic descriptions, see R. Baladie *Le Péloponnèse de Strabon* (1980); P.W. Wallace *Strabo's description of Boiotia* (1979).
[13] 14.1.24; 12.8.11; 12.8.15; 10.5.4.   [14] 17.1.7; 3.2.6; 2.5.12.
[15] 5.1.8; 4.5.3–4. Aquileia was the biggest city of Italy according to Herodian (8.2.2). For merchants trading between Britain and Gaul after the conquest, see Chastagnol (1981) and Hassall (1978).
[16] 5.2.5; 5.3.11; 12.8.14; 5.1.7.

Strabo expresses the viewpoint of a monetised society, in that he finds barter worth mentioning. The abstention from money found in Dalmatia is unique in those regions, but common among barbarians in general. In Albania by the Caspian Sea, the inhabitants are believed to live by barter and cannot count past 100. In the interior of Lusitania, people use barter or bits of silver to make their exchanges.[17]

Although Strabo's economic coverage is intermittent and geographically uneven, his local economic bulletins almost always provide valuable evidence. They are not accompanied by any overview of the relative importance of trade and agriculture in the Mediterranean economy. The residual assumptions of an educated class with agrarian expectations emerge when Strabo writes that the Massiliotes took to the sea because their territory was agriculturally poor. What Strabo says is generally consistent with there being a string of urban economies which could only be serviced by trading activity. To this extent, his scattered references are consistent with a world in which the existence of sea-borne trade could be taken for granted. Though navigable rivers served almost the same function as the sea (the Massiliotes grew rich on the tolls from the Rhone granted them by Marius), there is little in Strabo's work to suggest that inland regions away from rivers were often accessible to long-distance trade.[18]

2.3 Archaeology

Pottery can survive thousands of years under the ground or under the sea. Because it survives so plentifully, imported pottery can be used to trace the location and date of trade patterns. Where storage-vessels are concerned, these inferences can face difficulties, because the contents that were shipped did not always come from the same places as the containers. Alexandria's wine was mainly grown at Laodicea in Syria (from Strabo's categorical statement). But this is not reflected in finds of Laodicean amphorae amongst the vast accumulation at Alexandria, largely made up of Rhodian amphorae. Nevertheless Strabo certainly knew Alexandria at first hand. Therefore the likelihood is that Laodicean wine, through Laodicea's commercial links with Rhodes, travelled in the Rhodian amphorae which predominate at Alexandria.[19] Papyrus records indicating that goods from Asia and the Aegean came to Egypt from Syria, not direct, again show that written evidence can reveal important facts about trade which physical remains by themselves will not necessarily convey.[20]

Other potential difficulties in reading trade patterns from pottery arise when there are contradictions between different samples. For example, there are

---

[17] 7.5.5; 11.4.4.; 3.3.7.   [18] 4.1.5; 4.1.8.
[19] Strabo 16.2.9; Fraser (1972) 1.167; cf. J. Davies *CAH²* 7.1.274. For amphorae whose source was different from the source of their contents, see also Paterson (1982) 154–5.
[20] Fraser (1972) 1.150, n.24; 259 BC.

serious differences between the importance of imports of African olive-oil suggested in finds in Rome, and that implied in finds at Ostia, the port of Rome. Mediterranean amphorae of the early Principate found in Britain are typically different from those found on the Rhine, although this was the likely supply-route to Britain.[21]

Because it is abnormally resistant to destruction, pottery is not a secure indicator of trading volume. Even large-scale pottery remains if accumulated over centuries do not necessarily show that trade-volume was large in any given year.[22] And the exchange to which imported pottery belonged seems often to have been ancillary to exchanges of which no archaeological trace survives. Wine-amphorae could certainly represent a major cargo. But not all wine travelled in amphorae, and that tends to create gaps of unknown size in the archaeological record even here.[23] Large concentrations of imported pottery need not in fact show any significant primary trade in artefacts which could have been sustained without an accompanying trade in staples. Nevertheless, archaeological evidence is virtually unique in its ability to reveal patterns of long-distance trade (see chapter 3).

2.4 The historical context

Sea-borne trade was already an active feature of the Mediterranean economy in archaic times, as the growing number of wreck-finds clearly shows. But in this section, the limited intention is to look briefly at immediate precursors of Rome. Rome was one of a succession of powers which dominated the Mediterranean. Before her in the East were the Persians and the Hellenistic kings. Before Rome in the West were Carthage, the Etruscans and the Greek states in Sicily. Mediterranean trade was certainly vigorous under both Greeks and Phoenicians. While Rome was the first to control both East and West, very long mercantile traditions already existed in the world that Rome conquered.

2.4.1 **Carthage** Accounts from Carthage do not survive, but such tradition as exists clearly shows Carthage as very wealthy, and wealthy by reason of trade. In Pliny's list of inventions, the Phoenicians were the discoverers of trade (*mercatura*) and for Strabo they were the greatest of all sailors.[24] Diodorus using Timaeus writes that the Phoenicians voyaged continuously for reasons of trade, and became very rich as a result. Thucydides describes one of the Syracusans as invoking Carthaginian aid against Athens, saying that Carthage

---

[21] Panella (1984) 182; (1981) 77.

[22] Cf. French (1964) 190, n. 1. Monte Testaccio (cf. Peacock–Williams (1986) 4; 13) is an exception, but conditions in Rome, fed partly by tax-grain and tax-oil, cannot be generalised.

[23] For wine-shipment in barrels, see e.g. Strabo 5.1.8; 5.1.12; Herodian 8.4.4. See also Peacock (1978) 51 and Tchernia (1986) 138; 285 (cf. Pucci (1983) 115). [24] *NH* 7.199; Strabo 16.2.23.

has much gold and silver. Before her destruction Carthage was called the richest city in the world.[25]

Besides war-fleets, Carthage of course had a great many merchant-ships. Late in the Second Punic War, as many as 100 merchant-ships were sent to Italy in an abortive attempt to aid Hannibal.[26] The docks at Carthage had 220 ship-berths, a number almost paralleled at Cyzicus in the Black Sea, but at very few other ports.[27]

Carthage was the first Mediterranean power to voyage past the Straits of Gibraltar, and the trading zones which Carthage discovered she kept for herself. The celebrated story of the Carthaginian captain on his way to the Cassiterides who drove his ship on to the rocks rather than let the Roman ship behind find out where he was going, is directly echoed in the way that Carthage apparently excluded the Etruscans from the big island that she discovered in the Atlantic.[28] Gsell also saw Herodotus's effective ignorance of north Africa west of Carthage as a sign that the Greeks on whom Herodotus depended for his information were kept out of the western Mediterranean.[29]

The clearest evidence for private trading zones is the early treaties between Carthage and Rome. These explicitly lay down a dividing-line within the Mediterranean which the Romans may not cross for purposes of trade or settlement. Carthage debarred Rome from trading in Sardinia and Libya, but allowed trade on equal terms in Sicily, Carthage and Rome. But at some point a trading agreement with the Etruscans gave equal trading rights to Carthaginians and Etruscans alike.[30]

The standing of Carthage as a trading power is reflected in other evidence. By the end of the fifth century, Agrigentum on the south coast of Sicily had grown rich by supplying Carthage with wine.[31] Later, Carthage was importing much wine from or through Rhodes in the eastern Mediterranean.[32] Diodorus mentions the big commercial presence of Carthage in Syracuse. And Strabo writes of Carthaginians trading wine for silphium at their emporium in the Greater Syrtes.[33]

It is very difficult to say whether Rome took over the trading network owned by Carthage (other big Punic cities such as Utica were potential beneficiaries from her fall). But the markets served by Carthage largely survived, and the late Republic seems to have been a time of commercial expansion in the Roman world, not one of commercial atrophy (cf. chapter 1, n.47).

---

[25] Diod. 5.20.1; Thuc. 6.34.2; Polyb. 18.35.   [26] Appian *Hannib.* 549.
[27] Appian *Lib.* 96; Strabo 12.8.11.   [28] Strabo 3.5.11; Diod. 5.20.
[29] Gsell (1913–1930) 4.117. For the archaeology of Punic trade, see Gill (1988).
[30] Polyb. 3.22–24; Arist. *Pol.* 3.9.   [31] Diod. 13.81.4–5.   [32] Gsell (1913–1930) 4.153–4.
[33] Diod. 14.46.1 (398 BC); Strabo 17.3.20.

2.4.2 **The East before Rome** An effective overview of trade in the
Hellenistic world still seems to lie in the future.[34] What is clear are the signs of
great wealth in the eastern Mediterranean, some of it wealth from trade. Richest
of the Hellenistic kingdoms was probably Egypt. Egypt was where Carthage
turned for a loan at the time of the First Punic War, attempting to borrow 2,000
talents, and where Rome also turned for supplies when deprived of Italian grain
by Hannibal.[35] The East contained states whose prosperity was directly linked to
trade, such as Rhodes and Palmyra. Much of the trade of the eastern
Mediterranean depended on an axis of which Rhodes and Alexandria, and to a
lesser extent Delos and Syrian Antioch, were focal points.

Rhodes in the early Hellenistic period was said to owe her wealth to trade links
with Egypt; for example, the Laodicean wine which the upper classes in
Alexandria drank for preference was evidently shipped in Rhodian containers.[36]
By the second century BC, though her trade with Alexandria remained vigorous,
Rhodes was evidently in decline, with a trade shrinkage reflected in a fall in her
harbour-dues from four million to 600,000 sesterces per year as a result of the
opening of Delos as a free port in 167 BC. But in the first century, Rhodes still
yielded Cassius nearly 200 million sesterces (8,500 talents), representing
enormous assets for a city state.[37] Even lesser Greek maritime states still had very
substantial resources. By squeezing them to the utmost limits, Mithridates
obtained HS48 million from Chios, and Cassius HS36 million from Tarsus.[38]

The trade passing through Rhodes in her heyday was obviously very great. If
Rhodian customs duty was 2%, as generally assumed by analogy with practice in
other Greek states, and if the trade was mainly entrepot trade, as the Rhodian
complaint about Delos implies, its value would be about HS100 million sesterces
per year, even if duty was paid both on entry and on departure.[39] Trade volume
at Delos in the early third century BC was apparently of the order of HS1 million
per year, not in any way comparable with the Rhodian figure, though still not
insignificant.[40] Customs-dues lay at the heart of taxation in Greek states: when
Rhodes herself was damaged by an earthquake in 226—7 BC, two of the states
which helped her did so by exempting Rhodians from their customs-dues.[41] Any
Greek state which allowed centuries to pass before it levied customs-dues made
itself a laughing-stock,[42] obviously reflecting the important place of international
trade in the economy of the eastern Mediterranean.

---

[34] J. Davies *CAH²* 7.1.260–4, pointing out some limitations in Rostovtzeff's large-scale survey of half a century ago. For the Hellenistic grain-trade, see Rathbone (1982).
[35] Appian *Sic.* 1; Polyb. 9.11a (Fraser (1972) 1.152, 155).   [36] Diod. 20.81.4; see above at n.19.
[37] Trade with Alexandria: Fraser (1972) 1.164. Harbour-dues: Polybius 30.31 with Walbank *Commentary* 3.459–60. Cassius: Plut. *Brut.* 32.   [38] Appian *Mith.* 47; BC 4.64.
[39] For double duty, note Strabo's evidence for Egypt (17.1.13).
[40] Larsen *ESAR* 4.354–5.   [41] Thuc. 7.28.4. Polyb. 5.88–90.   [42] Strabo 13.3.6.

3 Regional coin-deposits and their implications

The illustration put forward in support of the Hopkins model uses a graph showing the dating concentrations of denarii minted in AD 40–260 found in different parts of the empire, based on publications of coin-hoards and stray finds. Shown logarithmically, the lines for different regions generally move in step for most of the period. This is taken as an indication that 'the whole Roman Empire was integrated into a single monetary economy'.[43]

3.1 Empirical problems

The argument would suggest that, if the empire were *not* integrated in monetary terms, chronological representation of the silver coin-issue would differ from region to region. If representation does not differ, or does not differ markedly, that should show integration.

Whether or not trade was the only process by which a homogeneous distribution might be achieved, as the model assumes, the method overlooks an empirical weakness. Most sizeable samples of coin in circulation will be cross-sections of coin issued over a long period, as is true of the typical Roman silver-hoard of the second century. Consequently, even if inflow of coin to a given area was in fact irregular, its irregularities will tend to be masked by the fact that what came in was already a cross-section spread over a long period of production.

3.1.1 Equally important is the fact that chronological concentrations within coin-finds provide no *quantitative* index of monetisation. If some areas were relatively under-monetised, chronological patterns as such will hardly show this.

Moreover, the extent of regional monetisation cannot be measured by the incidence of hoards (still less by stray coin-finds, since these often go unrecorded). Hoard-survival is affected by non-economic factors, and in the Principate it tends if anything to be inverse to the degree of local monetisation. Silver-hoards are common in 'insecure' and heavily garrisoned frontier regions such as Britain and the Danube, but rare in 'secure' and less militarised regions such as Africa and Spain.

3.1.2 The areas on which the diagram is based are mainly 'military' regions of the empire, whose access to specie is likely to have depended more on the transmission of army pay than on anything else (Germany, Britain and Gaul, the Balkans, Dura-Europos). The one clear exception, coin-finds from northern Italy, does not come from a province.

[43] Hopkins (1980) 112.

3.1.3 Aggregating the contents of many hoards into one creates erratic results, because hoards buried at different dates have different chronological profiles, as a result of coin-wastage. Wastage means that coin of Trajan, for example, forms a substantially larger part of hoards buried in AD 150 than it does of hoards buried in 195 or 230.[44] Because hoard burial-dates vary so widely, this effect creates internal distortions in the overall chronology that aggregated samples will show. Hence, even profiles based on hoards buried at a series of different dates which agreed with each other fully would not necessarily demonstrate real uniformity of circulation. And uniformity in itself would support the model only where the samples were clearly free from the effects of army payments.

3.1.4 The denarius was not a universal currency. Separate silver currencies were produced in Egypt and Asia. These do not appear to have travelled outside the provinces to which they belonged, to any noticeable extent, and they seem not to have been legal tender outside the province.[45] Cicero's profits of HS2.2 million as governor of Cilicia remained on deposit in Asia for at least a year. The sum was in local *cistophoroi*, which may have been a reason for its not being repatriated at once. Getting use of the money involved a 'permutatio' or currency-conversion.[46]

3.2 Regional coin-find evidence

More detailed analysis of regional finds of denarii suggests, in contrast to what the model argues, that under the Principate coin-populations in different parts of the empire possessed characteristics of their own, and that trade-flows were not such that these characteristics were erased.[47] This observation undermines the diagram-based argument, and it means that even if the regions utilised in the diagram were more representative of non-military areas, general similarities of chronology would not have the significance suggested.

[44] See for example Bolin (1958) 53, Table 3.
[45] Milne (1933) xvi; Christiansen (1988) 1.11; Broughton *ESAR* 4.882ff.; Burnett (1987) 87.
[46] *ad Att.* 11.1–2 = Shackleton Bailey 211–12, with editor's comments; *ad fam.* 5.20.
[47] Argued more fully in Duncan-Jones (1989B). As far as the choice of samples is concerned, there is little reason to think *a priori* that any one component of the range of types issued by the Rome mint will provide a better 'marker' than any other component. Examples using coin minted for particular individuals are chosen here solely because their details can often be extracted from hoard-publications even when the types have not been listed. Fully published hoards are still only a small minority, and large hoards which did not receive scholarly analysis at the time of discovery have frequently been dispersed, preventing any future analysis. For findings using fully published hoards, based on more detailed inferences from a smaller body of material, see Table 11 and Duncan-Jones (1989B).

Some straightforward examples can be stated briefly. These show on the one hand, coin-issues whose representation is relatively consistent in most areas; and on the other, coin-issues whose representation is subject to major geographical anomalies. The undoubted existence of both phenomena argues that the configuration must reflect patterns in the transmission of new coin, and that the mint's procedures caused some issues to be distributed evenly, and others much less evenly.[48]

3.2.1 An example of relatively even distribution is provided by the denarii of Sabina, Hadrian's empress, whose coinage belongs to the second half of his reign. We can relate the Sabina denarii to those struck for Hadrian, and express the denarii of Sabina as a percentage of the denarii in Hadrian's name. In an assemblage of 20 hoards each with a minimum of 100 coins of this reign, the coefficient Sabina/Hadrian shows a heavy concentration within the range 5% to 8% (Appendix 1). In 18 out of 20 hoards in this first assemblage, the coefficient falls within this range. The hoards in question are widely distributed: they include five from Britain, two from Germany, one from Gaul, two from Italy, one from Cyprus, one from Syria and a number from parts of the Balkans and eastern Europe.

In this assemblage, the distribution is relatively homogeneous (the mean and median averages are both 6%, the standard deviation 1.4). But in three further hoards making up an assemblage from a part of the empire not considered so far, the Black Sea, the result is completely different. Values for the Sabina/Hadrian coefficient here range from 11% to 17–18%. Two of the hoards are from lower Moesia, and one from east Dacia (Appendix 1). The median of 17% here is almost three times the median of 6% in the first assemblage, though that was drawn from a far wider area. The pattern found in most of the hoards is relatively consistent, but the extreme contrast found in one region argues a clear discontinuity in the transmission of new denarii to the provinces in the second half of Hadrian's reign.

3.2.2 The second example again suggests a norm, to which one part of the empire shows a clear exception. Denarii struck for 'Divus Marcus' by Commodus soon after his father's death, are equal to 8–12% of the total for denarii struck for Commodus himself, in an assemblage of eight hoards from Syria, Moesia, Poland and Dacia. But two hoards from Britain and Gaul give a completely different result, showing a quotient of 1% or even less (Appendix 1). The anomaly suggests a straightforward difference in distribution, whereby in

---

[48] For possible reasons see Duncan-Jones (1989B). Though it does not affect the present argument, if current orthodoxy should be wrong in thinking that Antonine denarii all came from one mint, some of the contrasts noted below could result from separation of mints.

north-west Europe percentage representation of the 'Divus Marcus' issue was only a small fraction of what it was in coin-populations further east.

3.2.3 Regional differences emerge even more strongly in the small issues struck late in Trajan's reign for Marciana and Matidia (with the same sample-threshold as before).[49] There is again a noticeable contrast here between East and West. In four hoards from north-west Europe containing over 600 denarii of Trajan's reign in all, no example of either issue occurs. And in three Italian hoards, representing over 1,900 denarii of Trajan, there is only one coin from this pair of issues. But in eastern Europe two out of five hoard-samples show examples of one or other issue. And in the Black Sea both available hoards contain examples, as do hoards from Syria and Egypt. In Syria and Egypt the find-rate is one coin of Marciana or Matidia for 150 coins of Trajan. In Italy the find-rate is only one for 1,900 coins of Trajan, and in the substantial samples from Britain and Gaul, the issues are missing altogether.

3.2.4 It is obvious that coins struck for Marciana and Matidia were relatively few, probably 1% of Trajanic denarius-output or less. But striking regional differences can also be seen in the mainstream coin-issues struck for Trajan himself. Six large hoards, for which detailed type-inventories are available, show a strongly contrasting pattern for a large issue struck in Trajan's name (*RIC* 147; shown as a percentage of denarii of Trajan's reign; hoard-locations are listed from East to West; see Appendix 1). The results show the relative importance of this issue in the West as approximately twice that in the East.

Table 11. *Representation of Trajan RIC 147 in different hoards*

Region	Percentage of denarii of Trajan	Location (see Appendix 1)
Syria	1.3	'Tell Kalak'
Lower Moesia	0.8	Reka-Devnia
Dacia	1.8	La Magura
Rhineland	3.3	Stockstadt
Britain (I)	3.3	Bristol
Britain (II)	4.0	Londonthorpe

3.2.5 The present regional differences reflect what were almost certainly discontinuities in the distribution of new coin from the central mint.

[49] Appendix 1 (C). For their coin-types, see Temporini (1978) 190–4.

Their importance here is that they imply that significant differences existed between regional coin-populations of the Principate, and that these differences were not erased by inter-regional exchange.

4 Monetary equilibrium and trade

4.1 Preliminary approach

Where inter-regional trading took place, this did not necessarily generate money-flows between regions on any scale commensurate with the volume of trade. Maximising the proceeds of maritime trade meant loading a ship with cargo on each leg of her journey, to be sold profitably at a later port of call. The second-century trading contract which Scaevola cites shows a two-way traffic in cargo, not in coin. The shipper borrows money with which to buy a cargo in Berytus.[50] He does so on condition that he will buy other cargo at his destination in Italy, and then repay the loan when he gets back to Beirut, after selling his second cargo. Money changes hands in Beirut when the loan is made and the first cargo is bought. Money will change hands again in Brindisi when the original cargo is sold, and when the second cargo is purchased. But the coin itself appears not to travel, since the money used in Beirut stays in Beirut, and the money used in Brindisi stays in Brindisi.

This is not to say that coin did not travel by sea commercially. We can see for example a commercial outflow of coin, particularly gold coin beyond the eastern frontier (n. 54). But it does not seem that inter-regional trading generally had as either its aim or its result significant transfers of specie. In so far as coin did percolate from one region to another through trade, its diffusion over long distances is likely to have been slow and relatively small-scale.

4.2 Development zones

There is an important limitation in what the model implies. The process of change envisaged is not that of fructifying underdeveloped parts of the empire. Instead, its logical result is that of promoting development in areas which were already relatively developed. The frontier provinces of the empire in which Rome's armies were mainly stationed (such as the Rhine, the Danube and Britain) were typically less urbanised and less wealthy. But their role in the model, since they housed armies paid in cash, is seen as that of market for goods which the wealthier 'civilian' provinces now exported in order to generate cash with which to pay their taxes. Similarly, the role of the 'civilian' provinces, whose larger tax-revenues presumably imply that they already produced a substantial surplus, is seen for the purposes of the model as being that of increasing production still further in order to generate money income from outside.

[50] *D.* 45.1.122.1.

4.2.1 When looked at individually, important areas of the empire do not seem to fit the premisses of the model. A prime case is that of Syria, the station of one of the largest provincial armies, but wealthy in its own right, containing cities whose splendour was almost proverbial, and set on a major trade-route. It is unlikely that Syria was starved of specie, and for this reason Syria is difficult to fit into a model in which 'military' provinces depend for coin on tax-revenues from elsewhere. In fact Syria almost certainly accounted for much of the extra 140 million sesterces added to Rome's annual revenues by Pompey.[51]

Not only Syria but other large parts of the Hellenised East, which seems always to have formed the wealthier half of the empire, already had a long history of large-scale urbanisation, and of the access to trade-based supplies that this usually implied (cf. section 2.1 above). When Vespasian held the East and Vitellius the West, Vespasian was said to be in a position to bring Vitellius to his knees by denying him Egyptian corn, and the 'vectigalia opulentissimarum provinciarum'.[52]

It is possible that the provinces whose state of development meant that they had larger tax-revenues were already, like Syria, commercially active, and that existing commercial activity was sufficient to offset any outflow of money paid as tax. Before the Principate, Cicero already said that Asia exceeded all other regions in her agriculture, her pastures and in her exports.[53]

4.3 How were monetary imbalances corrected?
If the model's trade-based mechanism cannot be sustained, the question still remains of how the available monetary stock was deployed so as to pay armies spread along the periphery, without denuding the interior of the empire of specie.

This has two main aspects. The first is, how did the government obtain enough specie? The second is, how was market liquidity maintained?.

4.3.1 Was the monetary system efficient in practice? The drain of precious metal out beyond the frontiers, seen in Pliny's statements about eastern trade, in the subsidies increasingly paid to frontier tribes and in the frequent monetary finds beyond the northern frontiers, shows no obvious regard for optimal deployment of bullion resources.[54]

It would be in keeping with this if long-term differences in regional liquidity were not always eradicated. Gaius writes of the chronic differences in interest-rates and in prices that exist within the empire from region to region. The

---

[51] Broughton in Frank vol.4 (1938) 4.565; Plut. *Pomp*. 45. For Śyria, cf. *CERP²* chapter 10.
[52] Tac. *Hist*. 3.8.   [53] *pro lege Man*. 14.
[54] Eastern trade: Pliny *NH* 12.84; 6.101. Subsidies: see e.g. Dio 71.12.1–2; 78.17.3; cf. 72.19.1; Jones (1974) 79. Coin-finds across the frontier: Crawford (1977); Wielowiejski (1980); Kolendo (1980).

underlying reality could be a cellular economy in which monetary anomalies were relieved only to a limited extent by fiscal or market mechanisms. The circulation-speed of Roman coin was much lower than any seen in coin of comparable size in recent periods.[55]

It is quite possible that the government was only partly effective in recovering coin paid out, and depended (because of inefficiency in the circulation-system, as well as because of normal coin-wastage) on a continuing input of 'new' metal, from mines or from private owners, to maintain its primary spending commitment to the army. Debasement of the silver coinage was likely to indicate that bullion supplies were short.

4.3.2 The army was not always paid in full, and not all payments were made in cash:

(A) There were very heavy clawbacks for food, clothing, etc. illustrated in surviving financial statements of soldiers serving in Egypt in the first century which show the soldier as retaining in cash less than half the payment nominally due to him (there was also a compulsory savings scheme). The amount of the deductions appears to over-represent their true cost, which may also have been offset by requisition.[56]

(B) Soldiers might potentially remain in the army well beyond their legal period of service at times when the government found difficulty in funding their discharge bonuses.[57]

(C) Army numbers were apparently allowed to dwindle under peacetime conditions, and mobilising the standing army for war generally seems to have meant an energetic recruiting-drive.[58] This policy effectively reduced outgoings on army pay.

This suggests a system that was in different ways prone to very wide variation and deterioration, whose overall tendency was to reduce the size of cash outgoings.

4.3.3 Pannonia and Syria were taxed in money (chapter 12) and taxation in money was possibly a general pattern in provinces which contained major garrisons.[59]

---

[55] Gaius D. 13.4.3; see also ERE[2] 134, n. 1. For the different circulation-speeds of gold, silver and bronze coin as measured by the rate of weight-loss, comparing Roman with later evidence, see Duncan-Jones (1989A).

[56] PGen Lat 1, etc. (cf. Watson (1969) 102–4; Speidel (1973)). Cf. also Pékary (1980) 106.

[57] Tac. Ann. 1.17.   [58] Brunt (1974).

[59] The vast sum said to have been lent in Britain by Seneca soon after the conquest may imply that as a Roman province, Britain had large-scale tax obligations in money (Dio 62.2.1).

4.3.4 Some government cash needs were met by indirect taxes collected in money (chapter 12, section 6), and probably by taxes in kind which were converted into cash in markets where there was enough liquidity to make that possible (chapter 12, section 5).

4.3.5 Recycling of silver currency from a central point does not seem to be confirmed by the numismatic evidence (3.2 above). Their regional peculiarities argue that local coin-populations remained separate from each other, and that any recycling of silver coin must have taken place at provincial rather than national level (cf. 4.3.3).[60] Input of coin to the provinces from outside would still have been necessary, to replace coin which disappeared from circulation through wastage and through normal inertia in the exchange system.

4.3.6 Any realistic view of currency transfers within the empire must take gold into account as well as silver. Silver was apparently the preferred means of payment in Republican Rome (chapter 12, n. 63); but under the Principate, when the empire possessed an abundant gold currency (cf. n. 62), long-distance money-shipments may often have been in gold, which was much lighter than silver, value for value. Roman authors however rarely give any details of payments. (Among exceptions are Plutarch's account of how the younger Cato shipped 7,000 talents from Cyprus to Rome, with cork marker-buoys on board in case the ship went down; his mention of treasure-ships sailing from Asia to Greece encountered by Brutus; and Caesar's description of Pompey's preparations for his final voyage, when he took on board a great weight of bronze coin for army pay, seized from the tax-farmers in Syria.)[61]

The relative infrequency of gold-hoards is not a good index of the importance of gold coin. At Pompeii, which provides by far the most important evidence not mediated by normal mechanisms of loss or 'hoarding', gold in terms of value accounts for about two-thirds of the coin found.[62] If, as is likely, large-scale monetary transfers often took place in gold, no positive confirmation is likely to emerge, because of the shortage of large-scale gold-finds.

5 Summary and conclusions

If inter-regional trade did increase under the Principate, it is doubtful whether stimulus from money-taxes was the cause. There are three immediate reasons:
(i) The extent to which direct taxes were levied in money seems to have been

---

[60] This is discussed more fully in Duncan-Jones (1989B).
[61] Plut. *Brut.* 24.3; *Cat. Min.* 38.1; Caes. *BC* 3.103.
[62] This emerges from analysis of the find-evidence tabulated by Breglia (1950).

limited (chapters 12 and 13). Though much remains obscure, the policy governing the format of provincial taxation is likely in general to have been conservative and pragmatic, rather than one whose innovations would exacerbate coin-shortage.

(ii) Regional samples of centrally minted coin retained distinct characteristics to an extent which undermines the claim that their composition reflects and was significantly determined by the action of inter-regional trade (section 3).

(iii) The mechanisms of long-distance trade did not necessarily create long-distance money-flows (section 4).

There are also difficulties of 'fit' between the model and the historical evidence. The premisses seem inapplicable to important areas of the empire in the East. And the areas in which the model posits growth are those which were already by Roman standards relatively developed, not those which were less developed.

In any case, the evidence for extensive trade in the Mediterranean in earlier periods (section 2.4) is so clear that, in the new conditions of peace that now existed throughout the Mediterranean, commercial stagnation would be much more surprising than commercial growth. Even so, the strongest motive forces behind growth in long-distance trade under the Principate often seem to have been governmental or official, the need to feed cities which grew both in size and in privilege, the need to ship tax-grain and tax-oil, and the need to supply a large and widely dispersed army.[63]

Unlike (say) Punic society, or Florentine society in the Renaissance, Roman society remained one with heavy ostensible prejudices against trade and traders.[64] A society in which senators were forbidden to own ships, and shopkeepers were admitted to the town council only if *honesti viri* were in short supply, was one which tried hard to separate involvement in trade from social position.[65] The persistence of these taboos does not suggest that they were there merely to be broken.

Trading fortunes built up in one generation seem to have been invested elsewhere or become submerged by the next.[66] The fact that even in the vital *annona* trade, positive discrimination was needed in order to maintain an adequate supply of large-scale shippers suggests a restricted scale of shipping operations in the free market.[67] Although lending money as an investment retained the utmost importance in Roman society, the effective silence of the

---

[63] Cf. Whittaker (1985) 56–7.   [64] For traders in the Roman East, cf. Pleket (1983).

[65] Livy 21.63.3, cf. Dio 56.27.3; D. 50.2.12.

[66] The freedmen's sons who were a characteristic feature of Italian town councils (Garnsey (1975)) had presumably given up any involvement in trade for activities which were more socially acceptable (cf. note 65). Dio Chrysostom's father seems to have been in effect a large-scale moneylender, but the son was a landed gentleman (*Or.* 46.5; 8; cf. Jones (1978) 6–7; 23–4).

[67] D. 50.5.3; Suet. *Claud.* 18.3–4; Gaius 1.32 (Garnsey (1988) 233–4).

evidence leaves it doubtful whether the very rich, who controlled a large part of all liquid resources, sought to invest in trade.[68] If they refrained, the governing reason may have been as much prudential (the hazards of voyaging) as social.[69] Market mechanisms sufficient to satisfy major needs certainly existed, but there is little to suggest that commercial success engendered the large operating-units seen in much later societies.

[68] D'Arms (1981) argues for commercial involvement of senators, but cf. Paterson (1982) 154, and Duncan-Jones *TLS* 81 (1982) 321. It is obvious that Plutarch found involvement in shipping-loans and other forms of business enterprise worth including in his account of Cato the elder because it was so atypical of what the Roman aristocracy did with its money (21.6). For the enormous size of some Roman fortunes, see *ERE*[2] Appendix 7.

[69] Sea-transport was considered so uncertain that Fronto could cite the danger of loss through shipwreck as a reason for not allowing wills from the provinces to be adjudicated at Rome (in a speech to the Senate; *ad M. Ant.* 1.6.5).

3
Separation and cohesion in Mediterranean trade

1 Evidence from Roman lamps

Signed Roman lamps ('Firmalampen') show some of the ways in which archaeology can increase our knowledge of trade. Their usefulness here is as a commercial artefact whose large numbers show identifiable distribution patterns. The patterns tend to suggest trading regions within the Mediterranean, divided by discernible boundaries. The boundaries imply restricted sailing patterns, and commercial zones which were more or less distinct from each other.

Pottery lamps, because they supplied household lighting by burning oil, were a standard artefact in the Roman world. Lamps produced in the western Mediterranean during the Principate survive in thousands. While many carry inventive pictorial designs, a large number are plain lamps whose main identification is a maker's name. The number of known signatures is roughly 2,000, a few being so common that they resemble modern trade marks.[1] Frequency-counts for a number of marques were published by Harris in an important study in 1980; present indebtedness to his survey will be obvious. This discussion utilises Harris's figures, analysing some of them in greater detail.[2]

There are serious uncertainties about how lamps of a particular marque achieved wide diffusion. At least four possibilities have been envisaged:

(1) Long-distance export from a central production point.

(2) Production in secondary areas under licence.

(3) Unlicensed production in secondary areas (pirating).

(4) Production in more than one area by lamp-makers who moved from one place to another.

The lack of sure information about where given specimens came from leaves these difficulties partly unresolved. In many cases, neither style, nor size nor fabric seems to offer a secure route to establishing where a particular lamp was

---

[1] Cf. Harris (1980A) 129.

[2] Harris (1980A). Some figures are partly provisional in cases where recorded holdings may have been affected by museum purchases from elsewhere. Some of Harris's totals for 'African' marques are significantly increased by Procaccini (1981). But in the regional samples chosen here for a highly generalised analysis, Harris's totals appear sufficiently large, and their patterns sufficiently coherent to warrant direct consideration.

produced.[3] Nevertheless, possibilities (3) and (4) are not convincing as prime explanations. Even if pirating could readily take place in a society without effective copyright, the organisation needed to flood different markets on the scale seen here does not seem consistent with operations which were mainly clandestine. Similarly, the evidence for diffusion over wide areas, and for large-scale production, is too strong to be convincingly explained by hypotheses about migrating potters who carried their trade marks with them. On the hypothesis that one in 10,000 of the lamps ever made has been recovered, which may still be optimistic, production would have run to several million lamps for the largest marque alone.

This leaves (1) and (2) as the main possibilities, that is, export of lamps, or export of designs leading to local production under licence. Local production in the provinces of 'standard' marques originating in Italy is an undoubted fact, shown most clearly by the number of lamp-moulds for 'Firmalampen' found in Pannonia.[4] But it is equally certain from underwater finds that the lamps themselves could be exported overseas in large quantities.[5] Harris concluded that localised production was the main explanation behind the wide diffusion of marques, and argued convincingly that Roman commercial organisation did allow for 'branch' manufacture. He discounts the possibility of significant export of the lamps themselves, on the ground that lamps were too cheap to be economic as a long-distance export.[6]

Though this argument has some force, it allows too little for the fact that a structure of trading voyages already existed within the Mediterranean, and for the fact that lamps occupied little cargo space. The point at which small goods like lamps became too cheap to be exported is not at all clear. Ten lamps would occupy not significantly more (possibly less) space than a modius of wheat (8.62 litres). Even at the low price of 1 as per lamp, cited by Harris from rather uncertain evidence, they would not be worth much less than a modius of wheat, which could cost roughly 10 asses, or HS2.5 in producing areas.[7]

Traders whose ships carried foodstuffs in one direction still needed goods for the return voyage, and could not necessarily fill their holds with high-priced luxury goods.[8] Modest African table-ware seems to have conquered the markets of much of the Roman world by late antiquity.[9] The fact that they were low-priced would probably have prevented lamps (and cheap table-ware) from ever

[3] Cf. Bailey (1980) 89–90; Harris (1980A) 136–7.   [4] Harris (1980A) 135.

[5] Bailey (1980) 92–3. Examination of the fabric by neutron activation analysis has now produced further positive evidence that lamps could travel considerable distances within the Mediterranean (M.J. Hughes in Bailey (1988) 483; the examples here belong to the East).

[6] Harris (1980A) 134.

[7] Harris (1980A) 136; *ERE*[2] 51. Now see also Bailey (1987). For some space-calculations for Greek lamps, see Gill (1987) 122.   [8] Cf. Harris (1980A) 136.

[9] Cf. Carandini (1983) and Fulford (1984).

Table 12. *Distribution of signed lamps*
(A) *Selected regional samples*

Region		Marques								
	ATIM	CRES	FORT	PHOE	STRO	VIB	CCLO	CIUN	COPP	IUNI
Vindonissa	17	—	49	11	15	—	—	—	—	—
Lauriacum	—	64	18	—	1	31	—	—	—	—
Dacia	9	9	168	—	30	1	—	—	—	—
Pannonia	50	258	541	5	37	98	1	—	—	—
Switzerland	17	2	67	17	32	2	—	—	—	—
Dalmatian coast	36	80	229	16	41	76	—	—	—	—
Aquileia	53	155	342	10	36	180	—	—	—	—
N. Italy	130	238	676	34	120	288	9	3	13	2
Germany/3 Gauls	67	8	347	19	108	15	8	6	27	5
Gallia Narbonensis	9	7	50	11	23	5	6	6	15	1
N. Africa	—	1	4	—	2	—	172	155	189	117

Note: The small samples for Carthage, Sabratha and Mauretania Tingitana reported separately by Harris have been included in the aggregate totals for N. Africa shown here.

(B) *Percentage distribution*

Region		Marques								
	ATIM	CRES	FORT	PHOE	STRO	VIB	CCLO	CIUN	COPP	IUNI
Vindonissa	18.5	—	53.3	12.0	16.3	—	—	—	—	—
Lauriacum	—	56.1	15.8	—	0.9	27.1	—	—	—	—
Dacia	4.1	4.1	77.4	—	13.8	0.5	—	—	—	—
Pannonia	5.1	26.1	54.7	0.5	3.7	9.8	—	—	—	—
Switzerland	12.4	1.5	48.9	12.4	23.4	1.5	—	—	—	—
Dalmatian coast	7.5	16.7	47.9	3.3	8.6	15.4	—	—	—	—
Aquileia	6.8	20.0	44.1	1.3	4.6	23.2	—	—	—	—
N. Italy	8.6	15.7	44.7	2.2	7.9	19.0	0.6	0.2	0.9	0.1
Germany/3 Gauls	11.0	1.3	56.9	3.1	17.7	2.5	1.3	1.0	4.4	0.8
Gallia Narbonensis	6.8	5.3	37.6	8.3	17.3	3.8	4.5	4.5	11.3	0.8
N. Africa	—	0.2	0.6	—	0.3	—	26.9	24.2	29.5	18.3

Table 13. Spearman correlations between distribution of six signed lamp-marques in ten regions north of the Mediterranean

Region	Switzerland	Vindonissa	Lauriacum	Dacia	Narbonensis	Germany/Gaul	N. Italy	Pannonia	Dalmatia	Aquileia
Switzerland	1.00	0.896	−0.45	0.687	0.971	0.971	0.000	0.000	0.088	0.000
Vindonissa	0.896	1.00	−0.53	0.662	0.812	0.928	0.116	0.116	0.058	0.116
Lauriacum	−0.45	−0.53	1.00	0.191	−0.41	−0.46	0.667	0.725	0.812	0.667
Dacia	0.687	0.662	0.191	1.00	0.638	0.696	0.464	0.551	0.638	0.464
Narbonensis	0.971	0.812	−0.41	0.638	1.00	0.886	−0.09	−0.03	0.086	−0.09
Germany/Gaul	0.971	0.928	−0.46	0.696	0.886	1.00	0.086	0.029	0.086	0.086
N. Italy	0.000	0.116	0.667	0.464	−0.09	0.086	1.00	0.943	0.886	0.086
Pannonia	0.000	0.116	0.725	0.551	−0.03	0.029	0.943	1.00	0.943	0.943
Dalmatia	0.088	0.058	0.812	0.638	0.086	0.086	0.886	0.943	1.00	0.886
Aquileia	0.000	0.116	0.667	0.464	−0.09	0.086	0.086	0.943	0.886	1.00

becoming *primary* objects of trade, for whose sake long voyages regularly took place.[10] But where voyages were already being made to meet food or luxury needs, it is extremely difficult to argue that goods which were low-priced, but saleable and compact, were not traded over long distances.

Harris assembles figures for ten marques, six of which are common in the north-west Mediterranean and its hinterland. The sample used here is based on the eleven largest regional samples in Harris's list, totalling 5,757 identified lamps. (Smaller samples for Spain and southern Italy are also referred to below in Table 16). The main patterns can be seen most clearly from the internal correlations between regions and between marques. (Where percentages are used in Table 12(B), these refer solely to the lamp-totals reported by Harris.)

The same correlation-test must be used throughout, to allow comparability. As some of the data are badly skewed, the conventional product-moment test (r^2) will not function reliably. Rank-order tests such as the Spearman test are less sensitive, but are not undermined by skewing. Using the Spearman test, significance at the 95% level (0.05) is achieved for these samples when the correlation exceeds 0.886 (lamp-marques, $n = 6$, Table 13) or 0.648 (regional samples, $n = 10$, Table 14).

2 North of the Mediterranean

Looking at the evidence first by region (Table 13), we find that four samples from the same broad area correlate strongly with each other. In each case, the three highest correlations are with the other three in the group. The strongest set of correlations reads:

(Group IA)

Switzerland–	Gallia Narbonensis	0.971
	Germany/Gaul	0.971
	Vindonissa	0.896

Four samples from a different area also show strong regional cross-correlations. Here again the highest three correlations are always with the other three in the group. Based on Aquileia, the correlations read:

(Group IB)

Aquileia	– N. Italy	1.000
	Pannonia	0.943
	Dalmatia	0.886

The two remaining samples, from Lauriacum and Dacia, do not show such strong correlations at any point (the maxima are 0.812 and 0.696), and they do not obviously belong to regional groupings within the material studied.

The distribution of lamp-marques (Table 14) agains shows two clear groupings.

[10] Cf. Gill (1987).

Table 14. *Spearman correlations between six signed lamp-marques in ten regions north of the Mediterranean*

Marque	ATIM	CRES	FORT	PHOET	STROB	VIB
Atimeti	1.000	0.476	0.884	0.653	0.896	0.628
Cresces	0.476	1.00	0.697	−0.13	0.539	0.891
Fortis	0.884	0.697	1.00	0.427	0.927	0.685
Phoetaspi	0.653	0.13	0.427	1.00	0.665	0.183
Strobili	0.896	0.539	0.927	0.665	1.00	0.624
Vibiani	0.628	0.891	0.685	0.183	0.624	1.00

FORTIS–ATIMETI–STROBILI (here called Group A) show distributions which are very highly correlated, in the range 0.927–0.884, where 0.648 is needed for 95% probability. VIBIANI–CRESCES (Group B) are likewise highly correlated (0.891). The sixth marque PHOETASPI appears more isolated: its closest correlations are with STROBILI (0.665) and ATIMETI (0.653), both in Group A.

Chronology helps to clarify the underlying pattern. The marques in Group A were being produced in Italy in the Flavian period: 24 unused lamps of STROBILI and 2 of FORTIS were found in a container at Pompeii buried in AD 79. ATIMETI, likewise found at Pompeii, has also been identified as Italian. One of the marques in Group B, VIBIANI, is identified by Bailey as Italian and as belonging to the Antonine or Severan period.[11] CRESCES is not included in Bailey's massive catalogue of Italian marques represented in the British Museum. But the close correlation between this marque and VIBIANI (0.891) in ten widely distributed samples seems difficult to explain except by common origin. Group A and Group B were evidently both Italian in origin, but were clearly not contemporary, despite periods of production which overlapped.

Two regional samples come from finds whose chronological limits can be roughly identified. Vindonissa seems to have been abandoned in AD 101, while Lauriacum in Noricum shows deposits datable to the third century.[12] These sites thus offer some guidance about which marques were in production at different dates.

In the sample at Vindonissa, ending under Trajan, there are apparently no lamps of Group B (CRESCES–VIBIANI). This group is also very scarce in the samples for Switzerland and Gallia Comata (CRESCES 1.5% and 1.3%, VIBIANI 1.5% and 2.5%). That may argue that these samples were predominantly early also.

At Lauriacum by contrast, two of the marques from Group A are missing or very rare (ATIMETI is unrepresented, and STROBILI only 0.9%). Even FORTIS is as low as 15.8%, less than half its lowest quotient anywhere else.

On the face of it, these comparisons suggest that by AD 100 Group B had not

[11] Bailey (1980) 274; 91; 102.   [12] Bailey (1980) 274; 275.

yet come into existence, or had not achieved wide diffusion, while by the third century the marques in Group A, very heavily represented at the earlier date, had either disappeared, or were in sharp decline. But this conclusion would only be categorical if, once in production, the same lamps were available everywhere. Some variants might turn out from fuller evidence to be regional rather than chronological.

To see how far the machinery of diffusion was efficient, it is worth looking at PHOETASPI, the sixth marque. Its concentrations do not closely follow those of the other five marques. PHOETASPI is generally fairly rare. But it achieves a significant presence in three samples, essentially from one part of the empire. They are:

Switzerland	12.4%
Vindonissa	12.0%
Gallia Narbonensis	8.3%

The strongest representation that PHOETASPI achieves anywhere else is only 3.3%, so the regional contrast is great. Neither Italian sample shows this marque in serious quantities (2.2% in N. Italy, 1.3% at Aquileia). The strong showing at Vindonissa might suggest that PHOETASPI belongs essentially to the late first century. Thus if it was an Italian marque, as Bailey concludes, it would appear to be one with very strong regional distribution outside Italy in the lands to the north and north-west.[13]

There are suggestions that diffusion of PHOETASPI was weaker further east, with figures of 1.3% at Aquileia, 0.5% in Pannonia, and none cited for Dacia. But this is confused by the marque's stronger showing in Dalmatia, 3.3%. These differences may be chronological, if PHOETASPI had disappeared or declined by the second century when the Romanisation of Dacia took place, and if the Pannonian sample is predominantly second century or later, as appears quite likely. In a similar way, percentage representation of PHOETASPI in the big Italian samples may be low partly because so much of those samples appears to belong to the second and third centuries.

The marque which offers the strongest regional contrast with PHOETASPI is FORTIS, whose percentage representation is surprisingly consistent. If representation of FORTIS as a percentage of the six 'northern' marques in Table 14 is indexed to the quotient for Aquileia, the result is that shown in Table 15.

FORTIS was very strongly represented throughout the areas in question during the first and second centuries. Its much weaker showing in the sample from Lauriacum, which is third-century at least in part, may argue that by this later date FORTIS had seriously declined. But late samples from other areas would probably be needed before this chronological conclusion could be definite.

---

[13] Procaccini (1981) 519 refers to production of PHOETASPI in the Rhone valley, echoing the high percentages seen above.

Table 15. *Representation of
FORTIS indexed to its representation at Aquileia*

Region	Index figure
Lauriacum	36
Aquileia	100
N. Italy	103
Narbonensis	108
Dalmatia	109
Switzerland	111
Vindonissa	121
Pannonia	124
Germany/Gaul	139
Dacia	176

This brief survey of Harris's 'northern' marques suggests clear concentrations by region and clear concentrations by marque. The ten regional samples fall into two main groups of four, one concentrated in Gaul (Group 1A), the other round the northern Adriatic (Group 1B). The six lamp-marques studied likewise fall into two, a group of three (Group A) and a group of two (Group B), which have very strong internal correlations.

But two other variables affect the interpretation of these results. One is chronology, whose difficulties have been mentioned. The other is provenance. Are we looking at widespread export of lamps over a very large area, or at widespread diffusion of trade marks and designs? The answer remains unclear; both phenomena certainly existed. But in most cases, export was probably important, since heavily modulated patterns of regional distribution like those which we can see in Table 12, could most readily be generated by variations in trading patterns.[14]

In the case of FORTIS, however, whose high percentage representation is remarkably consistent from region to region (Table 15), export of designs and local production must seem more likely. It has been argued that copies produced locally tended to be smaller, because of the reproducing technique employed. Harris's figures show a noticeable decrease in median size between the Italian sample for FORTIS from Aquileia and three out of four provincial samples.[15]

3 South of the Mediterranean
Diffusion outside the regions examined so far is also worth considering. Harris's table shows a definite contrast between north and south. In regions north of the

---

[14] Now see also Bailey (1987).
[15] Harris (1980A) Table II, p. 134; the size-trends in the figures for ATIMETI and STROBILI are less convincing.

Mediterranean, the six marques examined were very common in aggregate. To the south, in Africa, they were very largely unknown, and their place was taken by other marques and types, some of which were evidently produced there.

In broad terms, the contrast can be seen as a division between two areas in each of which local lamp production was relatively strong. But the difference also suggests a restriction in trade flows.

The four 'southern' marques (here called Group C) show a striking contrast with the first six, since they make up virtually all the signed lamps from Africa in the Harris sample (98.0%). But the 'northern' marques are very largely absent from Africa on these figures (Table 12). The difference in distribution is thus clear-cut.

Nevertheless, the African market for signed lamps was not entirely monopolised by the four marques in Group C. Procaccini gives details of at least two other significant marques, MNOVIUST and AUFIFRON.[16] There are 182 and 46 African examples respectively, making up 31% of Procaccini's samples of African finds; that however omits CCLOSUC, which accounts for 29% of Harris's sample of African lamp-finds. A workshop making 'MNOVIUST' (M. Nov. Iust.) has been excavated in Africa at Hadrumetum, though another has been found in Gallia Narbonensis.[17]

The distributions suggest that at least three of the marques in Group C were based in Africa. Their percentage representation is seen in Table 16.

The concentrations of the first three marques are obviously much stronger in the south than the north, and strongest of all in Africa.[18] There is more uncertainty about the provenance of COPPIRES (C. Oppius Restitutus). Harris noted that Restitutus is a common name in Africa, but that is not enough to be conclusive.[19] Procaccini, who reports the marque more fully, counted 426 specimens in Italy, against 185 in Africa. Though published lamp-finds are more numerous in Italy, this very strong Italian showing may support Procaccini's suggestion that the marque was in fact Italian-based. Pavolini dates COPPIRES to Domitian and Trajan, thus making it substantially earlier than the other Group C marques, which are late Antonine on his dating.[20] Export of lamps from Italy to Africa may be plausible at this earlier date.[21]

The remaining figures for Group C seem to make it clear that in the second century African lamp-marques were being widely distributed within the western Mediterranean. But they apparently did not spread beyond this area, to the northern Adriatic and the Balkans, since they are missing from the substantial samples for Aquileia, Dalmatia and Pannonia. Equally striking is the fact that the

---

[16] Procaccini (1981) Table 2.
[17] Harris (1980A) 132; Martin (1977) (Bailey (1987) 62, n. 12).
[18] Bailey (1980) 93–4 classifies CCLOSUC as Italian; but cf. 89–90.
[19] Harris (1980A) 132.   [20] C. Pavolini BCAR 85 (1975/6) 75, 129.
[21] For a pattern of imports to Africa in the first century rapidly declining in the second, see Guéry (1979) 32 (terra sigillata imported from Gaul).

Table 16. *Diffusion of 'southern' marques*

Region	CCLOSUC, IUNIALEXI and CIUNDRAC Percentage of local sample	Number	COPPIRES Percentage of local sample	Number
Pannonia	—		—	
Dacia	—		—	
Dalmatia	—		—	
Aquileia	—		—	
N. Italy	0.8	12	0.9	13
Germany/Gaul	3.1	19	4.4	27
Gallia Narbonensis	9.8	13	11.3	15
Spain	29.8	17	47.4	27
S. Italy (*CIL* x)	53.9	55	6.9	7
Africa	70.3	464	28.6	189

Note: The percentages refer to Harris's sample of ten marques of signed lamps for each area as shown in Table 12. The totals for Spain and for *CIL* x (not shown in Table 12) are 57 and 102.

marques predominant in these samples from the north-east (Table 14) seem to be virtually unknown in Africa. On Harris's figures, even FORTIS, the leader among signed lamps north of the Mediterranean, provides less than 1% of African finds of signed lamps (taken together, the Table 14 marques make up only 1.1% of these African finds).

Similar geographical boundaries are shown by the distribution of other lamp-types reported by Pavolini.[22] The sharp hiatus probably reflects limits in the trading pattern. Africa exported grain to Rome and presumably to other ports and islands in the western Mediterranean. But there is little to suggest that African trade links with either the northern Adriatic and the Balkans (marques in Group IB), or with the interior of Gaul (Group IA) existed on a significant scale at this time.

4 The East

Representation in the eastern Mediterranean of western signed lamps, whether Italian or African, appears to be very restricted. Lamps with 'brand-names' in Roman lettering may have been unattractive to Greek-speakers, but the Greek world in any case had its own tradition of lamp-making. Western lamps are

[22] Pavolini (1981) tav. 33–4.

hardly found in Greece and Asia.[23] Interestingly enough, one of the marques in Harris's sample does emerge in the east in Egypt, at least as a trade name.[24] The few PHOETASPI lamps found from Egypt do not belong to the same type as those in the west: hence they probably show local production or local imitation. But there would be no obvious reason for imitation in a distant province if the original were unknown there. These limited survivals thus almost certainly argue that examples of PHOETASPI made in the west were also being imported into Egypt.

The fact that the recipient in this case was Egypt apparently reflects the strength of Egypt's links with Italy. The shipping which plied between Alexandria and Puteoli or Ostia was much the most important contact between regional trading zones in east and west which otherwise are likely to have been largely distinct.[25]

5 Results

Correlation-tests provide clear evidence for association and dissociation between lamp-populations in different parts of the Roman world. These potentially identify both the areas in which particular marques were distributed, and the areas that they did not penetrate significantly.

It is clear that some lamps were traded, not produced locally. To the extent that this was so, distribution patterns will carry some reflection of trade patterns. In so far as lamps were produced in the regions in which they have been found, the layout of finds still shows regional limits in the way production was organised, which ultimately reflect limits in the long-distance trading pattern. The implicit boundaries, especially the sharp north–south differences within the western half of the empire, show limits in the trading pattern, and they do not support the view that, in trade terms, the empire formed a single integrated economy.[26]

---

[23] Bailey (1980) 277. For mass-production of lamps in the classical Greek period, see Gill (1987).

[24] Bailey (1980) 276–7.

[25] Rathbone (1983) argues that references to 'Aminean' and 'Hadrianic' wine in late papyri show imports from Italy. As long as the grain-ships were still running between Egypt and Italy, there should have been obvious capacity for imports to Egypt from Italy (cf. chapter 2, at n.14).

[26] And specific inferences about commercial interaction between east and west, based on demand for slaves in Italy in the second and first centuries BC and the rising curve of prices for slave-manumission at Delphi, seem to founder both on difficulties of proving a clear price-trend, and on the uncertain relationship between manumission-payments and sale-prices (see Duncan-Jones (1984)).

4
Stability and change

The literary sources that survive from the Roman Principate are so defective that any chronology that exists anywhere else is worth the effort of analysis. If extensive enough, documentary time-series usually embody some reality of the period from which they come. Stimuli that they reveal may include dynastic, fiscal and economic change.

The available sources include inscriptions, papyri and coins. All three survive in abundance, and all three contain obvious dated series. Inscriptions are in some ways the most useful, because they typically represent significant expenditures, in other words, discrete economic events.[1] In themselves, dated papyri and coins primarily show the functioning of government machinery which existed at all times, but they still have great interest as sources of chronological data. Examined by category, dated papyri can yield specific evidence about economic change,[2] and changes in coin-output can potentially mirror changes in government spending.

1 Building-series

1.1 Approaches to the evidence
Public inscriptions on stone from the Roman world provide some index of building activity, whether they refer to the construction of statues or to complete buildings.[3] Different ways of interpreting this evidence can be considered.

(1) One approach would regard town building activity as essentially an expression of political and social tendencies. Within the Roman empire, local populations sought to equip their towns with public buildings and statues in imitation of Rome and of each other, and members of local aristocracies aided that process by competitive spending, usually linked to local office.

(2) Another approach, while recognising these mechanisms, would see the

---

[1] The value of chronological data is not always understood, and dating indications are omitted altogether from some recent inscription indexes (cf. n.42).   [2] For example, see chapter 9.
[3] For the cost of statues, often substantial, see *ERE*[2] 78–9, 126–7.

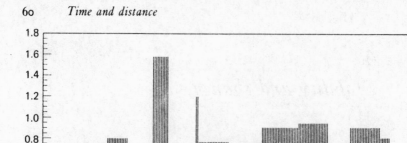

Figure 7. Spain: emperor-dated inscriptions per reign-year (*CIL* II)

incidence of building as being modulated and even determined by external change or fluctuation.

According to (1), decline or fluctuation in building activity might be due to simple self-regulating events, such as the completion of civic building programmes, the exhaustion of local resources, or the slackening of the cycle of competitive spending. According to (2), decline in building activity might incorporate responses to external change.

Neither approach necessarily explains everything in this evidence. Nevertheless, the second approach seems to be supported in some of the evidence below. In particular, reflections of dynastic change or political favour are sometimes implied by what we can see. The effects of events of the Principate, such as tax-concessions under Hadrian, plague under Marcus Aurelius (sections 2 and 3), and possibly fiscal oppression under Nero, also seem to emerge in the data analysed.

1.2 Inscription samples

A series of different samples have been assembled with the deliberate aim of studying overall contours, not in order to examine evidence piece by piece. The first sample, consisting of inscriptions from Spain comprising both statues and buildings, does not suggest strong variation between reigns (fig. 7).[4] The deep troughs coincide with reigns which were followed by *damnatio memoriae* (Nero, Domitian, Commodus). These should be discounted as evidence for building fluctuation, because the reigns were followed by deliberate destruction or

---

[4] Inscriptions dated by emperor listed in index to *CIL* II. Milestones are omitted, as in the other building samples below. For totals, see Appendix 2.

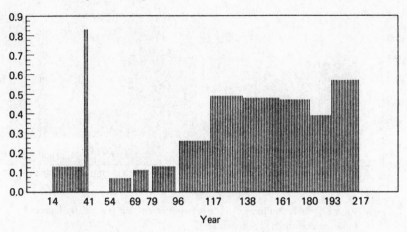

Figure 8. Syria: inscriptions per reign-year dated by local era (AD 14–217)

defacement of monuments. The peak under Nerva in AD 96–8 illustrates a common 'short-reign' effect, where heavy statue-building soon after the accession of a new emperor produces a high average if the reign ends quickly.

The one important variant is the peak shown in Vespasian's reign (AD 69–79). Vespasian made numerous grants of municipal rights to communities in Spain.[5] The exceptional peak in dedications almost certainly reflects a direct response to these concessions, and is therefore inspired by political change. The Spanish evidence otherwise approximates a 'steady state', discounting the artificially reduced figures for reigns with *damnatio*. However, the series does show a modest ascent during the Antonine period to a level maintained under the early Severan emperors. But there is no clear evidence of specific responses to change of emperor, except in the case of Vespasian.

This relative stability is echoed in some other series. In Syria (fig. 8) the annual building rate averaged by reign varies little in the century from Hadrian to Septimius Severus.[6] There is apparently a brief cessation under Caracalla, before the series resumes at lower levels under his successors. The main downward fluctuation, which falls in the reign of Commodus, again seems to be artificial.

In Syria however, in contrast to Spain, there is a sharp difference between the periods before AD 117 and the periods after that date. In the first century dated evidence is very scanty apart from an artificial 'short-reign' peak under Caligula. The sharp improvement after Trajan would probably be consistent with some boost or encouragement under the early Antonine emperors (see below). It is also

---

[5] Pliny *NH* 3.30; Josephus *contra Apion* 2.4. Galsterer (1971); Mackie (1983) 215–19. Vespasian's initiative produced the Flavian municipal charter now known in versions from different towns (cf. Gonzalez (1986)).

[6] J. Jalabert, R. Mouterde *Inscriptions grecques et latines de la Syrie* (1929–   ) (index to vols. 1–4).

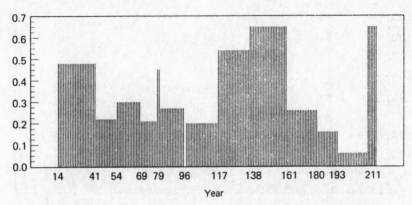

Figure 9. Italy: building dedications per reign-year (imperially financed building excluded) (Jouffroy data)

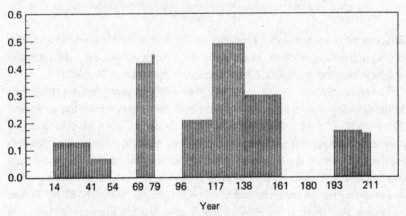

Figure 10. Italy: imperially financed building dedications per reign-year (Jouffroy data)

noticeable that Syria shows no sign of special concessions or special responses under Vespasian. The Syrian series is largely dated by local era, but emperor-dated series often show a similar pattern.

One case in point is building inscriptions from Italy (fig. 9).[7] Notable features here are a 'low' plateau from AD 41 to 117, followed by a higher level in the periods from 117 to 161. The early peak under Tiberius is unusual. But the peaks under Titus and to a lesser extent Caracalla appear to be versions of the 'short-reign' effect already mentioned.

Italy, in addition to the usual buildings financed by cities and private individuals, contributes data about buildings paid for by emperors.[8] Though the sample is small, its shape is relatively coherent (fig. 10). Again the gaps belong to

[7] Jouffroy (1986). Inscriptions from Rome and Ostia are omitted because atypical of Italy as a whole (cf. *ERE²* 351).   [8] Jouffroy (1986).

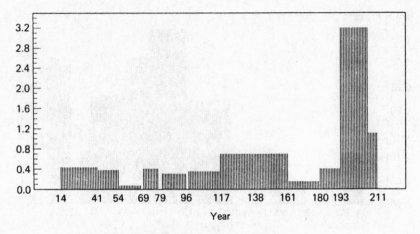

Figure 11. Lepcis Magna: dedications per reign-year (*IRT*)

the 'missing' reigns of Nero, Domitian and Commodus, and they do not necessarily signify breaks in building activity. The break under Marcus Aurelius, who did not receive *damnatio*, may reflect genuine changes, in view of the spectacular financial and military problems of his reign. The pattern in Italy is roughly 'Gaussian', suggesting a natural curve which starts at a low point, and reaches a steady crescendo half-way, before returning to its low point.

Africa also shows symptoms of relative stability. A notable example is provided by Lepcis Magna. Lepcis was the biggest city of Tripolitania, already wealthy in Caesar's day. It was the only Tripolitanian city where the governor was regularly present to dedicate monuments.[9] The data here (fig. 11) shows production of monuments (statues and buildings combined) which is roughly stable for the century from Tiberius to Trajan, with the familiar gap in Nero's reign due to *damnatio*. The reign of Hadrian brings a marked increase, and sets a higher level which is maintained under Antoninus Pius, but under Marcus Aurelius activity falls back. The Commodan level, though probably affected by *damnatio*, is still higher than that for Marcus.

The remarkable peak under Septimius Severus is closely linked to the fact that Septimius was a native of Lepcis, to which he gave new civic status as well as large monuments.[10] The level of building activity appears to rise at this point to approximately five times its previous highest level. But there is a sharp fall under Caracalla immediately afterwards, and the later Severan period (not shown) sees a return to the much lower levels of the first century.

Sabratha in Tripolitania, a sister-city of Lepcis, has also left a dated series of

[9] *IRT* p. 73ff. Inscriptions dated by emperor, together with those dated by governor are listed in the index. For the wealth that Lepcis gained from oil and its export, see Mattingly (1988).

[10] See chapter 11, p. 179 n.27.

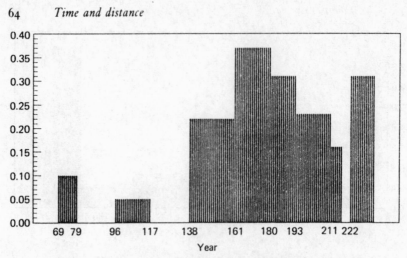

Figure 12. Sabratha: dedications per reign-year (*IRT*)

building inscriptions, though based on a much smaller sample (fig. 12).[11] First-century levels appear to be relatively low; but there is again a surge in the mid-second century, this time under Antoninus Pius, not under Hadrian. The peak is reached under Marcus Aurelius. This stands in direct contrast to the pattern at Lepcis. Contrasts are even greater in the reign of Septimius Severus. Instead of showing a five-fold increase, the Sabratha figures actually fall at this point. They recover, however, under Alexander Severus, again in contrast to the contemporary showing at Lepcis, where the level of activity in this reign appears to be very low.

It is worth comparing these big ports in Tripolitania with a third African city. Thugga, a hill-town in northern Zeugitana set well inland, was a fairly small secondary town, whose remains happen to be extraordinarily well preserved.[12] Here the data selected consist of building dedications, excluding statues. The sample therefore registers large-scale expenditures only. The sample is small, but it is still capable of showing a relatively stable picture (fig. 13). The Julio-Claudian averages are comparable with those reached for much of the Antonine and Severan periods.

But there are two striking exceptions. Building activity appears to stop in the second half of the first century, and resumes only under Hadrian, when there is an apparent return to the Claudian level. The blank shown by Nero's reign could be due to *damnatio*, though in other cases *damnatio* does not appear to have destroyed all the evidence. But here it may point to specific developments which had adverse long-term as well as immediate effects.

Thugga lay in the *pertica Carthaginiensis*, a region which enjoyed substantial tax privileges, if not outright immunity from direct taxation.[13] Thugga was also

[11] *IRT* index.   [12] See chapter 11, p. 178.   [13] See chapter 11, p. 178 n.27.

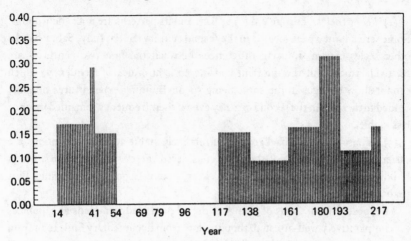

Figure 13. Thugga: building dedications per reign-year

close to a number of large private estates, some of which are known to have been seized by Nero.[14] These estates re-emerge in our evidence half a century later, of course under imperial ownership.[15] Possibly tax-immunity as well as ownership of land suffered from Nero's attentions to this part of Africa (which may have included the bizarre hunt for African treasure described by Tacitus).[16] The stark pattern shown in the Thugga building-series makes a major check at about this time seem quite likely. Thugga, not yet a fully-fledged Roman community, depended for virtually all its buildings on private generosity. When the building-series resumed, the benefactors included *conductores* of the nearby imperial estates.[17]

An important step towards Roman status for Thugga came under Marcus Aurelius; the *pagus*, one half of the double community at Thugga, was given the right to receive legacies (AD 168); the *civitas* received the title 'Aurelia', probably also at this time.[18] The building peak achieved soon afterwards under Commodus seems to reflect the advance in civic status. Any peak under Commodus defies the usual effect of *damnatio*, though buildings and building inscriptions resisted destruction better than statues. In the Severan period, frequency-levels at Thugga return to those of the Antonine period before Commodus.

1.3 Conclusions

The building-series show the following characteristics:

(1) The building rate per year averaged by reign remains stable for long periods, judged from the reigns whose evidence is not distorted by *damnatio*.

[14] Pliny *NH* 18.35. See chapter 8, p. 141 n.54.   [15] Cf. Kehoe (1987).
[16] *Ann.* 16.1–3. For building at Thugga, cf. also Jacques (1984) 758–60.
[17] *ERE*² no. 12, cf. Carcopino (1922) 31.   [18] *CIL* VIII 26528b; Gascou (1972) 159; 160.

(2) Nevertheless, change did take place, and its patterns are not synchronous. Some series show a peak located in the second century (Syria, Italy, Sabratha). In other series (Spain, Lepcis), differences between the first two centuries are relatively small. But the quotient considered is an index of frequency, which cannot show changes in the sums being spent. Building expenditures possibly tended to increase in the second century even if their frequency remained more or less stable.

(3) Where there is a background of relatively stable activity, exceptions are easier to isolate. In most of the areas considered there is an apparent surge in building starting with Hadrian (Syria, Italy, Spain, Lepcis) or Antoninus Pius (Sabratha).

The most obvious focus of change is the reign of Hadrian. Hadrian's policies are comparatively well-attested, though more from documentary finds than from anything in surviving authors. They show direct concern for the fiscal and economic well-being of the empire, as well as exceptional involvement by the emperor in local affairs. By the usual standards of Roman taxation, Hadrian's measures show economic liberalism. Several features are worth singling out.

Hadrian made a general remission of unpaid taxes amounting to HS900 million early in his reign, described as the largest remission made up to his time.[19] He also laid down that tax-farmers should not be forced to renew their contracts against their will, which would only make the contracts more difficult to assign in future.[20] In Egypt, Hadrian carried out a drastic reduction of taxes on crown-land in his reign, and a postponement of money-taxes some eighteen years later.[21] Hadrian also seems to have substantially reduced the payment demanded from mine-operators starting new concessions in government-owned mines.[22]

A surprisingly large number of chance survivals show detailed provisions by Hadrian affecting the economic life of the empire. For example he issued a law encouraging the cultivation of disused or virgin land, together with the growing of olives and vines, the 'lex Hadriana de ruderibus agris'. This is known from inscriptions in Africa, but it may be echoed in the mention of a 'rescriptum sacrum de re olearia' in an inscription from Spain.[23]

Hadrian also made detailed regulations for money-changing at Pergamum (Dittenberger's identification of this incomplete inscription as Hadrianic is generally accepted).[24] And he stipulated (or re-enacted) that a minimum proportion of the olive-oil produced in Attica should be sold in Athens rather than exported.[25] At Coronea in Boeotia, Hadrian regulated the drainage of land and made provisions for flood-barriers, which he partly financed.[26]

---

[19] *ILS* 309. See Duncan-Jones (1964A) 143, n.116; for earlier tax-remissions, see Gabba (1962) 65.
[20] *D.* 49.14.3.6; see also Dio 69.16.2.   [21] Smallwood (1966) 460; 462 (*ESAR* 2.108, 522).
[22] Smallwood (1966) 439.   [23] *FIRA* 1.102; *AE* 1958, 9.
[24] *ESAR* 4.892–5.
[25] Smallwood (1966) 443.   [26] Fossey (1982), nos. 4, 6, 7 (*SEG* 32 (1982) 460ff.)

Hadrian also promoted building activity and urbanisation by direct example in different parts of the empire. Some cities were provided with buildings, and even building materials from the imperial quarries.[27] His long series of peacetime visits to the different provinces of the empire, which were unique in their time, acted as a spur to further building activity and urbanisation.[28] Hadrian was even willing to hold local magistracies and to promise buildings in their honour.[29] Although Antoninus Pius did not maintain the same stimuli, the impetus that Hadrian gave to municipal building generally persisted for some time.

Thus it is possible to see some widespread events which promoted building activity. But discontinuities are also clearly visible. The three African series each show peaks in different reigns, under Marcus Aurelius, Commodus and Septimius Severus. The expectation that the advent of an African emperor would have a general impact on building throughout the province is not borne out here.

It can be argued that what generated such peaks was not so much economic advance as a dialogue between emperor and subject, whose content might be as much political as economic. The encouragements given by Hadrian were partly fiscal. But the later peaks at the three African cities considered seem to reflect political favour.[30] That is apparently also true of the peak under Vespasian in Spain, which coincided with grants of new municipal rights (see n.5). Nevertheless, building speeds could be very slow, and some buildings dedicated under one emperor might have been begun under a predecessor.

Evidence for municipal building constitutes direct evidence for wealth, and for the persistence of a building industry. But peaks in building activity which materialise only under political stimulus can be regarded as artificial in economic terms. The will to build could even exist independently of the capacity to do so. When inspecting cities in Bithynia, Pliny the Younger found several large-scale building projects which had been more or less abandoned unfinished.[31]

2 Egyptian documentation

There are important contrasts when we turn to Egyptian evidence. Dated documentation is many times more abundant here than in any other province. But what Egyptian evidence primarily reflects is levels of bureaucratic activity. The very large database from papyri and ostraka assembled by Bureth is

---

[27] *IGRR* 4.1431. See Millar (1977) 421.

[28] For itineraries and dates, see most recently Syme (1988B).

[29] *HA* Had. 19.1–2; cf. *ERE*[2] 88 and n.4. Though there was ample precedent for emperors holding honorary local magistracies (Liebenam (1900) 261–3), Hadrian, both by visiting the towns and by his elaborate generosity, carried this very much further than before.

[30] For Lepcis and Thugga see nn.9 and 18. Sabratha was apparently made a colony by Antoninus Pius or Marcus Aurelius, Gascou (1972) 82. Thugga, created colony by Gallienus, constructed public baths in his reign, as did its neighbour Thubursicu Bure, created colony at some point in the third century, perhaps under Gallienus (*ERE*[2] 115 no.64; *CIL* VIII 15267; 25998).

[31] Pliny *Ep.* 10.37–40.

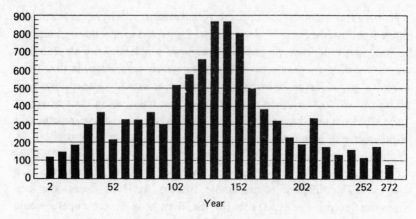

Figure 14. Volume of Egyptian documentation by ten-year periods, AD 2–
281 (Bureth): citations of the emperor dated by year

utilised here.[32] Bureth's decennial summaries show a striking picture (fig. 14).
Documentation per decade is relatively stable for the seven decades from 32/41 to
92/101, apart from an apparent check during the reign of Nero. In a documentary
context, the check can hardly be due to *damnatio*.

But document-totals in the second century show a steep climb for four decades
from 102/111 to 132/141. After a peak maintained in 142/151, a decline in the next
decade is followed by a sharp crash, which reduces the index to the level of the
start of the century. The fall then continues into the later decades of the third
century.

The second-century peak in the Egyptian documents partly coincides with
peaks in the building-series. This means that a time when many provincial cities
were constructing more monuments was also a time when offices in Egypt were
recording more transactions. These transactions were often tax-payments, and as
such were due every year whether documented or not. Other typical documents
included loans, sales and land-leases; economic events like these were probably as
perennial as tax-payments. Hence fluctuation in the volume of records does not
measure fiscal or economic activity, so much as simple variation in how much was

[32] Bureth (1964). Where Bureth's data has been analysed independently (fig. 15 onwards), the co-
ordinate studied is the number of documents in which imperial titles occur. Bureth's summary by
decade (fig. 14) is based on the number of mentions of imperial titles, which can recur several times
in the same document. Bureth starts each decade from the second regnal year (41/2 instead of 40/
41). As most documents dated by a regnal year fall in the second of the Julian years with which that
year overlaps (see below), Bureth's decades approximated by Julian year start from AD 52 and so
on (totals by regnal year, AD 138–180, in Appendix 3).
   Totals for regnal years have been converted to totals for Julian years by an adjustment of one-
seventh: the proportion of tax-payments per regnal year falling in the previous Julian year is 13.7%
in one large sample from Karanis of AD 171–4, and 15.1% in another (*apomoira paradeisou*,
$N = 804$; *geometria*, $N = 597$; Day (1956) Table 4, pp. 34–5).

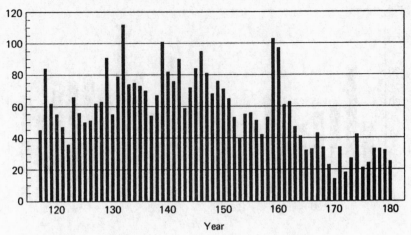

Figure 15. Documentation in Egypt: number of documents
(totals by regnal year)

recorded. The inefficiency of local record-offices in Egypt was already causing
official concern by the late first century AD.[33]

Further patterns can be seen when second-century evidence is looked at in
greater detail. An overview from Hadrian to Marcus Aurelius shows recognisable
cycles, as well as short-term fluctuation, some of it due to scattering in the source-
material (fig. 15). When a new emperor succeeds to the throne, this tends to bring
a peak within a year of his accession. Peaks are seen in 118, the first full year of
Hadrian, and in 139, the first full year of Antoninus Pius. But the pattern does not
occur in 161 or 162 at the accession of Marcus Aurelius, who had been a junior
colleague of Antoninus Pius for more than a decade. Where it occurs, the peak
following accession may show tightening of bureaucratic procedures.

Another pattern reflects the census. In Egypt the census ran on a fourteen-year
cycle, and generated special documents which were not produced at other
times.[34] Apparently because of inertia in the system, many census-declarations
belong to the second year of the cycle.[35] The census years in this period were 118,
132, 146, 160 and 174 (to use the nearest approximations by Julian year). In figure
15, local peaks are accordingly seen in each of these years.

Yearly trend figures are more difficult to assess. Using the coefficient of
variation to measure fluctuation from year to year (Table 17) both parts of
Hadrian's reign appear relatively consistent at levels close to the average (fig. 16).
Later there are two periods of heavy variation, the second half of Antoninus Pius
and the first half of Marcus Aurelius; there is also a period of exceptionally

---

[33] *SP* 219; 422.   [34] Hombert–Préaux (1952).
[35] Hombert–Préaux (1952) 91–4 show about 90% of declarations as falling in the second regnal year
of the census-cycle.

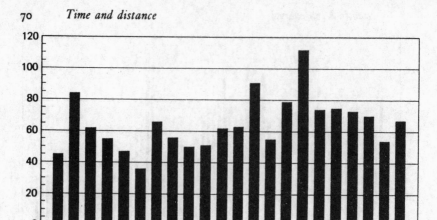

Figure 16. Volume of Egyptian documentation under Hadrian
(totals by regnal year)

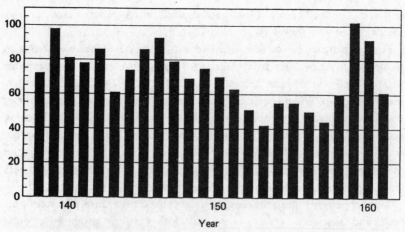

Figure 17. Volume of Egyptian documentation under Antoninus Pius
(approximate totals by Julian year)

slight variation, the first half of Antoninus Pius. The decade of the 150s sees a trough running as far as 157, followed by a strong recovery to the highest previous levels of the reign, both in 159 and in 160, the census year (fig. 17). In the first half of Marcus Aurelius, the strong variation is caused by a steep decline from the initial levels, which continues throughout the 160s (fig. 18).

The average document-total (Table 17) shows a significant increase in the second half of Hadrian and first half of Antoninus Pius, but a virtual collapse under Marcus Aurelius. The highest total achieved in this reign is only just above the minimum for the first half of Antoninus Pius. And the minimum under

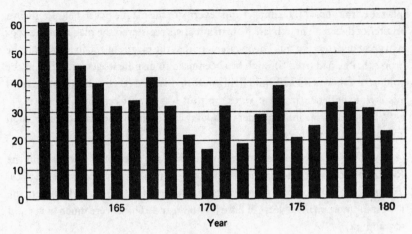

Figure 18. Volume of Egyptian documentation under Marcus Aurelius (approximate totals by Julian year)

Marcus Aurelius (14 documents in the regnal year 169/170) is far below the lowest totals seen in the two previous reigns. Looked at more closely, the reign shows falls in the years 161, 163, 164, 165, 168, 169 and 170 (figs. 15 and 18). The recovery in 167 is relatively minor, and the subsequent fall is very extreme. The document-total for the three years from 169 onwards (71) is less than the average for single years between 130 and 150.

Changes in Egypt at this time have been connected with the impact of the

Table 17. *Inter-annual variation in the volume of emperor-dated documents*

	Coefficient of variation (V)	Document-total per regnal year		
		Mean	Maximum	Minimum
Hadrian				
regnal years 1–11	22.8	56	84	36
12–22	24.2	73	112	53
Antoninus Pius				
regnal years 1–12	15.4	79	101	59
13–24	31.6	62	103	40
Marcus Aurelius				
regnal years 1–10	39.4	39	63	14
11–20	24.9	29	42	18
Median average	24.6	59	92.5	38

Note: For years divided by death, the document-total utilised is the figure for the full year by the Egyptian calendar (thus Hadrian 22 + A. Pius 1 = 12 months).

plague of the 160s.[36] The impact and severity of the plague nevertheless remain a matter of debate. Though late Roman annalists registered the plague of the 160s as a great disaster, Cassius Dio's statement that the plague of 189 in Rome was the worst that he had lived through has been used to dispute its severity. But in the mid-160s Dio was a small child living in Bithynia, and hardly able to assess from his own experience an event whose impact was almost certainly uneven.[37]

Without entering into arguments about the intensity of the plague, it is enough to note two things here.

(1). A downward fluctuation more serious than any previously seen within the Roman period takes place in the volume of Egyptian documentation in the 160s. The totals registered in the regnal years 164/165 and 165/166 (32 and 33) were the lowest for more than 60 years. Those for 168/9 and 169/70 were much lower still (23 and 14).

An epidemic is reported at Smyrna in 165. In the winter of 165/6, plague broke out in the camp of Lucius Verus's army at Seleuceia on the Tigris. Plague had reached Rome by 166. The great physician Galen also observed its effects among the troops at Aquileia in the winter of 168/9; and he declined to go on the subsequent expedition against the Marcomanni for 'health reasons'.[38]

The ancient biographer of Marcus Aurelius writes that plague-losses created the utmost difficulty in army recruitment: by his account slaves, gladiators and brigands were now accepted for the army.[39] Direct evidence from Egypt certainly points to a striking change in recruitment. An inscription shows that in 168 legionary intake relied very heavily on men who were camp-born, and thus technically illegitimate and without a citizen *origo*.[40] In a list only a generation earlier, legionaries in Egypt almost all came from cities.[41]

[36] Bagnall (1985).

[37] Dio 72.14.3–4 with Gilliam (1961) 231; for objections, see Millar (1963) 13, n.6. Later citations of the plague under Marcus in Eutropius 8.12; Jerome p. 205 Helm (AD 168); p.206 (AD 172); Orosius 7.15.5 (Gilliam (1961) 232–3). Gilliam's rigorous discussion carries agnosticism to extremes in wondering whether the plague ever reached Egypt (241). Immunity for Egypt is virtually inconceivable when the province had so many trade-contacts with the east, with Syria and with Rome, quite apart from garrison-troops recruited in the eastern Mediterranean. Ammianus wrote that the plague spread contagion and death everywhere from the Persian frontier to the Rhine and the Gallic provinces (23.6.24).

Littman–Littman (1973) use Galen's description to deduce that the plague was smallpox.

[38] Citations in Gilliam (1961) 227–30.   [39] *HA* Marc. 21.6–7; also Orosius 7.15.6, 7.27.7.

[40] Fullest text (without commentary) in Wright (1942) 33–8, cf. *ILS* 2304 (part of the inscription was used to resurface the drive of an English country house in the nineteenth century). Of 42 men of named origin, 24 appear to be from the camps (typically described as 'castris', 'kastr' or 'c'). The figure 13 given for camp-born by Forni (1974) 389 is an evident misprint. For the sons of legionaries and their status, see Vittinghoff (1971) 310–11. If recruited as legionaries, these sons were normally inscribed in Pollia, which apparently did not exist in its own right as a tribe to which any provincial city belonged.

In a Balkan list of men recruited in the following year (AD 169, *CIL* III 14507), the percentage of legionaries recruited from the camps is negligible. This shows that recruitment from the cities continued in some areas, and suggests that, where possible, it was still preferred.

[41] *AE* 1969–70, 633, recruits from AD 133/4.

Table 18. *Lycian funerary*
inscriptions by date (AD 162–171)

Year	Number	Year	Number
162	1	167	4
163	1	168	2
164	1	169	6
165	2	170	1
166	2	171	3

Further clear signs of a massive check in the late 160s can be seen in the dated discharge certificates ('diplomata') of auxiliaries and fleet veterans, which survive from frontier provinces, and particularly from the Balkans. In the two decades from AD 148 to 167, diplomas dated to within 1–2 years run at an average of 2.45 examples per year. The next ten years, from AD 168, by contrast produce no closely dated diplomas, and only 3 are found in the decade after that, an average of 0.3.[42]

Dated funerary inscriptions in the recently published series at Lycian cities, though very few, suggest some clustering of deaths in the late 160s (Table 18).[43]

(2). The volume of documentation in Egypt (measured by dated citations) did not recover from the abrupt check under Marcus Aurelius. Totals per decade instead continued to fall for most of the next century. As already seen, the fastest collapse took place at the beginning. Although the empire was also subject to great military and presumably fiscal strains at this time, the coincidence in date between a plague serious enough to be remembered centuries later, and the decline in Egyptian documentation, is too close for a connection to be ruled out.

3 Coin-series

Although there are no surviving mint-records from Rome, extant coin-hoards include some so large that their totals year by year are likely to reflect the volume of coin being produced. Chief among such hoards is the one found at Reka-Devnia in Bulgaria (formerly Marcianopolis in Lower Moesia), from which over 80,000 denarii were reported in the list published in 1934.[44]

This hoard contains almost 11,700 denarii struck under Marcus Aurelius. These immediately show a coherent pattern when analysed by date (fig. 19). The

[42] Figures calculated from the list provided by M.M. Roxan *Roman Military Diplomas 1978–84* (1985) 121–7.

[43] *TAM* 5.1. The index ignores the dating evidence. MacMullen (1986) provides an analysis by 20-year periods.

[44] Mouchmov (1934). The Reka-Devnia hoard is more than ten times bigger than the next largest silver-hoard covering this period (from printed evidence). The figures quoted are based on analysis of Mouchmov's inventory, collating his list of Cohen types with *RIC*, and using datings from *RIC*.

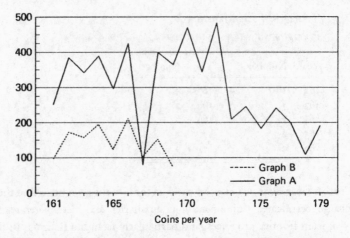

Figure 19. Annual denarius-output, AD 161–179: Marcus Aurelius (graph A) and Lucius Verus (graph B) (coin-totals from Reka-Devnia hoard)

year-dated evidence comes from coins struck for male members of the dynasty, which make up more than half the Reka-Devnia sample from this reign. Coinage for empresses and princesses, though plentiful at this time, does not normally have year-dating.

The pattern in figure 19 shows two prime features. Coin-output appears to alternate regularly between years of high output and years of low output. This is true of coin struck for Marcus almost throughout the reign, and the alternation does not stop until 178. The coin struck for Verus tracks these movements closely, following the same biennial cycle.

Secondly, a massive check in the coin struck for Marcus occurs in the year 167. The biennial cycle predicts 167 as a year of 'low' output, but the total for Marcus at this point is far below the predicted level. Table 19 shows that output for Verus in 167 contains no obvious abnormality; but output for Marcus seems to fall to approximately one-quarter of the average for 'low-output' years of the 160s. Output recovers fully in the next year (fig. 19), and maintains its recovery for several years afterwards.

This check in mainstream coin-output, shown as brief but acute, occurs in 167, the year after the first mention of plague at Rome in surviving sources (see 2.0 above). Possibly the check reflects a short-term impact of plague on either the supply of metal, or on the operation of the mint. But the change is not obviously reflected in the evidence for Verus. The coinages of Marcus and Verus are separated not only in these coinage-totals for 167, but also in differences in average weight and fineness.[45] Possibly the coin struck in 167 used reserves that

---

[45] Hoard-analyses now in progress suggest differences in average weight and/or fineness between denarii struck for different members of the imperial house within a given reign; these seem to go back at least as far as Vespasian.

Table 19. *Denarius-totals at Reka-Devnia in 'low-output' years under Marcus (AD 161–169)*

Years	Marcus	Verus
161	251	95
163	341	157
165	296	123
167	79	101
169	364	72 [posthumous coinage]
Median average	296	101

Note: The totals for 161 do not represent a full year, because Marcus and Verus became emperors in mid-year.

were higher in the 'Verus' sector of the mint than in the 'Marcus' sector. If for example the plague affected shipping movements, mining activity or tribute-payments, shortage of precious metal in Rome would be a possible result.

The pattern in figure 19 also raises the wider question of how a biennial output-cycle came into being. A regular pattern of explicit year-dating on the coinage only starts in the middle of the second century, under Antoninus Pius. But the denarius coinage of the second half of his reign (in the huge Reka-Devnia sample) does not imply that any regular alternation of 'high-output' and 'low-output' years was taking place at that time. From the very restricted information available, the biennial pattern under Marcus seems to be peculiar to his reign.

On the hypothesis that regular fluctuation in minting may have mirrored regular fluctuation in spending, there are several types of recurrent expenditure that might explain what was happening to mint-output.

(1.) *Congiaria* or cash-handouts to the Roman plebs. But in six cases out of seven, the known dates of the *congiaria* under Marcus Aurelius do not coincide with the 'high-output' years shown in figure 19.[46]

(2.) *Donativa* or handouts to the troops. Our knowledge of *donativa* under the Principate is very incomplete. Unlike *congiaria* to the plebs, which had some local interest for ancient chroniclers of the city of Rome, donatives do not normally figure in the late annalistic sources. But full *donativa* were enormously costly, and there is nothing to suggest that they could have been taking place as often as every two years in this period.[47]

(3.) *Praemia militiae* or bonus-payments made to army veterans on their retirement. Discharge of legionaries in the mid-second century seems to have taken place only in alternate years. The known dates, which include AD 160,

[46] Van Berchem (1939) 156.
[47] *HA* Had. 23.12 and Ael. 6.1–3 (not in the discussion of donatives in Campbell (1984)).

locate this cycle in even-numbered years.[48] The peaks in figure 19 likewise occur in even-numbered years. This correlation suggests a possible connection between the number of denarii struck in years of 'high' output and the need to pay *praemia militiae*.

4 Conclusions

The chronological data considered here are usually less effective in revealing long-term trends than in suggesting changes or deviations in the short term. Nevertheless, building-series (as far as can be judged from samples of very limited size) seem to have inherent tendencies towards stability. In approximate terms, peaks in the series tend to coincide with some political concession whose effects were felt locally. A clear landmark is provided by Hadrian's policies, which evidently gave a stimulus to building, in both short and medium term.

The dated Egyptian documents and the annual coin-totals provide much more sharply focussed indices, which are capable of reflecting events that took place in specific years or in short groups of years. The case chiefly illustrated here is the apparent impact of the plague under Marcus Aurelius.

Time-series evidence may, for obvious reasons, often be limited in what it can reveal. But unlike the literary tradition, it is not mediated by the values of the society from which it comes, and as a neutral source, it has a definite value as a historical tool. It is potentially capable of supplementing and quantifying what is known, particularly in areas that lie outside the preoccupations of the literary record.

[48] H. Nesselhauf *CIL* XVI p.187.

PART II

DEMOGRAPHY AND MANPOWER

5
Age-awareness in the Roman world

1 Introduction

In many 'traditional' societies, age-reporting shows serious distortions.[1] Preference for particular digits tends to be stereotyped, leading to obvious peaks and troughs in the overall age-pattern (fig. 20). Distortions which are not systematic cannot be directly identified. But in a population which reports age correctly, ages will not be concentrated at multiples of a particular digit. Where such concentrations do exist, they argue limited age-awareness, and they probably imply that some age-information was contributed in ignorance.

The typical preference is for ages ending in 5 or 0; this is found in many cultures at widely different dates. On the face of it, heaping at 5s and zeros could be a minor distortion, merely implying that correctly known ages were often rounded off to the nearest convenient multiple of 5. But age-distributions show that populations which round ages heavily are also prone to other forms of numerical distortion, such as exaggeration.[2] Serious exaggeration disrupts age-reporting very thoroughly, because as well as creating fictitious longevity at one end of the scale, it transfers some of the lower ages into higher age-cohorts. The result is large-order distortions, much greater than those which would be involved in rounding off true ages to multiples of 5.

In Roman evidence, age-declarations by the same individual at different dates typically show internal discrepancies, which are sometimes serious. A case in point is Aurelius Isidorus of Karanis in Egypt, a well-to-do landowner of the time

---

[1] The main source-material is tombstone-ages assembled by Szilagyi (see Tables 22–6, 29–31). Most of the material comes from the Principate. Szilagyi divides his data between the first two centuries AD and the subsequent period. But tombstones are often very difficult to date, and this chronological division is not really convincing (see Duncan-Jones (1977) Appendix II).

[2] Read as tabulations of $l(x)$, African tombstone-ages show the percentage of survivors at 20 still alive at 80 as being high (Cirtan colonies M/F 22.9%/19.2%; Celtianis 28.7/29.9; Thugga 25.6/ 21.1). Life expectation at birth in the Roman period is in most cases unlikely to be above 30 (chapter 6), but these African results would lead to quotients between 50 and 60, assessed by the Princeton South model. Outside Africa, the percentage of tombstones containing age-statements is too low to allow the same test, and is often skewed towards lower ages. But Pliny's figures for northern Italy, from Vespasian's census, show that age-exaggeration was also prevalent there (NH 7.162–4).

Table 20. *Age-reporting by Aurelius Isidorus*

Age-declaration	Implied birth-year	Discrepancy with preceding date
35 April 297	262	—
37 April 308	271	+ 9 years
40 August 308	268	− 3 years
45 pre-June 309	264 (or earlier)	− 4 years
40 June 309	269	+ 5 years

Source: PCair Isid p.394.

Table 21. *Other conflicting age-declarations in Egypt*

Age-declaration	Discrepancy with previous age
(A)	
36 on 25 October 107 BC	—
30 on 16 August 104	−9 years
35 on 12 April 101	+2 years
40 on 18 November 99	+ 3 years
(B)	
45 on 27 February AD 310	—
50 on 3 April 317	−2 years
58 on June 327	−2 years
and still 58 in October 328	− 1 year.

Source: A. Calderini *Rass. it. ling. litt. class.* 2 (1920) 316–26.

of Diocletian. His ages reported in documents preserved in his family archive are shown in Table 20. Of the precise ages, no two are consistent. If Isidorus knew his date of birth, he did not relate it to his present age.[3]

Two more cases from Egypt are cited by Calderini (Table 21). Most of the ages in these three examples are multiples of 5. These defective age-declarations relied overwhelmingly on multiples of 5. The results were almost always inconsistent, and they imply that what lay behind the round numbers was guesswork by the individual.

[3] For birth-certificates in Roman Egypt, see Montevecchi (1973) 180, Carter (1967) and BGU XI 2020. Isidorus, who was called *agrammatos* and had to declare his property through an intermediary, was evidently illiterate (PCair Isid 4; 5; Youtie (1971A) 172). The Egyptian evidence in general shows a substantial proportion of the propertied class as signing documents through intermediaries, apparently because they could not do otherwise (Calderini (1950)). Over two-thirds of the citizens who applied for the corn-distribution in third-century Oxyrhynchus were illiterate (cf. J.D. Thomas *CR* 26 (1976) 111). In theory illiteracy in Greek need not have meant illiteracy in demotic (cf. Youtie (1971A), (1971B)); but cases in point are lacking, and official documentation in demotic dies out early in the Roman period.

Table 22. *Age-heaping by individual Egyptians who declare their age*

0	5
1	—
2	—
3	—
4	—
5	4
6	1
7	1
8	2
9	—

Source: Tables 20 and 21.

In general, the age-rounding quotient is a relatively sensitive index which follows clearly marked regional and social patterns. It is misleading to see age-heaping as something which existed in isolation. Stylisation of ages is a visible symptom of a wider ignorance, one of whose results was functional innumeracy. It may point to wider innumeracy, and it is almost certainly connected with illiteracy (see section 7 below).

2 Assessing deviation

In theory, age-heaping may take the form of concentration on any of the 10 digits: 6 was favoured in Roman Egypt, 1 in Roman Africa, and 7 is very frequent in returns from present-day Iraq.[4] But in the Roman age-evidence in general (as in most of the parallel evidence), preference for multiples of 5 overshadows everything else (fig. 20). This distortion is so marked that differentiation between samples remains virtually the same whether the test is the standard deviation, which assesses all digital abnormalities, or a test based only on multiples of 5.[5]

It has been suggested that preference for 5s in the Roman evidence might specifically reflect the 5-year *lustrum* used in conventional Roman time-reckoning.[6] But if that were so, it should tend to make 5 and 0 of equal importance. In reality their frequencies differ in the Roman evidence, more so than in a number of modern samples (Table 23).

[4] Egypt, see n.10; Africa, Harkness (1896) 62–4; Iraq *Demographic Yearbook*, (1963) 670.

[5] A series of tests produced this result; no complete analysis by standard deviation has been carried out.

[6] Cf. Etienne–Fabre (1970). Dating by consuls and corresponding lack of a sequential dating-system were potential obstacles to efficient age-reckoning. But under the Principate, most dating in surviving inscriptions and documents is by emperor, which provided a sequential index for each reign. Continuous eras were even better, but the one substantial test-case, Mauretania

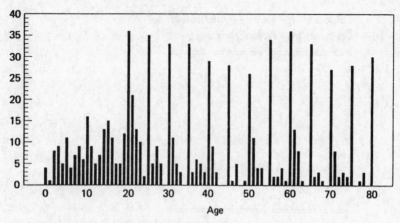

Figure 20. Tombstone age-reporting: male ages of death in the Cirtan colonies (ages 81–120 not reproduced)

Table 23. *Ages ending in 5 as a proportion of ages ending in 0 (range 23–82)*

	Male and female (percentage)
Roman Empire	
1. Africa	90.9
2. City of Rome	84.0
3. Italian cities	76.3
4. Spanish cities	71.8
Modern evidence	
5. Ceylon 1963	106.7
6. Brazil 1950	94.4
7. Guatemala 1950	94.3
8. Mexico 1970	93.9
9. Nicaragua 1963	92.0
10. Egypt 1947	86.5
11. Iran 1966	80.8
12. Morocco 1960	71.7

Sources: 1–2: Harkness (1896); 3–4: Szilagyi (1962) 301; (1963) 147; 5–12; see Table 33.

The measures adopted for assessing representation of 5s is based on a percentage. (1) The percentage of ages divisible by 5 is calculated. (2) The quotient of 20%, representing the normal level, is subtracted, so that what is left is the deviation. (3) This residue is expressed on a scale from 0 to 100, by multiplying by 1.25. Thus a sample where multiples of 5 make up 40% of the ages will register as: $(40–20) \times 1.25 = 25$.

This reckoning is applied to each of the four decades in the 40-year age-period from 23 to 62 inclusive. The consolidated index is an average of the resulting four figures (sample-sizes quoted here always refer to the age-group 23–62 unless otherwise stated). An additional procedure of this kind is needed in order to minimise contamination of the rounding-quotient by peculiarities in the age-pattern. That readily occurs if the sample is analysed as a single unit, since rounding is inherently heaviest in the upper age-cohorts, but samples vary considerably in the proportion belonging to these cohorts.[7]

3 Class differences in age-rounding

Roman tombstones generally reveal little about occupation or rank, and the number of social comparisons is limited. But where social groups are identifiable, some sharp differences can be seen (Table 24).

The gradation between members of the town council and other identifiable groups is very big, roughly three-fold, while almost all other differences are relatively small (for local differences in Africa, see Table 30). Such a striking variation is likely to reflect prime educational differences, suggesting acceptable levels of age-numeracy among town councillors, but low or extremely low levels in the main social groups.[8] The small sample of Christian tombstones shows a striking decline in age-awareness at Carthage (this difference is even stronger in the female samples; see Table 25). Another substantial variation is the difference at Rome between land-troops and civilians, suggesting somewhat better age-awareness among soldiers (a difference which is much reduced at Lambaesis).

Available evidence for studying social differences among women is less revealing (Table 25). The main gradation in the female patterns is the fact that quotients for women in citizen samples from Puteoli and Carthage are substantially below those in the other social groups. The difference probably argues some advantage in the social composition of the age-samples (though the

Caesariensis, with widespread use of continuous numbering by years of the province in its inscriptions, fails to show any corresponding advantage in terms of age-accuracy (see Table 29; *CIL* VIII 5, pp.179–82).

[7] For 'unitarian' analyses of age-rounding and the problems that arise from them, see Duncan-Jones (1977) Appendix I.

[8] This strong social trend is extended by evidence from the Senate, although the sample is extremely small. A group of 16 tombstone-ages of men from senatorial families from 20 upwards shows no excess rounding (multiples of five are 3 out of 16, or 19%; listed in Eck (1981)).

Table 24. *Male social differences*

Social groups	Rounding index (sample in brackets)
Italy	
Town councillors	15.1 (75)
Civilian citizens and *incerti*	42.8 (904)
Fleet-troops (Italy and Rome)	47.2 (299)
Freedmen and slaves in Italy	49.5 (117)
Rome	
Land-troops	37.9 (408)
Civilians and *incerti*	48.4 (1271)
Freedmen	47.4 (295)
Slaves	48.5 (132)
Africa	
Town councillors and office-holders	17.5 (34)
Carthage citizens	42.8 (123)
Carthage freedmen, slaves and 1-name	49.7 (141)
Lambaesis soldiers	54.4 (270)
Lambaesis, other free males	56.4 (189)
Carthage Christian tombstones	58.5 (38)

Sources: Italy and Rome: Szilagyi (1962) 298–301; (1963) 133–41; 149–50; Levison (1898) 29; 44. The main data from Szilagyi come from his samples for 'small' communities in Italy, and Ostia, Puteoli, Aquileia and Mediolanum. Africa: Szilagyi (1965), (1967); Carthage: Duncan-Jones (1980A).

Table 25. *Female social differences*

Social groups	Rounding index (sample in brackets)
Rome	
Women of citizen birth and *incerti*	48.9 (1003)
Freedwomen	52.9 (279)
Slaves (ages 23–52)	(58.8) (89)
Italy	
Puteoli: women of citizen birth and *incerti*	34.2 (118)
Carthage	
Women of citizen birth and *incerti*	33.1 (117)
Freedwomen, slaves and 1-name	62.0 (87)
Christian tombstones	69.6 (38)

Sources: Rome: Szilagyi (1964) 131; 149; 150. Puteoli: Szilagyi (1963) 134–5; Carthage: Duncan-Jones (1980A).

Table 26. *Age-rounding by freedmen and slaves*

Social groups	Rounding index (sample in brackets)
Males	
Freedmen in Rome	47.4 (295)
Slaves in Rome	48.5 (132)
Freedmen and slaves in Italy	49.5 (117)
Carthage freedmen, slaves and 1-name	49.7 (141)
Females	
Freedwomen, Rome	52.9 (279)
Slaves (ages 23–52), Rome	(58.8) (89)
Freedwomen, slaves and 1-name, Carthage	62.0 (87)

Source: Tables 24 and 25.

quotients are still twice those for town councillors in Table 24). By contrast, the very small status-variation seen at Rome argues that whatever sub-group provided the citizen ages for males and females in this case was not socially advantaged.[9]

The rounding-quotients contain some reflection of the expected social hierarchy, in that town councillors, as has been seen, round age much less, and slaves and ex-slaves round ages somewhat more heavily than citizens of free birth. Rounding-quotients for men of servile origin are reasonably consistent (Table 26).

In so far as these figures reflect educational standards, they suggest that the advantages necessary for correct age-awareness were largely confined to a very small social elite, and that the rest of Roman society, slave and free, lacked those advantages.

4 Sex-differences in age-rounding

In traditional societies of the past and in present-day developing countries, access to literacy tends to be more restricted for women than for men (Table 33). In a significant number of cases, knowledge of age as reflected in the age-rounding index shows the same hierarchy (Tables 32 and 33). Tombstones can be a blurred source of data about the individual, because their age-information may potentially come from the person arranging the burial, not from the deceased. But the trend seen here suggests that either women themselves were the source of data, or that, within the family, awareness of female ages was less precise than awareness of male ages.

[9] For the very large proportion of freedmen, whose status is not always explicit, in inscriptions from Rome, see Solin (1971) 135–6; Taylor (1961) 118 and 123; Weaver (1972) 83–6.

Table 27. *Sex-differences in age-rounding by region*

Region	Male rounding	Female rounding	Female excess over male (percentage)
Italy outside Rome	42.6	41.8	−1.9
Gaul	44.1	43.1	−2.3
Rome	47.0	50.2	+6.8
Africa and Numidia	51.4	52.2	+1.6
Mauretania	51.6	54.1	+4.8
Dalmatia	53.3	56.0	+5.1
Spain	56.6	58.4	+3.2
Moesia	57.2	73.3	+28.1
Germany	57.3	20.7	−63.9
Dacia	61.2	65.0	+6.2
Pannonia	64.8	75.9	+17.1
Noricum	82.1	77.3	−5.8

Source: see Table 29.

Table 27 shows that in the Roman evidence age-deviation is usually greater for females. In two-thirds of the samples in Table 27, the age-rounding quotient is higher for females than for males. Two of the exceptions, Italy and Gaul, are cases where the rounding index is relatively low. The sex-variation here is slight. The remaining cases are frontier provinces where the rounding-index is exceptionally high (Germany and Noricum; the female sample from Germany is 45, only one-eighth of the male sample). The underlying reason for these exceptions is likely to be sampling variations, and social discrepancies between samples for males and females.

Bigger sex-variations emerge when we look at some specific social groups (Table 28). These figures indicate that sex-variation in rounding widens in groups which are socially disadvantaged. The Christian evidence is difficult to assess, but added to the data in Table 27, it suggests that sex-variants tended to increase where rounding-quotients were inherently high.

5 Regional differences
Authentic regional variations in age-awareness are difficult to establish decisively, because social differences were potentially powerful enough to override them. For example, the Egyptian data in Table 29 might belong to a higher social milieu than regional samples from the West.[10] As it stands, the Egyptian funerary evidence indicates better age-awareness than in correspond-

---

[10] Sexes have to be combined in the Egyptian figures because the source of data does not separate them; see Duncan-Jones (1979A).

Table 28. *Sex-variation in age-rounding within smaller groups*

Social groups	Male	Female	Female excess over male (percentage)
Freedmen at Rome	47.4	52.9	+11.6
Slaves at Rome	48.5	58.8	+21.2
Freedmen, slaves and 1-name, Carthage	49.7	62.0	+24.7
Christian tombstones at Carthage	58.5	69.6	+19.0

Source: Tables 24 and 25.

Table 29. *Regional variation in Roman age-rounding from funerary records*

Region	Rounding (male) (sample in brackets)	Rounding (male/female) (sample in brackets)
Egypt, tombstones (Tenis)	—	27.1 (69)
Egypt, tombstones (Terenuthis)	—	27.8 (89)
Egypt, mummy labels (Panopolite nome)	—	36.6 (242)
Italy outside Rome	42.6 (1213)	—
Gaul	44.1 (311)	—
Rome	47.0 (2337)	—
Africa and Numidia	51.4 (3110)	—
Mauretania	51.6 (298)	—
Dalmatia	53.3 (358)	—
Spain	56.6 (721)	—
Moesia	57.2 (193)	—
Germany	57.3 (350)	—
Dacia	61.2 (134)	—
Pannonia	64.8 (489)	—
Noricum	82.1 (206)	—

Note: The evidence comes from tombstone inscriptions unless otherwise stated.

Sources: Egypt: Duncan-Jones (1979A); West: Szilagyi (1961–7). The Italian index is based on the Szilagyi 'small' communities, together with Aquileia, Milan, Ostia and Puteoli (Szilagyi (1962) 301, 133–4, 298–9). The data for Mauretania come from Levison (1898) 60, because Szilagyi conflates Mauretania with Africa.

ing samples from the West. The material is drawn from three different parts of Egypt, Terenuthis in the Delta, Tenis, a town between Oxyrhynchus and Antinoopolis, and the Panopolite nome in the Thebaid. The far south, perhaps predictably, shows the highest level of age-rounding. Current ages recorded by the record-office at Tebtunis in the Fayum in the first century AD have a much higher rounding-index of 49.6 (N = 130). This figure is closely comparable with the tombstone samples from the western Mediterranean; this sample from a bureaucratic source is not likely to be economically or socially select.

There is a noticeable 'ethnic' feature in Egypt, the excess representation of ages ending in 6. As a fraction of ages other than multiples of 5, 6 should make up 12.5%. In the mummy ages the quotient is 18%, and in the Tebtunis sample 27%. But the exaggeration is missing from the tombstone samples at Tenis and Terenuthis, and this reinforces the suggestion of social selection in their low rounding-quotients.[11]

The amounts of tombstone data from the Latin West appear very large in aggregate, but in reality they still represent minuscule samples of the population from which they come. They are spread across a number of generations, and the larger regional samples each represent a population running into millions at any given time. In very crude terms, if Africa Proconsularis had a mean population of the order of 6 million, and the actual span of the evidence was at least 10 generations, then a working sample of 3,000 males, as shown in Table 29, would represent one age-figure for every 10,000 male inhabitants. Sampling on such a small scale can still produce statistically valid results, if the sampling techniques are known and are rigorously controlled. But the samples are at the mercy of what happens to survive, and that may be skewed in ways which cannot be detected.

Nevertheless, traces of a hierarchy can be seen in the Latin tombstone quotients. Mediterranean regions appear in general to have had lower rounding-quotients, while frontier regions had higher quotients. Some corresponding difference in educational levels may be plausible. But all these bulk figures show much heavier age-rounding than the small samples from the curial class. The city of Rome fails to stand at the top of the hierarchy. This is essentially a reflection of the social character of surviving tombstone evidence from Rome, in which people of slave origin predominate, as they may have done in the population itself.[12]

6 Local variation

The best forum for studying local variation in rounding-levels is Africa, a region endlessly fertile in Roman tombstones containing age-information. Unlike other parts of the empire, Africa in fact reveals very few tombstones from the Principate which lack an age-statement.[13] At least in part, the variant is chronological, reflecting the late start made in the production of Latin tombstones in the African provinces.[14]

The African evidence can be divided schematically into three sectors, based on distance from Carthage (Table 30).

[11] Duncan-Jones (1979A).   [12] See n.9. Cf. Tables 24 and 25.   [13] Kajanto (1968) 9.
[14] Dating tombstones even approximately is often very difficult. But a useful symptom of the date at which specifying age became the fashion is the very small number of ages in epigraphy from Pompeii, which ends in AD 79.

Table 30. *Local variation in citizen age-rounding in Africa and Numidia*

Area	Males (sample in brackets)	Females
Carthage	42.8 (123)	33.1 (117)
Zone 1 (towns 1–200 km from Carthage)	39.4 (560)	38.0 (440)
Zone 2 (towns 201–300 km from Carthage)	46.4 (689)	47.9 (627)
Zone 3 (towns 301–400 km from Carthage)	59.2 (1574)	60.4 (1200)

Note: Zone 1: Sicca and Ucubi, Thugga, Mactar, Uchi Maius, Mustis, Masculula, Maxula, Thibursicum Bure, Simitthus; zone 2: Thubursicu Numidarum, Madauros, Theveste, Ammaedara, Thibilis, Calama, Thala, Thagaste; zone 3: Lambaesis, Cirtan colonies, Celtianis, Tiddis, Sigus, Mastar, Arsacal, Thamugadi.
Sources: Szilagyi (1965) 315ff.; (1966) 235ff.; (1967) 27; for Carthage, Duncan-Jones (1980A).

Table 31. *African age-rounding in the largest local sample in each zone*

Area	Males (sample in brackets)	Females
Sicca and Ucubi (zone 1)	25.6 (172)	33.3 (135)
Thubursicu Numidarum (zone 2)	41.5 (183)	53.6 (162)
Cirtan colonies (zone 3)	57.3 (389)	59.4 (350)

Source: Szilagyi (1965) 316; 320; 309.

Table 30 shows that age-awareness deteriorates with increasing distance from the capital, itself a well-known centre of learning.[15] All the female figures, and three of the four figures for males, show this clear hierarchy. The one exception is caused by the inclusion in the sample for zone 1 of Sicca and Ucubi, another noted educational centre.[16] Figures for Sicca are shown in Table 31. Both sets of figures in the Table again show that age-awareness appears to decline very sharply with distance from the capital. Part of the male age-pattern reported from the Cirtan colonies is illustrated in figure 20, showing extreme stylisation, which of course intensifies in the coverage of ages from 81 to 120 (omitted from the figure for reasons of space).

7 Other historical evidence

Set against the Roman tombstone ages, the later European evidence (Table 32) has a built-in handicap, because it is based on general surveys of society, not on

[15] Cf. Audollent (1901) 691ff.
[16] *RE*, s.v. Sicca; Cabrol–Leclerq *Dict. d'arch. chrét.* s.v. Kef. Sicca was the birthplace of Arnobius, the medical writer Caelius Aurelianus and the rhetorician Tuticius Proculus (P. de Labriolle *Dict. hist. eccl.* 4.548; *RE* s.v. Caelius Aurelianus; Birley (1967) 132–3).

Table 32. *Age-rounding in later European evidence (ages 23–62)*

Evidence	Male/Female	Male	Female
1. Town of Florence, 1427 census	—	24.6	39.7
2. Florence territory, 1427 census	—	49.3	55.8
3. Pistoia census 1427	42.4	—	—
4. Pozzuoli census 1489	—	72.9	70.6
5. Sorrento census 1561	—	60.7	73.6
6. Geneva deaths 1560–1600	54.5	—	—
7. Geneva deaths 1601–1700	44.5	—	—
8. Geneva deaths 1701–1800	23.4	—	—
9. Liège deaths 1740	26.2	—	—
10. Paris deaths c. 1750	15.3	—	—

Sources: 1–2: Herlihy-Klapisch (1978) 656–62; 3: Herlihy (1967) 283–6; 4–5: Beloch (1937) 1.29–31; 6–10: Mols (1956) 3.203–6 (mis-scaled so that 20 is shown as 19, etc.).

Table 33. *Age-rounding and illiteracy in twentieth-century censuses*

Place and date of census	Rounding (ages 23–62)		Excess female rounding (percentage)	Illiteracy from age 15 (percentage)	
	Male	Female		Male	Female
1. Egypt 1947	74.9	80.4	7.3	68.5	91.3
2. Morocco 1960	53.1	67.4	26.9	78.1	94.0
3. Iran 1966	35.8	44.2	23.5	67.2	87.8
4. Iraq 1957	26.1	32.2	23.4	76.1	94.7
5. Nicaragua 1963	22.6	24.0	6.2	49.9	50.8
6. Turkey 1965	21.8	42.6	95.4	35.5	72.6
7. Guatemala 1950	20.9	32.3	54.5	65.6	75.6
8. Ceylon 1963	19.5	27.6	41.5	14.6	36.1
9. Mexico 1970	12.7	16.0	26.0	20.6	27.0
10. Brazil 1950	10.5	12.9	22.9	45.2	55.8
Average	29.8	38.0	27.5	52.1	68.6

Sources: 1: *Demographic Yearbook (DY)* 1955) 276; *World illiteracy at Mid-century*, UNESCO (1957) 53; 2: *DY* (1963) 660; *Compendium of Social Statistics 1967*, UN Statistical Office (1968) *(CSS)* 311; 3: *DY* (1971) 223; (1970) 588; 4: *DY* (1963) 670; *CSS* 323; 5: *DY* (1971) 200; *CSS* 317; 6: *DY* (1971) 244; (1970) 589; 7: *DY* (1955) 301; (1960) 438; 8: *DY* (1971) 218; (1970) 587; 9: *DY* (1971) 199; (1970) 586; 10: *DY* (1955) 313; *CSS* 319.

Table 34. *Correlation between coefficients for age-rounding and illiteracy*

	Spearman correlation	Probability (percentage)	Product-moment correlation	Probability (percentage)
Males	0.791	> 95	0.595	> 90
Females	0.709	> 90	0.721	> 98

Source: Table 33.

information from monuments which only some could afford. In spite of this, part of the Renaissance evidence still equals or surpasses Roman levels of age-accuracy. The best case, the figure for males in the Florence census of 1427, is superior to almost all the Roman figures, with the one exception of Roman town councillors (Table 24; the Egyptian tombstone-samples also approach this level, Table 29).

Whatever regional and national variants may have influenced them, these later figures as they stand show progressive improvement from the fifteenth to the eighteenth century. The initial comparison makes it clear that at its best, age-awareness in post-medieval Tuscany was already substantially better than in any bulk sample from the Roman West.

8 Age-rounding and illiteracy

Statistics from developing countries in the twentieth century allow quotients for age-rounding and for illiteracy to be juxtaposed.[17] Some results are shown in Table 33.

These figures refer to ten populations in which a noticeable age-rounding tendency and heavy illiteracy exist side by side. On average, age-rounding distortion is less than in most evidence from the Roman world, though sometimes still quite high. There is some relationship between age-rounding and illiteracy, which shows signs of being high enough to be statistically significant (Table 34). Table 33 shows that there is at least a *de facto* association between age-rounding and illiteracy in some modern populations. Table 34 suggests that the relationship is in some degree systematic. Although age-rounding levels are typically well below Roman levels, they are accompanied in these twentieth-century samples by a degree of illiteracy which is in some cases very high.

It can readily be argued that these comparisons involve too many cultural variants to allow direct analogy with Roman conditions. But the indications that age-rounding and illiteracy are in some sense allied phenomena are difficult to reject. Comparisons within the Roman period which reveal enormous variation

[17] For literacy cf. Cipolla (1969); Harris (1983); Marrou (1965); Goody (1977).

in age-awareness must also reckon with the likelihood of some corresponding, though not necessarily commensurate, difference in literacy. The case of the Egyptian landowner seen at the beginning of the chapter is a warning against thinking that wealth always carried with it either numeracy or literacy.

9 Conclusions

The survey shows that age-awareness in the Roman empire was seriously defective, despite the fact that most of the data comes from economically select groups whose members could afford stone tombstones. Modern parallels suggest that defective age-awareness is often accompanied by a low level of literacy, and that the two deficiencies can express similar forms of ignorance. The gradations in the Roman evidence also show quite separately that there were large social and geographical variants in age-awareness. These gradations in some sense quantify differences by class and by region, in a way that other sources can rarely achieve.

6
Roman life-expectancy

This brief survey considers three pieces of demographic evidence from the Roman world. They consist of a register of town councillors, an actuarial table from a Roman lawyer and a body of age-statements from tombstone inscriptions and papyri.

1 The album of Canusium

The complete list of the town council at Canusium in southern Italy as it stood in AD 223 is both a source for Roman municipal history of almost unique value, and a potential source of demographic information.[1]

The key to any demographic interpretation is the age at which office-holding began. The inscription lists a standard Roman town-council of 100 members, of whom 68 had held at least one magistracy. Its contents allow two possible reconstructions. The standard legal age for entry to the town council and to the junior magistracies was 25.[2] In a society where life-expectancy was far below modern western levels, the legal age-threshold was quite likely to function in practice as both minimum and maximum. The pressures were if anything for age-thresholds to be lower: when tombstones break their customary silence about the age of magistrates, it is often to reveal a case in which office was held below the legal minimum age.[3]

Town magistracies were normally held in parallel by two colleagues, like the original consulships of Rome. Canusium had *duoviri* as its chief magistrates; because offices were held in sequence (see below), there would only have been enough candidates for the duovirate if the lower magistracies, the quaestorship and aedileship, were also collegiate. The album lists 9 men at the level of quaestor (the current holders, together with the surviving ex-quaestors who had not yet

---

[1] The standard publication is *CIL* IX 338; for a fuller publication, with a photograph of the original, see M. Chelotta, R. Gaeta, V. Morizio, M. Silvestrini *Le epigrafi romane di Canosa* I (1985) no.35. Office-holding at Canusium as shown in the album has been examined by Garnsey (1974); Jacques (1984) 508–25; Horstkotte (1984).

[2] *ILS* 6089, 54 and other sources in Liebenam (1900) 269.

[3] Cf. *JRS* 67 (1977) 196 and Liebenam (1900) 269. Cf. also Jarrett (1972) and Morris (n.8 below).

risen any higher); 19 at the level of aedile, the intermediate post; and 40 at the senior level of *duovir*, 7 of whom had held the post in a quinquennial year, making them 'duoviri quinquennales'; and 4 more were honorary *quinquennales* ('adlecti inter quinquennalicios').

The number of surviving office-holders is 68. In itself that suggests that, under the prevailing demographic regime, a regular annual intake of 2 magistrates per year at age 25 produced 68 survivors. The 4 *adlecti* were appointed to the most senior rank without having held the qualifying office, and that might suggest that their careers contained other irregularities.[4]

In the most extreme case, all 4 might through social advantages have obtained positions of seniority without holding the quaestorship. If that were so, they would not belong to the population of ex-quaestors whose survival-rate is in question here. Though such irregularities were not excluded, we do not know whether they were frequent. The law laid down that local offices should be held one after the other in order of seniority.[5] The city was entitled to ask that its office-holders held all the magistracies in the local career, and the very common expression 'O(mnibus) H(onoribus) F(unctus)' in inscriptions of the later Principate tends to argue that complete local careers were the norm for those who survived long enough to hold all the magistracies.[6]

Two reconstructions of the demographic regime can thus be made. One of them, reconstruction A, assumes that the list contains 68 quaestors and ex-quaestors. The other, reconstruction B, assumes that there are only 64, and that the 4 men adlected to a senior post had bypassed the quaestorship. Reconstruction A appears to be better supported by the evidence for patterns of office-holding cited above.

This produces 68 survivors from an annual intake of 2 men per year holding the quaestorship at approximately the age of 25. That implies that expectation of life at 25 (e 25) is 34 years. The closest fit in the Princeton Tables (South) is with Level 6, where expectation of life at birth is 31.7 years ($e(0) = 33.995$). Infant mortality at this level is 278 per thousand.[7]

Reconstruction B instead provides 64 survivors, implying life-expectation at age 25 of 32 years. The closest fit here is with Level 4 (e 25 = 31.979). Here life-expectation at birth is 27, and infant mortality is 329 per thousand.

The essential conclusion is that if the Canusium figures refer to a stationary population, they are consistent with a mean expectation of life at birth for males of about 32 years (or, on a less well-supported interpretation, about 27 years).[8]

---

[4] Cf. *JRS* (1977) 196.   [5] Liebenam (1900) 269.   [6] Cf. *ILS* 3, pp.689-90.
[7] Coale–Demeny (1983).
[8] Since a qualifying age of 25 means any age between 25 and 26, using 25 years and 0 months as the baseline is potentially imprecise. But by this date any age from 24 upwards was legally acceptable, (see sources cited by Morris (1964) 317; for inclusive counting, see *ERE*[2] 118 (264) and 378)).

1.1 Age-thresholds

The Princeton South Tables are based on Mediterranean populations from Italy, Spain and Portugal, but they cannot be pressed beyond a certain point as a model for Roman demographic structures.[9] Where there are great contrasts in typical mean longevity, age-structures may potentially diverge in important ways. Nevertheless, rough outlines of the age-structure underlying office-holding at Canusium can probably be gained from the Princeton model.

At Canusium, men of quaestorian rank made up 14.06% of office-holders, *aedilicii* 29.69% and *duoviralicii* 56.25%. These percentages in the age-structure for Princeton South Level 6 (r = o) are as follows:

Category	Age	Percentage of men over 25
First group (*quaestoricii*)	25.00–29.91 years	14.06
Second group (*aedilicii*)	29.91–41.34 years	29.69
Third group (*duoviralicii* and *adlecti*)	41.34– years	56.25

The Princeton model suggests that in practice the age-thresholds for the higher magistracies may have been approximately 30 years for the aedileship, and 40 or 41 for the duovirate. But it is not known whether there were formal age-thresholds for the higher magistracies at Canusium, or at Italian cities in general under the Principate. If there were no formal thresholds, it need not be the case (assuming appointment by election rather than by seniority) that all *aedilicii* were older than all *quaestoricii*.

Another detail of the Canusium list affects its implications for age-classes. Three senior *duoviri* are named as having held the duovirate twice. This means that the list contains a maximum of 43 tenures of the office, rather than the 40 implied by the number of individuals on the list. Present conclusions about the number of survivors from the quaestorship do not seem to be affected, since the number of men entering the cadres of office-holders was limited to the two holders of the quaestorship each year. But had there been no repeated duovirates, the distribution of the office-classes would be different, with more ex-duovirs and fewer *aedilicii*. Fluidity of this kind probably argues against any attempt to detect formal age-thresholds behind the Canusium figures. Nevertheless, the

Given a legal threshold of 24 years, the true baseline for a reconstruction should be 24.5 years (since the individual had equal chances of finding that his 24th birthday fell 1 day or 364 days before the annual municipal elections). Given a legal threshold of 25, the true baseline should be 25.5 years for the same reason. But we cannot estimate which threshold, 24 or 25 years, was more common in practice, and 25 years and o months is therefore an acceptable approximation.

[9] Coale–Demeny (1983) 12.

figures clearly imply a mean interval of approximately four years between quaestorship and aedileship, and approximately ten years between aedileship and duovirate.

Several minor areas of imprecision remain.

(1). Some men could have held the quaestorship after the age of 25. This would raise the implied level of life-expectancy.

(2). Some magistrates, through social influence like that reflected in the adlections 'inter duoviralicios', could conceivably have omitted a junior office. This would reduce implied life-expectancy.

(3). The pattern shown by a single document might be affected by fortuitous changes which cannot be allowed for (such as epidemics of unusual severity, or political disturbances).

These potential sources of distortion cannot be controlled or allowed for in any demographic use made of the Canusium evidence. Minor distortions would alter the implications, without changing them beyond recognition: thus a hidden error of $+/-$ 2 years in the assumed age of quaestors would change projected life-expectation at birth by $+/-$ 3 years.

2 The Ulpian Table

The one Roman document which explicitly refers to survival-rates comes from a Roman legal source. A jurist of the early third century, Aemilius Macer, gives figures for expected survival at particular ages, citing Ulpian as his authority. They represent the factors officially used in 'grossing up' the value of bequeathed life-annuities for legal purposes. Ulpian's figures are shown in Table 35.[10]

It might readily seem that figures from a legal context should have some official standing. But numerous observations are needed to produce an efficient descriptive life-table, as well as some knowledge of sampling technique. The fact that the Ulpian figures give the same survival-quotient for age-spans of five years or even longer makes it very unlikely that these requirements were satisfied.

We can explore the implications of the figures by assigning the survival-rate to the mid-point in each five-year period, and supplying rates for the remainder of the period by linear interpolation. This produces relatively consistent results (Table 35).

Applying these figures to the standard age-thresholds used in modern life-

---

[10] *D.* 35.2.68. pr. Frier (1982), 214–19 discusses the context at length, arguing that despite inclusion of this text mentioning the lex Falcidia in the Digest title on that law, its true context must be the levying of 'vicesima', the 5% inheritance tax, referred to here as a gloss for 'Falcidia'.

But it is difficult to see the stated context as implausible. The lex Falcidia preserved 25% of an estate for the legal heir as a rigid minimum, thus requiring a precise valuation. If the portion not left to the heir happened to include life-annuities, the legality of the will under the lex Falcidia could only be established by valuing the annuities. In order to do this, the expected duration of the annuities had to be worked out, which gave the Ulpian Table its obvious purpose.

Table 35. *Survival-rates in Ulpian*
Ulpian figures from age 20

Age	Survival (years)	Single-year equivalent age
20–24	28	22.5
25–29	25	27.5
30–34	22	32.5
35–39	20	37.5
40	19	
41	18	
42	17	
43	16	
44	15	
45	14	
46	13	
47	12	
48	11	
49	10	
50–54	9	52.5
55–59	7	57.5

Table 36. *Implied survival-rates at standard age-thresholds*

Age	Survival (interpolated from Ulpian)
20	29.5
25	26.5
30	23.5
35	21.0
40	19.0*
45	14.0*
50	9.7
55	8.0
60	5.0*

*Survival-rate stated by Ulpian, not interpolated

Table 37. *Median life-expectancy I*

Age	Frier Table 5	Ulpian (interpreted in Table 36 above)	Frier/Ulpian difference (percentage)
20	28.17	29.5	⁻4.5
25	25.32	26.5	⁻4.5
30	22.49	23.5	⁻4.3
35	19.72	21.0	−6.1
40	17.16	19.0	−9.7
45	14.70	14.0	+5.0
50	12.35	9.7	+27.3
55	10.09	8.0	+26.1
60	8.10	5.0	+62.0

tables, and supplying survival-rates by interpolation, the implications of Ulpian's figures can be shown more fully (Table 36).

2.1

Frier has analysed and defended Ulpian's figures at length in a detailed study, partly in the light of selected modern census-data from Mauritius in the 1940s, and partly in the light of the life-table in Princeton West model 2. Like Dupâquier, he interprets Ulpian's data as figures for median life-expectancy, or probable length of life, not mean expectation of life ($e(x)$), familiar as a coefficient in modern life-tables.[11] This interpretation is convincing, since it is unlikely that Ulpian can have aimed at, or have seen the need for, a measure which can be calculated only by totalling all lives lived within the sample utilised.

By a series of calculations, Frier constructs a full model life-table starting from Ulpian's figures, but including sophisticated supplements and elaborations.[12] The results depart somewhat from the starting-point, if we accept the figures in Table 36 deduced by linear interpolation. The main discrepancies are shown in Table 37 (median life-expectancy is calculated from Frier's figures for $l(x)$). For the five age-groups from 20–24 up to 40–44, Frier's implicit target is approximately 5% below the point of reference. There are further discrepancies of larger size between Ulpian's figures (as derived in Table 36) and the two models which Frier uses as a starting point. These are shown in Table 38. This Table shows that, for the age-range where Ulpian's data best approximates other series, both the models consistently fall below Ulpian's figures for life-expectancy. That makes life-expectancy in Ulpian significantly higher than in the models. But the consolidated model that Frier derives, using Ulpian as the

---

[11] Frier (1982); Dupâquier (1973). See also Jacques (1984) 497–500.   [12] Frier (1982) Table 5.

Table 38. *Median life-expectancy II*

Age	Princeton West Level 2 (males)	Mauritius 1942–4 (males)	Ulpian (Table 36) percentage difference from Princeton	Ulpian percentage difference from Mauritius
20	27.45	28.37	+7.5	+4.0
25	24.69	25.03	+7.3	+5.9
30	21.94	21.87	+7.1	+7.5
35	19.29	18.79	+8.9	+11.8
40	16.86	15.80	+12.7	+20.3

Table 39. *Ulpian's figures compared with two model life-tables: median life-expectancy at specific ages*

Age	Ulpian (Table 36)	Princeton S(1) (e(o) = 19.9)	Difference (Ulpian/PS(1)) (percentage)	Princeton S(3) (e(o) = 24.7)	Difference (PS(1)/PS(3)) (percentage)
20	29.5	32.39	−9.0	38.81	−16.5
25	26.5	29.93	−11.5	32.78	−8.6
30	23.5	27.08	−13.3	29.61	−8.5
35	21.0	24.01	−12.5	26.11	−8.0
40	19.0	20.82	−8.8	22.57	−7.8
45	14.0	17.63	−20.6	19.17	−8.0
50	9.7	14.48	−33.0	15.82	−8.5
55	8.0	11.52	−30.6	12.64	−8.8
60	5.0	8.76	−42.9	9.68	−9.5

starting-point, contains the opposite difference. Here life-expectation at birth (e(o)) is 21.11 years. The corresponding figure for Mauritius is far above this (32.25 M), and the consolidated (MF) model for Princeton West (2) does not fall below it.[13]

2.2

If comparison is based on the Princeton model derived from Mediterranean populations, it could instead be argued that life-expectancy in Ulpian's figures is notably low. Comparisons with the Princeton South model are shown in Table 39. The last column of the Table shows that for the initial five age-cohorts, the

[13] Frier's Table 5 does not differentiate between the sexes. In Princeton West (2) e(o) = 20.444 (M)/ 22.500 (F). For a suggestion that the South model would fit his figures better, see Frier (1982) 251, n.84.

Ulpian figures roughly follow the curve of Princeton S(1). The Ulpian readings are all well below the corresponding Princeton readings, and they show a median difference for these five cohorts of −11.5%. The last column shows the differences between Princeton South (1) and Princeton South (3), where the median difference for the first five cohorts is −8.5%.

Life-tables for expectation at birth significantly below 20 years are not readily available. But in crude terms Table 39 suggests that the Ulpian figures are at least as far below Princeton S(1) as Princeton S(1) is below Princeton S(3). The implied mean life-expectation at birth in Ulpian's population ($e(0)$) would appear from the comparison to be well below 20 years.

Any such finding is disquieting, since the implied reproduction rate would be very high, perhaps higher than any rate securely observed in recent times.[14] Argument based on the Princeton South model thus leads to three possible results.

(1) The population reflected in Ulpian's figures had a very low expectation of life at birth, significantly less than 20 years, but was not necessarily self-sustaining, because of the very high birth-rate required.

(2) Ulpian's figures were not based on accurate demographic observation; those given for age-cohorts over 50 are difficult to credit on any interpretation.

(3) Differences between the Roman demographic experience reflected in Ulpian's figures, and that of recent populations reflected in the model life-tables, are too wide to allow one to be interpreted in terms of the other.

Possibilities (2) and (3), which are not mutually exclusive, are effectively negative. Whether the first possibility, that the implied life-expectation was in fact very low, is plausible depends on the social context that the figures refer to.

2.3

If the Ulpian data describes a real population, argument from the Princeton South model suggests a demographic regime far removed from the pattern at Canusium. Yet the Ulpian figures belong to a world of property-transfers among those rich enough to bequeath life-annuities, and that world too is essentially upper-class.

But examined in detail, the context contains a crucial social difference. In many cases, probably the majority, the subjects of Ulpian's calculation can only have been slaves or ex-slaves. The life-table was produced to assess the value of bequests of maintenance annuities in money or in kind (*alimenta*).[15] The plentiful

---

[14] The GRR for a stationary population in Princeton S(1) is 3.23, approximately 6¼ live births per adult female on average.

[15] This of course specifically referred to maintenance grants which ceased on the death of the recipient, not to perpetual grants for supporting a number of children, on the pattern of Trajan's *alimenta*.

evidence for such bequests shows that the beneficiaries of life-annuities were typically members of the dead man's household.[16] That meant slaves, or more commonly ex-slaves.[17] Senators might provide for whole troops of their household staff in this way. In Pliny's case, these provisions seem to reflect genuine concern for the well-being of dependants who might otherwise face destitution.[18] One magnate even bequeathed his house at Arles for his freedmen to live in till the end of their days.[19]

Thus if Ulpian's table was empirical, it should reflect life-expectancy in the population of servile origin to which it would usually have applied. Considered in this way, the quotients for earlier ages in Table 36 may be relatively plausible. But the figures remain very crude.

3 Ages in inscriptions and papyri

The demographic data in the Canusium album and the Ulpian Table does not depend on statements by individuals about their own age. But the moment that we start to use such data, new problems begin. Where available, successive age-declarations by the same individual often show quite arbitrary discrepancies. Whether because of vagueness or because of innumeracy where age was concerned, a man of property might shed as much as five years between one age-declaration and the next.[20] These cross-checks, where available, clearly show that bureaucratic requirements were rarely matched by the knowledge needed for accurate age-declarations. Even where statements cannot be separately checked, the very high incidence of stylised and exaggerated ages points to serious limitations in age-awareness (see chapter 5).

Similar clashes between bureaucratic expectations and the limited capacities of the population at large were a feature of British India. Census-takers there freely recognised that much of the age-data that they collected had little or no value.[21] Whether Roman officials fully understood the problem is less obvious. The elder Pliny, writing as a veteran administrator of high rank, cites a series of impossibly high ages declared in Italy in the census of Vespasian. But it seems clear that he believed the figures.[22]

If private age-information outside the upper elite of Roman society tended to be fallible, peculiarities can be expected almost wherever we find age-data dependent on individuals. Ages from tombstones and census-declarations tend

---

[16] See Pliny's will supporting 100 of his freedmen (*ILS* 2927) and juristic evidence cited in ERE², 30 and notes 1–5; p.29, n.8; p.341, Appendix 5.

[17] Slaves not freed in the will were normally bequeathed with the estate, and so would be maintained thereafter by their new owner. It was primarily freedmen belonging to the owner's household at the time of his death for whom provision might be needed.

[18] Compare Pliny's letters about his household, his nurse and his physician (8.16; 6.3; 10.5–7), and the bequest to his freedmen (n.16).   [19] *D.* 33.2.34. pr.   [20] Chapter 5, p.80.

[21] Cf. J. Hutton in *Census of India 1931*, 1.1.81–5.   [22] *NH* 7.162–4.

Table 40. *Median life-expectancy at age twenty*

Princeton South (1) (male/female)	Egyptian census documents (male/female)	Egyptian tombstones (Terenuthis)	African tombstones (Sicca) (male)
33.5	17.5	23.5	32.3

to be highly stylised, with strong biasses toward multiples of 5 and 10 (and even to other digits: 6 was another favourite in Egypt, as was 1 in the Roman Maghreb).[23]

Much of the tombstone data is also biassed towards representation of particular parts of the age-spectrum, the age of early deaths being recorded, while later deaths lack any figure.[24] Serious biasses are present even in regions where virtually all tombstones carry an age-figure, as in North Africa.[25] Comparisons with model life-tables show that these figures contain marked age-exaggeration. The signs are unmistakeable even in the samples where digital distortion is lowest. At Sicca Veneria, where male age-rounding is lower than in any other substantial local sample, the proportion of survivors at 20 alive at 80 is implied as 16.7%; in Princeton South (1) the proportion is 1.9%.[26]

Age-data from census-declarations, because it comes from an official context, might seem more reliable than private statements on tombstones. But such data still almost always depended on the individual, whose grasp of his own age tended to be poor. Age-statements in papyri still show much age-rounding, and it seems to be only in cases where official birth records were specifically utilised (as in poll-tax lists based on age) that age-rounding disappears.[27]

It is worth noticing a few implications shown in Table 40.[28] The Egyptian examples there suggest levels of life-expectancy far below the most modest projections in the Princeton South model (column 1). But their accuracy and

23 Chapter 5, p.81. Other sources which have been cited in this context include ages estimated from skeletal remains (cf. Frier (1983)), and ages deduced by indirect means from tax-declarations (Samuel (1971)). Both sources appear uncertain, ages from skeletal remains being generally imprecise (cf. Brothwell (1981)).

24 For an important basic discussion, see Hopkins (1966); see also Clauss (1973), Kajanto (1968) and Ery (1969). Tombstone data from the city of Rome (cf. Harkness (1896)) provides a prime illustration of the distortion in question.   25 Kajanto (1968) 9.

26 Accepting for this comparison the common convention which treats a tabulation of tombstone-ages at death as if it were a life-table showing survivors at age (x). The tombstone sample from the 4 Cirtan colonies, used extensively by Frier, possesses one of the highest rounding coefficients on record, and is very unlikely to have any serious value as demographic evidence (see chapter 5, fig. 20 and Table 31). The fact that heaping of Roman ages into 5s, essentially through ignorance, resembles the quinquennial divisions used in life-tables (invoked by Frier 236, n. 56) does not do anything to remove distortions.   27 See Duncan-Jones (1979B) Table 4.

28 Census-data, Hombert–Préaux (1952) 159–60; Terenuthis, Boyaval (1976) 235; Sicca, Szilagyi (1965) 316.

linearity cannot readily be assessed. If old people are under-represented, the quotients will do little more than reflect this fact. Consequently these co-ordinates do not provide any demonstration about life-expectancy in Egypt.

The tombstone sample from Sicca in Africa, where age-rounding was exceptionally slight, shows a quotient closely approaching that of Princeton South (1). But as mentioned, exaggeration of higher ages is clearly seen here, and it is essentially arbitrary to think that inability to state age correctly was limited to the higher age-cohorts.

There are in effect two levels of scepticism about the demographic value of this data. At the first level, without necessarily questioning the validity of tombstone-age data as such, we could question their statistical value, both because of their likely non-linearity as a sample of ages at death, and because they represent a random scatter of data from a very long period. The one attempt that has been made to check the demographic patterns shown by tombstone-ages against reliable records of births and deaths in fact showed wholesale distortions, which meant that the tombstone-ages failed to represent the demographic patterns already known.[29]

Scepticism at the second level must also take in the inconsistencies and stylisations seen in age-reporting by individuals (chapter 5), and it would lead to the conclusion that evidence which depends on individual age-statements is inherently suspect as a source of demographic information.

4 Conclusion

The album of Canusium may show life expectation at birth in the upper class at a town in southern Italy in the early third century AD as approximately 32 years. The evidence from the Ulpian Table is much more open to debate. Assessed by a Mediterranean model, its quotients appear very low. But the Table was evidently applied to a population of mainly servile origin. The tens of thousands of age-statements in inscriptions and papyri are subject to palpable distortions; despite their numbers, the samples are in reality very small indeed, granted the period of many generations from which they come. Though age-statements should at least indicate whether an individual considered himself young or old, their value as a basis for any systematic inference about life-expectancy is almost certainly very slight.

To draw overall conclusions from this variegated evidence about the demographic regime of Roman society is hardly possible. An uncontroversial working assumption about Roman life-expectation at birth places it within a range between 20 and 30 years.[30] Big nutritional differences, apart from anything else, almost certainly meant major class-variants in survival-rates. An upper-

---

[29] L. Henry's study of French provincial tombstones of the 1830s, Henry (1959) 327–9.
[30] Cf. Hopkins (1966) 263.

class figure for life-expectation at birth of over 30 years, and what may be a servile figure below 20, suggest possible elements in the range of variation. The extent of variation between town and country remains imponderable, though the fact of heavier mortality in large urban centres of the Mediterranean in the pre-modern period is one which the Roman world can hardly have escaped.[31]

[31] Cf. Brunt (1971) 134, 385, arguing from later parallels. The seasonality of death in the city of Rome plainly indicates peaks in infectious disease (Duncan-Jones (1980B) 78 n.): in the late Roman period, Christian tombstones dated by month (N = 2125) show a period of three months, from August to October, during which the average monthly death-rate is 80% higher than in the rest of the year.

7
Pay and numbers in Diocletian's army

The Beatty papyri originally consisted of two long rolls containing a day-to-day transcript of high-level correspondence sent to Panopolis in AD 298–300 by the authorities governing the Thebaid. The long series of letters, whose frequent refrain is the failure of subordinates to carry out instructions, gives the most graphic impression of Roman provincial government in action; and the dossier is in its way as important as Pliny's correspondence with Trajan two hundred years earlier.

The letters used here describe payments to ten different army units stationed in the Thebaid, which together made up a large part of the garrison of southern Egypt. Because they contain instructions to pay, the letters specify unit, amount, type of payment and period covered. If in a single case either the rate or the number of recipients can be convincingly identified, much wider information about unit-strengths and military spending under Diocletian potentially becomes available.

In an important pioneering discussion, A.H.M. Jones analysed the payments in money, using smallest round-figure denominators and common denominators. His results suggested that unit-strengths were relatively high, but that the basic rates of army pay (*stipendium*) late in Diocletian's reign were still what they had been early in the third century.

His interpretation, although based on ingenious analysis, and orthodox in some of its results, is not entirely convincing (Appendix 5).

(1) The interpretation does not take into account payments in kind detailed in the first papyrus (to one of the units whose money-payments are also shown), whose implications sharply conflict with those deduced by Jones from the later payments in money. Where Jones does make use of parallel sources for a given unit, the resulting estimates are somewhat inconsistent.

(2) His interpretation implies that despite the third-century inflation, the basic rate of army pay under Diocletian was still what it had been under Caracalla.

* This discussion has been revised without being substantially changed. A preliminary summary has been added as an aid to following the argument.

The present reconstructions start instead from the payments in kind. Two crucial cases (the *ala* at Thmou, and the *lanciarii* at Ptolemais Hormou) contain parallel details of payment in kind and payment in money. The new estimates obtained from these two sources agree to within narrow tolerances (0.01% for the numbers implied by barley rations and wheat rations at Thmou; 0.12% for numbers at Ptolemais Hormou from oil allowance compared with donative). The wheat:barley totals for the cavalry at Thmou are within 0.01% of an exact ratio of 1:4.5, and the rations implied for two months are simple round figures (5 modii per man, 5 artabas per horse).

Where the two cases overlap, the relatively low numbers implied by the rations in kind argue that the donatives cannot have been as small as Jones assumed. The rates for an officer, which are known explicitly, seem to have applied elsewhere, and this makes the unit-strengths indicated by donatives correspondingly lower than in Jones's synopsis.

Stated briefly, the conclusions are that the basic rate of army pay was probably six times higher under Diocletian than at the end of the first century AD under Domitian; that all the legionary units here corresponded to quingenary vexillations; but that the auxiliary strengths were much below levels known earlier (as are many details of unit-strength implied in other evidence from the late Empire (Appendix 4)); and finally, that despite large payments of donative, the real value of military pay under Diocletian was seriously below that in earlier periods.

1 Discussion

Size and pay are crucial to our perceptions of the Roman army. Documents of the mid-Principate throw some light on both, but mysteries increase in the third century.[1] The reign of Diocletian provides what amounts to a sudden flood of information from one part of the empire, which however is not easy to interpret.[2]

1.1 The payments in grain

The first Beatty papyrus records payments in kind to what was evidently one of the troop units whose receipts in money are listed in the second papyrus.[3] 'The

---

[1] Cf. Watson (1969), Speidel (1973), Jahn (1983) and (1984).

[2] For military developments in this period, cf. Ritterling (1903), Grosse (1920), Várady (1962), Hoffmann (1969).

[3] *P Beatty Panop* edited by T.C. Skeat. The span of time covered by the letters authorising payment was 28 January–1 March 300: 2.249; 270. Virtually all the payments were made in arrear. For the supply system at work, and the considerable distances involved, see Bowman (1978). The examination of Egyptian dry measures carried out in *CAM* is important to part of the present argument. The arguments in Shelton (1981) for refusing to recognise the choenix as a quantifying device, or to accept as artabas measures quantified by non-standard numbers of choenices, remain unconvincing (cf. Duncan-Jones (1979B) 368; for the Pharaonic evidence in that discussion, see now Spalinger (1987) 309–10).

soldiers under the prefect Papas, stationed in the fort of Thmou' were assigned as allowances in kind for the Egyptian months of Thoth and Phaophi (29 August–27 October) 2,610 Italic modii of barley and $128\frac{7}{8}$ artabas of wheat. The two payments were authorised on 24 September 298 (1.392–8). Sixteen months later, on 30 January 300, 'the cavalrymen under the command of Besas, decurio of the ala I Hiberorum stationed at Thmou' were paid 73,500 denarii as *stipendium* for the 4 months due on 1 January 300, and 23,600 as *annona* for the 4 months starting on 1 September 299 (2.36–42). As Skeat concluded, both documents refer to the same detachment: it was thought unnecessary in the first document to individuate the detachment of troops at Thmou by name, implying that there was only one detachment there. But the barley payment indicates that they were cavalrymen. The *ala I Hiberorum* is referred to at Thmou in another Diocletianic papyrus, and also figures as the garrison of this fort in the *Notitia Dignitatum*.[4]

The barley allocation is defined as 2,610 Italic modii (22,494 litres).[5] The official fodder ration (*capitum*) in a sixth-century military papyrus was 4 choenices (3.2 litres) of barley per horse per day.[6] Applied here, this rate produces a total of exactly 116 rations.[7] Assuming that as in other official papyri of the early fourth century, the tax-artaba of $4\frac{1}{2}$ Italic modii was being used, the wheat allowance of $128\frac{7}{8}$ artabas for the cavalrymen equals 116 shares of 5 Italic modii,

[4] *PBeatty Panop* xxvi; *POxy* 2953; *ND* Or. 31.46. For a Diocletianic date for the Egyptian information in the *Notitia*, cf. Price (1976) 144.

[5] For the Italic modius as 8.6185 litres, see *CAM* Appendix.

[6] *POxy* 2046 (see Jones (1964) 3.192, n.44; cf. *RE* s.v. Capitum). The allowance is $\frac{1}{10}$ artaba per day; the artaba used there has 40 choenices (1.58 and note), implying an allowance of 4 choenices = $\frac{3}{8}$ of an Italic modius = 3.232 litres (cf. *CAM* 43–4). The barley ration for cavalry horses in a Ptolemaic papyrus of 169 BC was 3 choenices per day (*SB* 6.9600). But inserting this figure in the present document creates seriously irregular totals for wheat rations, for *stipendium* and for *annona*. Cavalry under the mid-Republic apparently received far more, citizen horses 12.1 and allied 8.6 litres of barley per day (Polybius 6.39; for the Attic medimnos as 6 Italic modii, see *CAM* n.16). But other late evidence shows much lower levels. The stone measure labelled as a 'capitum hordei' at Cuicul in Numidia has a capacity of 5.7 litres, indicating a lesser original capacity, allowing for the internal bronze measure that is missing (Albertini (1920)); probably set up *c.* AD 386, following the instructions about public tax-measures in *CTh* 12.6.21.

Barley was not the only ingredient in horse feed: the cavalry in *POxy* 2046 also received daily rations of hay. Chaff was also important (cf. e.g. *PBeatty Panop* p.177). In the U.S. Cavalry, a 1,000-pound horse was fed 10 pounds of grain (7.3 litres if barley) and 11 pounds of hay per day (Thomas (1974) 223, 230).

[7] For accounting purposes 2 months = 60 days. $60 \times \frac{3}{8}$ Italic modii = $22\frac{1}{2}$ Italic modii. 2,610 / $22\frac{1}{2}$ = 116.

[8] See e.g. the long account in *PPrinc Roll* of AD 310–324 (2.4; 4.4; 6.4; 8.12); *PThead* 31 (319–20). *PLips* 97 shows the *metron modion (xyston)* with 48 choenices (Duncan-Jones (1976B) 259. The artaba of 48 choenices = $4\frac{1}{2}$ Italic modii in *PLond* 1718 (*CAM* 44–4). $4\frac{1}{2} \times 128\frac{1}{8}\frac{1}{24}$ = 579.94 modii; (the further 1/72 artaba needed for an exact result was omitted). The ratio of wheat to barley is none the less stated as 1:4.5 with an error of 0.01%. The precision is almost as great in sixth-century figures for wheat and barley issued to *numeri* at Hermopolis, where the target ratio is 1:4 (240:958$\frac{1}{4}$ = 1:3.99; Johnson–West (1949) 223). In Polybius, wheat:barley ratios are 1:3$\frac{1}{2}$ (citizen cavalry) and 1:3$\frac{3}{4}$ (allied cavalry; 6.39).

to within 0.01%.[8] This wheat ration for a two-month period is relatively low, but the troops received cash for *annona* as well.[9]

The interpretation reveals a very simple reckoning: for the two-month period, men got 5 modii and horses got 5 artabas ($128.875 \times 4.5 = 580$ modii (within 0.01%); $580/116 = 5$. $2610/4.5 = 580$ artabas; $580/116 = 5$).

1.2 Annona

Jones did not refer to these payments in kind, but argued from the total 32,866 (Table 51 line U) that the usual payment for *annona* for 4 months must have been $66\frac{2}{3}$ denarii per head and therefore exactly 200 per year. It followed that the *annona* total for the Thmou garrison at the beginning of AD 300 (Table 51 line B) gave a total of 354 men. This proves to be an almost exact multiple of the total indicated by the payments in kind sixteen months earlier (116×3.05). Radical changes are always conceivable where so little is known, but the possibility that numbers remained the same should also be considered. On a 'steady state' view, the rate of *annona* should be 200 denarii per man for 4 months in place of $66\frac{2}{3}$. That leads to a total of 118 recipients, an insignificant increase. The lesser hypothesis, that numbers remained stable, is easier to credit. There are indications of small garrisons in the second papyrus (Table 41) and in other evidence of the period (Appendix 4).

1.3 Stipendium

The rate of *stipendium* becomes intelligible at this point; 73,500 denarii represents 118 shares of 622.9 denarii as payment for 4 months. If there were 118 men, the plausible rate of 600 denarii emerges, assuming that the small excess of 2,700 denarii was absorbed by higher grades. The excess is enough, for example, to make 2 men *duplicarii* (2×600) and 5 *sesquiplicarii* (5×300).[10] Taken overall, the figures for Thmou suggest annual payments to cavalrymen (*alares*) in AD 300 of 600 denarii for *annona* and 1,800 for *stipendium*. Their salary is still only $\frac{1}{30}$ of the

[9] Table 41 line 8. The suggestion that the unassigned 100 artabas of wheat in the next letter (1.399) were additional provisioning for Thmou (Jahn (1984) 73) does not yield any regular figures, and it makes wheat rations exceed barley rations by a substantial number, if the 4-choenix barley ration applies here. Even if as Jahn suggests the army was short of horses at this moment, which is unverifiable, barley entitlements would probably have remained the same (cf. Jones (1964) 683).

Another conjecture, that there were more supplies to come from other districts for the same period, is unconvincing (i) because of the exact alignment between shares of barley and shares of wheat in the figures as they stand, and (ii) because the recipients and the period covered by the payments are both specified, indicating that the payments were made as quittance for the rations due for that period.

For reduced provisioning in kind, it is worth noting that the bread ration at Rome fell in 369 from 50 to 36 ounces per day. Since wheat produced 25–6 pounds of bread per modius (cf. Pliny *NH* 18.66–8), this presumably meant a cut from the old wheat ration of 5 modii per month to one of 3.6 (cf. *CTh* 14.17.5; Jones (1964) 696).

[10] The 223 cavalry of the *cohors XX Palmyrenorum* at Dura in 223/5 included 5 decurions, 7 *duplicarii* and 4 *sesquiplicarii* (Rom. Mil. Rec. 47).

54,000 evidently paid annually to the one officer described in the papyri (the *praepositus* of the *equites promoti* of the *legio II Traiana*; 2.201).

1.4 The donatives

There are two rates of donative in the papyrus. One (here called type A), given for the birthday or accession day of an Augustus, was about twice the amount of the other (type B), given for the consulship of the Caesars. But their ratio was 25:12, not 2:1 as Jones maintained (see 1.5 below).

The papyrus tells us that the *praepositus* of the *equites promoti* of the *legio II Traiana* received type A donatives of 2,500 denarii (Table 51 lines L-M). Jones assumed that because the recipient is an officer, his donative was higher than that of the rank and file.[11] But as Skeat noted, there seems to be no evidence for proportioning of payments to rank in what is known of *donativa*.[12] The rate shown here, equal to 10,000 sesterces in the currency of the Principate, is already attested in earlier evidence. Donatives at this rate are said to have been given by Octavian to his troops in 43 BC, unsuccessfully demanded by the Danube legions who supported Septimius Severus, and given to the praetorians by Caracalla. At the joint accession of Marcus Aurelius and Lucius Verus, the praetorians were even promised double this amount.[13]

Thus it appears possible that donatives were homogeneous and did not vary within a unit according to rank.

1.5 The payments in oil

The combination of donatives and payments in kind in the references to the *lanciarii* of the *legio II Traiana* allows us to test this hypothesis. If the *lanciarii* received the same type A donatives as the officer recorded elsewhere in the papyrus, there would have been 439 shares (Table 51 lines P-Q; 1,097,500/2,500 = 439). The unit also received as part of its 'salgamum' allowance 3,596 pounds of oil for 2 months (Table 51 line S).[14] The rate per head if there were 439 men equals almost exactly $\frac{1}{11}$ of a sextarius per day.[15] This is close to the rate

---

[11] Jones (1964) 3.188.

[12] *PBeatty Panop* xxviii; cf. Watson (1969) 108–14. Jones's donative figures are followed in essentials by Jahn (1984) 57.

[13] Appian *BC* 3.94; *HA* Sev. 7.6; Herodian 4.4.7; *HA* M. Ant. 7.9; Watson (1969) 113–14. See also Campbell (1984).

[14] The papyrus lists 3,596 pounds of oil and 3,596 Italic sextarii of salt. Although the measures are transposed by Skeat (*PBeatty Panop* xxvii and 149 *ad* 2.247–8), the information, repeated in letters despatched on different dates, is evidently correct as it stands. There is other explicit evidence for the official usage shown here: the Codes contain a direct parallel where oil is reckoned by weight (in pounds) and salt in capacity-measure (modii) (*CTh* 8.4.17; AD 385). Moreover metrological sources frequently measure oil in pounds (*MSR* 2.176 s.v. elaion; 190 (4)); and salt is measured by capacity-measure in a Trajanic customs tariff (*SB* 4.7365).

[15] The Italic sextarius = 1 1/2 pounds of oil (*MSR*, n.14), so 3,596 pounds = 2,397 1/3 sextarii. For accounting purposes 2 months = 60 days; 2,397 $\frac{1}{3}$/60 = 39.9555; 39.9555:439 = 1:10.987.

of $\frac{1}{10}$ of a sextarius per day attested as an army oil ration in sixth-century papyri.[16] The results are almost exact (a rate of $\frac{1}{11}$ produces 439.51 shares).

Jones's interpretation gave this unit a much larger, but shifting, membership; 878 men for the two donatives on 20 November and 22 December 299 (type A); 843 for that on 1 January 300 (type B); and 899 for the *salgamum* allowance for the 2 months from November 299 onwards (Appendix 5). These figures differ by nearly 7% overall, and none of them is compatible with an oil allowance close to the attested rate. Even the smallest yields only $\frac{1}{21}$ of a sextarius. The present interpretation places the oil allowance close to an attested rate and makes the projected unit-strength effectively constant. The type A donatives yield 439 shares, type B yields $439\frac{1}{16}$, and the oil allowance yields $439\frac{46}{90}$. The overall variation is less than 0.12%.

This reconciliation offers support for the underlying hypothesis. The 2,500 denarii given as donative to the *praepositus* of the *equites promoti* appears to have been the standard type A rate for legionary or equivalent troops. The corresponding type B donative must have been $\frac{12}{25}$ of type A, from the respective totals for the *lanciarii* (526,875:1,097,500). This makes the rate 1,200 denarii.

1.6 Numerical results

The rates of payment deduced are:

> *stipendium* (*alares*): 1,800 denarii per year
> *annona* (*alares*): 600 denarii per year
> *donativum* (type A for legionaries and equivalent): 2,500 denarii
> *donativum* (type B for legionaries and equivalent): 1,200 denarii
> oil allowance: $\frac{1}{11}$ sextarius per day

2 Establishment

These rates can be applied to other evidence in the papyri. The results are shown in Table 41.[17] *Cohortales* seem to have been paid one third less than *alares*, since their *stipendium* is about twice their *annona*, not three times (Table 41 lines 8 and 10).

Some of these unit-strengths agree quite closely with other evidence.[18] It is

[16] *POxy* 2046; 1920. See also n.6. The recipients were *symmachoi*, who were messengers rather than regular troops (Jones (1964) 3.191). The regular troops, *stratiotai*, received 1/8 of a sextarius; but their daily allocations appear generous by ancient standards: 4 pounds of bread per day, 1 pound of meat and 2 *xestai* of wine.

[17] It is assumed here (with Jones (1964) 3.188–9) that *alares* and legionaries were paid the same at this date (one of the two possibilities canvassed by Speidel (1973)). The strength that ensues for these legionaries (572, line 2) is close to that of a *vexillatio*. Jahn (1984) 70 also reads legionary salary as 1,800 denarii.

[18] Some untidy fractions are posited here. But they may reflect deductions at source (cf. n.67 and Speidel (1973)). Three of the totals fall just short of very large round figures: 2,496,250 (line 1) is

possible none the less that *stipendium* figures (lines 2, 8 and 10) are slightly inflated by extra payments to *duplicarii* and *sesquiplicarii* (cf. n.10 above). Line 1 shows a legionary *vexillatio* drawn from two legions whose suggested strength is 1,000 men (998½ shares). Vexillations with a nominal strength of 1,040 (*vexillationes milliariae*) are attested in second- and third-century inscriptions.[19] Their numbers seem to be identified there because they were above the normal level, which as with *alae* and cohorts was probably about half this strength. John Lydus writing under Justinian makes the *vexillatio* a unit of 500; Hyginus had spoken of a unit of *vexillarii* as having 600 men.[20] The Lydus evidence is closely supported in line 3 which suggests a *vexillatio* of 506. Line 4 shows a *vexillatio* with 554. There are roughly as many in the detachment of 'soldiers from legio III Diocletiana with the governor of the Thebaid', whose total is reconstructed as 572.[21]

The main legionary units (lines 1–4) thus agree with totals known from other sources. The remainder (lines 5–6) are less easy to evaluate. But if the *lanciarii* of the *legio II Traiana* were 439 men (line 5), their numbers produce a combined total very close to 1,000, taken in conjunction with the 554 in the *vexillatio* of the same legion (line 4). The number of *equites promoti* of *legio II Traiana* approaches the strength of a *centuria* of 80 men (77, line 6).[22]

Two of the auxiliary totals can easily be compared with other evidence. Line 8 shows an *ala* with a suggested strength of just under 120 men. Line 7 shows a unit of *equites sagittarii* numbering 121.[23] But the *ala* is usually taken as being quingenary. Arrian gives it 512 men, and John Lydus 600.[24] The cohort of 164 men listed in line 10 is likewise far below totals known elsewhere. Hyginus gives the auxiliary cohort 6 centuries apparently of 80 men, pointing to a total

0.15% short of 2.5 million; 1,386,250 (line 4) is 1% short of 1.4 million; and 1,097,500 (line 5) is 0.23% short of 1.1 million. Some payments may also have taken into account previous overpayments like that apparent in 2.31, where 21,000 is reclaimed. For a case where army ration allocations lead to a fractional total of recipients, see *POxy* 1920.1.3 note.

[19] *ILS* 2726; 531. Drawn from 'eastern legions' according to the papyrus, the unit here was evidently the vexillation of *III Gallica* and *I Illyrica* (both of which were stationed in Phoenice in *ND* Or. 32.30, 31) recorded shortly afterwards in an inscription from the present fort (*ILS* 8882, AD 315/6). Coptos = Potecoptos (*PBeatty Panop* 2.162 note). [20] *De mag.* 1.46; *de mun. cast.* 5.

[21] Jones estimated its numbers at 1,716 (Jones (1964) 3.210, n.171).

[22] Hyginus *de mun. cast.* 1. A detachment of Palmyrene cavalry in Egypt referred to in a document of AD 271 apparently numbered 75 (*POxy* 3115; the editor's first interpretation, which assumes the barley ration of 4 choenices per day, appears preferable to the second, based on Ptolemaic evidence; see n.6 above).

[23] Though it need not be directly relevant, both figures are close to the strength of 120 found for the *equites* in a *cohors quingenaria equitata* (Hyginus 26–7). A unit with 487 men accounted for, 111 of them *equites*, is a possible case in point (Thomas and Davies (1977), AD 213/6).

[24] *Tactica* 18, cf. Cheesman (1914) 26–7; Lyd. *de mag.* 1.46. The three *alae* with average complements of 145 men listed in an Egyptian inscription of the beginning of the Principate would appear to have been under strength (*ILS* 2483, with new reading in *CIL* III p.2297; Mommsen *Eph. Ep.* 5, p.8).

Table 41. Revised interpretation of payments in PBeatty Panop 1–2

	Suggested number of shares	Form of payment	Total (denarii)	Conjectured rate per head (denarii)
Legions				
1. *Vexillatio* eastern legions at Potecoptus	998½	Donatives (type A)	2,496,250	2,500
2. Soldiers of *leg. III Diocl.* with governor of Thebaid	572⅙	*Stipendium*	343,300 (4 months)	1,800 per year
3. *Vexillatio leg. III Diocl.* at Syene	506	*Salgamum*	(8,280 pounds of oil (4 months))	($\frac{1}{11}$ sextarius per day)
4. *Vexillatio leg. III Trai.* at Apollinopolis Superior	554½	Donative (type A)	1,386,250	2,500
5. *Lanciarii leg. II Trai.* at Ptolemais	439/439½	Donatives (types A and B); *salgamum*	1,097,500: 526,875; (3,596 pounds of oil for 2 months)	2,500; 1,200; ($\frac{1}{11}$ sextarius per day)
6. *Equites promoti* of *leg. II Trai.* at Tentyra	77⅗	Donative (type B)	93,12[5]	1,200
Other cavalry				
7. *Equites sagittarii* at Potecoptus	121	Donatives (type A)	302,500 × 2	2,500
8. *Ala I Hiberorum* at Thmou	116 (AD 298); 118 (AD 300)	Rations; fodder; *stipendium; annona*	(128⅞ art. wheat; 2,610 modii barley); 73,500 (4 months); 23,600 (4 months)	(2½ modii per month; 11¼ modii per month); 1,800 per year, 600 per year

9. *Ala II Herc. dromedariorum* at Toëto and Psinabla	21½ (?)	Donatives (type A)	53,750 × 2	2,500
Cohorts				
10. *Cohors XI Chamavorum* at Peamou	163¾ 164⅓	*Stipendium*; *annona*	65,500 (4 months) 32,866 (4 months)	1,200 per year; 600 per year

Note: For references see Table 51. The two main rates of donative, and the oil allowance, are deduced from line 5 in conjunction with other evidence. Rates of *stipendium* and *annona* are deduced from line 8 in conjunction with other evidence (detailed argument above). The suggested number of shares in line 9 is implausibly low, especially since the unit was divided between two forts. But it is difficult to see why a camel *ala* should have received a lower donative than the rest. However the figures for this unit may be incomplete, since overpayment had been made to some of its members in the previous month, and 21,000 denarii was reclaimed (2.31). The presence of 100 *kameloi despoitikoi* at Elephantine is recorded in A.D. 295 (*POxy* 43 recto II. 1.6; cf. W. Ensslin *Aegyptus* 32 (1952) 168–9).

approaching 500. Individual auxiliary cohorts known from documentary evidence under Trajan and Antoninus Pius totalled 546 and 505 men.[25]

Thus there are very big differences between these two auxiliary totals and strengths attested elsewhere. But small garrisons in late Empire forts are also shown by other evidence (see Appendix 4). In some cases a single unit might man two forts, as shown in line 9 of Table 41.

The present interpretation suggests that the legionary units in question were quingenary vexillations; that the unnamed unit of legionaries was also about this size; and that the auxiliary units in question show a very sharp reduction in size when compared with corresponding units in earlier evidence.

But the number of units in Egypt was now very heavily inflated, by comparison with Egyptian garrisons of former years. A summary put forward recently reads as follows:

	Early second century AD	Diocletian
Legions	1	13
Alae	4	22
Cohorts	9	12
Equites	—	10

Remarkable growth is suggested by these figures. But the term 'legion' could mean fewer men in the fourth century, perhaps only one-sixth of the numbers in a legion of the Principate (Appendix 4), or even a unit as small as one of the quingenary vexillations implied in the Beatty papyri. The small auxiliary units in the Beatty findings evidently belong to a similar pattern.[26]

2.1 Remuneration

The most interesting pay figure is the rate for *stipendium*, read as 1,800 denarii for legionaries and higher auxiliaries (*alares*), and 1,200 for lesser auxiliaries (*cohortales*). Two centuries earlier under Domitian, legionary pay was increased to 300 denarii.[27]

Septimius Severus subsequently increased army pay by an unknown amount which was evidently substantial; Caracalla increased it by another 50%; and Maximinus is said to have doubled it. The upper limit set by the figure given for

---

[25] Hyginus *de mun. cast.* 27–8; 1; Rom. Mil. Rec. 226; 64.

[26] See M. Speidel cited in Sijpestein (1986) 168. The present findings (see also Appendix 4) cast doubt both on Jones's view that 500 was a minimum unit-size, and on the global estimates of army manpower which use this as one of the multipliers (Jones (1964) 680; 682). Because the only surviving ancient estimates of global army size refer to later periods, it is difficult to relate them to the Diocletianic evidence. But there are seeming discrepancies between their impressive totals, and the much smaller figures reported for armies on campaign (the two do not necessarily agree in the way suggested by Jones (1964) 684–5).   [27] Cf. Watson (1969) 89–91.

the cost of Caracalla's increase by the hostile Dio seems to preclude the possibility that Severus's increase can have been as much as 100%. An increase of 33% or 50% would suit Dio's total better.[28]

Successive increases of 33–50%, 50% and 100% would raise the legionary rate from Domitian's 300 denarii to 1,200–1,350 denarii. This is still short of the Beatty figure for *alares* by 450–600 denarii, and a further increase of 33–50% in the intervening period would be needed to reach the Beatty level. If Severus had increased pay by $\frac{2}{3}$, this gap would be 20%.

Despite these changes, it is clear that in Diocletian's time, basic pay (*stipendium*) had not kept pace with inflation. Using Egyptian figures, which belong to a closed monetary area where prices may have risen more slowly than elsewhere, the official valuation of an artaba of wheat in the 290s had risen by a factor of at least 27 from the second-century level.[29] Comparing the figure in the Price Edict of AD 301 with a typical price of the Principate, the cost of wheat had risen by a factor of 67 or more.[30]

Stipendium alone had apparently risen by only a factor of 6 over the same period. But there were now apparently regular donatives as well. The soldiers in the Beatty papyri received donatives for the birthday and accession days of Diocletian, the senior Augustus, as well as for the consulship of the Caesars in 299. Jones argued from this a regular pattern of donatives for both birthday and accession day of all four Tetrarchs, making eight donatives per year.[31] But it is quite possible that only the Augustus and Caesar of the East would have been honoured in this way in the donatives for eastern troops, making a total of four regular donatives per year.

On Jones's reconstruction, legionary *stipendium* would have been 600 denarii per year, and the eight donatives would have brought in a further 10,000 denarii, making 10,600 denarii per year. If legionaries, like the *alares* at Thmou, also received cash *annona* (200 denarii on Jones's reckoning), and 30 Italic modii per year, their total pay in wheat-equivalent would be 192 Italic modii.[32]

This compares with 400 Italic modii at an earlier date, relating legionary pay under Domitian to a typical wheat price of the Principate of 4 sesterces per Italic modius.[33] But Jones's view that there were as many as eight regular donatives per

---

[28] Develin (1971) 687–95 at 692, arguing from Dio's statement (78.36.3) that Caracalla's increase cost 70 million denarii per year. Jahn (1984) 68 nevertheless maintains that Septimius doubled salaries. The salary of 781¼ denarii in third-century pay accounts is incorporated into his schema, on the assumption that 31¼ denarii were a supplement to the basic rate (*ChLA* 446; 495; Jahn (1983) 225).
[29] *POxy* 3048; see chapter 9 nos. 63 and 64. [30] Cf. *ERE²* 50–1, 66n.
[31] Jones (1964) 3.188. Jahn (1984) 58 argues for 7 donatives in AD 300, amounting to 500 folles for a soldier and 1,000 for an officer.
[32] Converted at 1 modius Italicus = 2/3 modius castrensis = 66 2/3 denarii in Diocletian's Price Edict (*ERE²* 66 and Duncan-Jones (1976D); Jahn (1980) prefers the smaller of the alternatives outlined there, reducing the modius castrensis in the Edict by 8%). [33] Cf. *ERE²* 50–1.

year may as suggested be optimistic; and if there were only four, total remuneration in wheat on his figures would fall to 117 Italic modii. That suggests very serious deterioration compared with the figure for the Principate, even though the salary of the Principate had been partly offset by deductions.[34]

On the present reconstruction, assuming four regular donatives per year, the corresponding figures (for *alares* and probably for legionaries) would be:

stipendium	1,800 denarii
donatives	10,000 denarii
annona	600 denarii
wheat	30 modii

The total wheat-equivalent by the same reckoning would be 216 Italic modii. There is still an obvious deterioration by comparison with the Domitianic figure. But the decline is much less extreme than in the more plausible version of Jones's estimates. The Beatty figures bear out Diocletian's widely publicised view that military purchasing power was under threat, and clearly show that donatives were now more important than *stipendium*, as is suggested by the word-order in Diocletian's reference to 'donativum . . . stipendiumque'.[35]

This pay structure seems to have had an alarming consequence for officers. Donatives at a flat rate would benefit the rank and file much more than the officer (even the Jones reconstruction allows very limited status-differentiation for donatives). The Roman world was accustomed to the most extreme differentials of army pay depending on rank: in the Principate the extremes of pay within the legion may have differed by a factor of as much as 67.[36] The Beatty evidence suggests a severe contraction of money differentials between officers and the rank and file. Taking the *praepositus* of *equites promoti* whose remuneration we know (Table 51 lines K–M) and a legionary *miles*, the ratio of their *stipendia* would be 30:1 (54,000:1,800). But the ratio of their gross pay would only be about 5:1, unless the officer also received greatly enhanced living-allowances. Later in the fourth century large-scale payments in kind had certainly become the main remuneration for officers. They could also gain heavily from the well-known abuse of *stellatura*, drawing compulsory contributions from the men under their command.[37]

3 Conclusions

The Beatty papyri give a uniquely detailed view of the payment and strength of part of the late Roman army. They describe a brief moment in the breakneck

---

[34] *PGen Lat* 1 with Speidel (1973); *ChLA* 446, 495, showing much smaller deductions at later dates (Jahn (1983) Table 1).
[35] S. Lauffer *Diokletians Preisedikt* (1971) 95, 1.8. The same word-order in Ammianus 17.9.6: 'nec donativum meruit nec stipendium'.   [36] Cf. Brunt (1950) 71.   [37] Jones (1964) 643–5.

inflation of their time, and payment at the money rates implied cannot have survived unaltered for very long. Consequently, what is most important here is the insights into unit-strength. The present analysis points to legionary vexillations of a normal size of 500–600 (in contrast to the milliary vexillations posited by Jones). But they imply very small auxiliary units. Evidence from a single province at a particular date need not always reflect practice in the empire as a whole. But these low strengths are supported by other evidence for garrisons from the late Empire, suggesting a proliferation of small or fragmented units.

The findings about pay are compatible with what is known about third-century pay increases, and they throw some light on pay policy in the period up to Diocletian. They fully bear out other evidence for the importance of donatives. But the papyri also probably suggest that, as things stood in AD 299–300, the real value of army pay and allowances had declined. This supports Diocletian's complaints about the impact of price changes on his soldiers.

PART III
AGRARIAN PATTERNS

8

Land and landed wealth

A detailed map of landholding in the Roman world would show many differences. We should see state land, imperial land and city land, as well as a host of properties of different size in full private ownership. This chapter briefly considers juridical differences before investigating the underlying reality of landholding patterns. Because of the layout of the evidence, an exhaustive treatment would be strongly biassed towards Egypt, but a wider approach is possible in a short discussion.[1]

1 Ager publicus

Land generally fell into one of six categories (if the nuances of legal title and the more complex situation in Egypt are set on one side).[2] The first type is *ager publicus*, land belonging to the *populus Romanus*, the Roman state. Such land, if cultivated, was generally in the hands of private tenants of the state. The extent of *ager publicus* was originally immense, since Rome normally expropriated the land of conquered peoples, at any rate in theory.[3] But the amount diminished as cultivable land was gradually assigned to veterans, civilian colonists or purchasers. As late as Trajan's time, *ager publicus* made up almost a quarter (22%) of peripheral holdings in a list of lands owned by private individuals and cities at Veleia in the far north of Italy. Not all of it was necessarily cultivated, since Veleia lay in a mountainous and infertile region; some may have been pasture.[4] In a

---

[1] For an attempt to establish how far Egyptian patterns of land division into large and small units follow a statistically 'normal' pattern, see Hansen–Schiöler (1965).

[2] The sequence here places registers of private owners, which require the longest discussion, at the end. For further description, cf. Weber (1891). For the position in Egypt, see for example *PBour* 42; nn.47–8 below; Westermann (1920) and (1922); Hohlwein (1938) at 35–53.

[3] See e.g. Siculus Flaccus 157L. Jones (1960) 143–9. Cf. *Atti* (1974).

[4] Identifying types of land use from the list of estates is very difficult. Though *saltus* is associated with *montes* in *oblig.* 48, the term does not obviously refer to any one particular type of terrain or exploitation when used in the Veleian register (*CIL* XI 1147; de Pachtère (1920) 60, etc. consistently associates *saltus* with pasture and forest land). The jurists use the term inconsistently to denote a large estate (Ulpian *D.* 11.4.1.1; Proculus *D.* 41.2.27), or pasture land (Ulpian *D.* 33.7.8.1; 19.2.19.1, etc.). For the Agrimensores, *saltus* could mean a unit of designated size (800 *iugera* according to Varro *r. r.* 1.10.2, 5,000 *iugera* according to Siculus Flaccus 158.20L), although it merely denotes a large estate in Agennius Urbicus (Thulin 45).

similar list from Ligures Baebiani in southern Italy, *ager publicus* forms 10% of peripheral holdings.[5]

2 Imperial land

A second category was land owned by the emperor. Though a few regional figures are available, the emperor acquired land in such varied ways that the scale of imperial landholdings must have varied greatly from one region to another.[6]

The Baebian and Veleian land-registers, which belong to a relatively early phase in the history of imperial accumulation of property, show the emperor as owning respectively 12% and less than 1% of peripheral holdings.[7] Two centuries later, Constantine was able to give the churches of Rome landed property in Italy and Sicily with a rental of nearly 15,000 solidi; their total area was probably of the order of 100 km².[8] Figures from the fifth century show the emperor as owning substantial amounts of provincial land. In North Africa, about 18% of the total area of Zeugitana and 15% of Byzacena was imperial land.[9]

3 City land

There was a practice of endowing new city foundations with some directly owned territory, whose revenue could be put towards the cost of running the city. At the end of the Republic, Augustus made enormous compensation payments to cities for land which he gave to veterans. He paid out HS600 million in Italy and HS260 million in the provinces (*Res Gestae* 16.1).[10] In Gallia Narbonensis, the veteran settlement of Arausio, which Augustus colonised, owned at least 7,330 *iugera* (18.4 km²), more than one seventh of the territory listed in incomplete registers of

---

[5] Veleia: *CIL* XI 1147; Ligures Baebiani: *CIL* IX 1455. References to neighbours (almost 700 at Veleia, although only 58 at Ligures Baebiani) seem to provide a usable index of the scale of landownership, taken en masse. The seven largest Veleian landowners received 76 mentions as neighbour, an average of 10.9 (accepting Bormann's identification of Cornelia Severa as daughter and heir of L. Cornelius Severus, cf. Duncan-Jones (1964A) 141, n.104). The seven smallest landowners receive only seven mentions as neighbour (*CIL* XI, pp.229–31). The estates of known value which are also 'neighbours' are on average worth much more than those which are not: the two differ by a factor of 4.22 at Veleia and by 2.92 at Ligures Baebiani. The Veleian and Baebian landholdings are tabulated by value in *ERE*² 211–15; for neighbours at Veleia see p.196 and n.4, together with lists in *CIL* XI, pp.229–31, and *CIL* IX, p.13.

[6] See Crawford (1976) and n.54 below.

[7] See n.5.

[8] Assuming 6% gross rental (cf. *ERE*² 133) and average land value of 5 solidi per *iugerum* (it cost 5½ in a sixth-century sale at Faventia in northern Italy, Jones (1964), 822). Liber Pontificalis cap. (M.G.H., *Gest. Pont. Rom.* I 47–72).

[9] Jones (1964) 415–16.

[10] The *Res Gestae* imply that city lands were used for the veteran settlements as a whole; in his earliest land settlements, Augustus/Octavian had evidently attempted to evict many private landowners, who may in some cases have been holding city land as *ager vectigalis* (Dio 48.6.8; Appian 5.12–13).

the Flavian period. As more than one-third of the remaining territory appears to have been cultivated, the town's share of cultivated territory was about one-fifth.[11] The towns of Veleia and Ligures Baebiani (neither of them a veteran colony) seem to have owned much less. At Veleia 5% and at Ligures Baebiani 3% of peripheral holdings were owned by the city. In addition, 2% of the land actually declared for loans at Ligures Baebiani belonged to the city; while 12% of the land declared at Veleia was the property of another city, Luca.[12]

At Arausio in Narbonensis, city land was leased to private individuals on what were evidently perpetual leases, in return for a low rent or vectigal.[13] The *vectigalia* attached to some private estates at Veleia suggest that they included city land, which would increase the apparent total there.[14]

In the stringent condition of the mid-fourth century, the state began to absorb local assets. Civic lands as such were confiscated by Constantius II. Though temporarily restored by Julian, they were once more confiscated by Valentinian and Valens. Valens however returned one third of the revenue to the cities from AD 374 onwards.[15]

4 Sacred land

Ownership of land by temples was widespread in the Greek world, but rare outside the Greek parts of the empire.[16] In the Hellenistic period large parts of the islands of Delos and Rhamnos are known to have belonged to the temple of Apollo.[17] But in the Roman period, few direct indices of scale are available for any region. Strabo mentions impressive totals for temple slaves in parts of Asia: 6,000 slaves of the temple of Ma at Pontic Comana (Strabo 12.3.34), and nearly 3,000 at the temple of Zeus at Morimene in Venasa (12.2.6). According to Diodorus, the temple of the Mothers at Engyum in Sicily owned 3,000 head of cattle and much arable land in the first century BC (Diodorus 4.80.5).

[11] From the evidence published by Piganiol (1962) 104ff., which includes editorial restorations, not all of which can be accepted, out of a total of 50,630 *iugera* whose status can be determined in the three cadasters, 15,803 or 31.2% was 'returned to the Tricastini', a neighbouring tribe; but virtually all of this land appears to have been uncultivated. Out of 9,961 *iugera* of land in this category whose condition can be determined 9,566 *iugera* or 96% are described as uncultivated.
[12] *CIL* XI 1147, ob. 43; IX 1455.3.23.
[13] Piganiol (1962) 57–60. For the explicit leasing of municipal land to private tenants in perpetuity see *AE* 1967, 531 (Apollonia) and juristic evidence in Bove (1960), 65ff. (Gaius 3.145; *D.* 6.3.1 pr.-1; 39.4.11.1). For subleases for 5 years or other short periods, see Hyginus 116–17L, Siculus Flaccus 162L.
[14] See list in *ERE*[2] 313, n.3. For *ager vectigalis* as municipal land, see Crook (1967) 158.
[15] Jones (1964) 146–7; 732.
[16] One exception was the temple of Diana Tifatina, endowed by Sulla with land, whose boundaries Augustus and Vespasian confirmed (de Franciscis (1966)). For the Greek world, Guiraud (1893) 362–81; Jones (1940) 309–10; Rostovtzeff (1957) 655–7; Jones (1974) 28–9. Broughton (1951) effectively contested theories of the omnipresence of temple land in Hellenistic Asia, already questioned by Jones. For Egypt, cf. Evans (1961).   [17] Kent (1948).

In Italy the only figures are effectively pre-Roman. In a Hellenistic inscription from Heracleia, the lands of the temple of Dionysos measured 3,320 square schoeni; those of the temple of Athena covered more than 930 schoeni. The size of the local schoenus is uncertain, but the total area is evidently between 4 and 7km², [18] suggesting that a sizeable part of the territory of Heracleia was owned by temples.

Sacred land in the Roman provinces began to be expropriated early. Sulla and Pompey seized temple treasure in Asia and Greece; and Augustus took over temple land in Egypt. [19] But temple land still survived at a much later date. Constantine appears to have confiscated the lands which existed in his day. They were soon restored by the pagan emperor Julian, but were again confiscated (finally, it appears) by Jovian in the late fourth century. [20] Meanwhile however, the Christian church had begun to receive massive amounts of property, both from Constantine and from private sources. [21]

5 Land assigned by the state (*ager assignatus*)

Much of the *ager publicus* that Rome acquired by conquest was redistributed as land grants to individuals. [22] To some extent this created stereotyped allotment patterns. But the size of allotments varied from one distribution to another. Livy suggests that the figure could even be arrived at by dividing the number of colonists into the amount of land available (35.9). Two other main reasons for variation in plot size were compensation for differences in the fertility of land, and social biassing in favour of men of higher standing. [23] Distributions within a few years of each other could still vary greatly. For example in 181 BC infantry veterans settled at Aquileia received lots of 50 *iugera* (12.6 hectares), while in 173 Latins (politically inferior by definition) who were given *viritim* grants of land on the territory of the Boii received only 3 *iugera* each (Livy 40.34; 42.4).

Though land grants continued under the later Republic and Empire, their size is not well-documented. The last explicit figures refer to allotments by Caesar to civilians with 3–4 children in the Ager Campanus and Ager Stellas. The units planned here were respectively 10 and 12 *iugera* (2.5–3 hectares) (Cicero, *ad Att.* 1.16.1; *de leg. agr.* 2.85). The most massive land allotments of all, those of Augustus when the scale of armed forces was drastically reduced at the end of the

---

[18] R. Dareste, B. Haussoulier, Th. Reinach *Recueil des inscriptions juridiques grecques* I (1891), no.12. For dating, see Sartori (1967) 39; for estimates of the Heraclean schoenus varying from 33.32 to 39.6 metres, see Sartori 41. Cf. Ghinatti–Uguzzoni (1968) 98–9; 182.

[19] Larsen in Frank vol. 4 (1938) 365; Johnson in Frank vol.2 (1936) 122. Appian indicates that Antium, Lanuvium, Nemi and Tibur were richest in temple treasure after Rome in the second century AD (5.24). For temple treasure in Africa, see *ERE²* 110, nos.381–2.

[20] Jones (1964) 415–16; 732–3.

[21] See n.8 above. Jones (1964) 894–910; 933.   [22] Cf. e.g. Salmon (1969); Frederiksen (1973).

[23] Siculus Flaccus 156L; cf. Brunt (1971) 295, n.8.   [24] Brunt (1971) 332–42.

civil wars, are not documented in detail. Brunt's reconstruction suggests that the allotments to veterans in 30 and 14 BC, on which Augustus spent HS860 million (600 million in Italy, the rest in the provinces), went to 155,000 men (*Res Gestae* 16).[24] This implies an average of HS5,500 per head, and interpreted in the light of Columella's land-price of HS1,000 per *iugerum*, it leads to an average holding as low as 5½ *iugera*. But Columella's price for ordinary land appears exaggerated, perhaps by two-fold for Italy and probably by a larger factor for the provinces.[25]

The cash retirement bonus of HS12,000 which was substituted for land in 13 BC (Dio 55.23.1) would be worth roughly 20–25 *iugera* on this arithmetic. That suggests, on the face of it, a considerable advance in generosity in a context where, because of Augustus's financial difficulties, such an advance is not very likely. But the size of the earlier land allotments remains uncertain, because compensation to cities may have been limited, and the numbers of recipients cannot be closely established.

This was not the end of direct allocation of land to veterans, since veteran colonies, whose creation implies specific land grants, continued to be founded.[26] Later Egyptian figures give the size of some actual veteran landholdings. At Philadelphia in the Fayum in AD 216, 18 veterans held an average of 13.23 *arourae* (14.5 *iugera* or 3.7 hectares); the list also shows 11 soldiers with an average of 13.12 *arouras* each (14.4 *iugera*).[27] The median averages are lower, 9.25 for veterans, 11.4 for soldiers, and the patterns are very dispersed (the coefficients of variation are 91.3 and 67.5).

Figures from the late Empire (*CTh* 7.20.3) suggest land allotments of more generous size, though they were apparently made from deserted land, whose profitability may often have been marginal. Under Constantine veterans received a yoke of oxen, 100 modii of seed corn, and 25 folles for expenses, in addition to an unspecified quantity of land. The implications of these amounts are not consistent. The quantity of seed appears the only usable index. Allowing for fallowing,

---

[25] Brunt (1971) 337, n.3; cf. *ERE*² 48–52, 345, 347–8, 366. The value added by the state and type of cultivation is an important variable that cannot be taken into account. Columella's calculations (*de r. r.* 3.3) purport to refer to the provinces as well as to Italy, but the passage contains improbabilities (*ERE*² 40 n.5, 39–50, 376–7; see also MacVe (1985)). Brunt suggests that the release of so much cash into the land market would have increased land-prices substantially. This is certainly likely in a free market (it is illustrated at a later date in Pliny *Ep.* 6.19). But Hyginus states that Augustus paid compensation 'secundum reditus' (197.17L), suggesting that the price was assessed by applying a fixed multiple of revenue, and was not necessarily the owner's asking price. This procedure could have reduced the inflationary effects created by the release of such large funds. De Neeve (1985) argues against Columella's land–price, and against all attempts to deduce average land-prices in Italy.   [26] Cf. Forni (1953) 39ff.

[27] Individual area figures for this section of *PYale* 111 145 (awaiting publication) were kindly communicated by Professor J.F. Oates. Of the land owned by soldiers and veterans 13% was orchard-land, the rest corn-land. In the list as a whole, orchard-land is 16% (Bowman (1985) 151).

100 modii of seed should point to an area of 40 *iugera* (10.1 hectares).[28] But the amount of seed may still be no more than a convenient round figure.

6 Privately owned land

6.1 The layout of private property

Land being the principal source of wealth in Roman society, differences in land ownership often coincided with differences in wealth. The usual processes of transfer of wealth appear to have been by inheritance, by bequest and by marriage.[29] Inheritance could enlarge landholdings in cases where owners died without issue and left their property to other landowners, or it might fragment them by dividing a property among several heirs.[30] Where the mechanism enlarged landholdings, it would not usually do so by adding conveniently adjacent plots. Consequently, large landholdings typically contained several non-adjacent components. A wealthy man whose land lay entirely in one district would often own a number of farms, like Sextus Roscius whose HS6 million at Ameria was made up of 13 farms bordering the Tiber. The very rich would typically own land in more than one district, like Pliny who farmed on a large scale both at Comum and Tifernum Tiberinum, or his contemporary Aquillius Regulus who owned land in Umbria and Etruria.[31]

Although there were perennial shortages of liquidity in the Roman world, great wealth potentially conferred large enough cash reserves to allow estates to be reconstituted on a less scattered basis. Pliny was evidently alive to the possibility of enlarging his main holding at Tifernum by buying adjacent property because it was adjacent (*Ep.* 3.19.2–3).[32] But because it was continually renewed by inheritance, the pattern of random location was generally too strong to eradicate, and it remained dominant in large-scale landowning.

[28] Jones (1964) 636. References for sowing quantity of 5 modii (43.65 litres) per *iugerum* (0.2517 hectares) and fallowing in alternate years in Italy in *ERE²* 49, nn.2 and 5.

[29] Cf. e.g. Crook (1967) 118–32. The view that most property was acquired by purchase, not by inheritance, based on the fact that the writers on agriculture give advice about purchase, is quite unconvincing (Le Gall (1974) 40).

[30] Thus Pliny evidently received the landed property of his uncle as well as that of his parents. Various cases of fragmentation among heirs occur at Veleia: four properties for example were split between the third and fourth largest landowners in the list (*CIL* XI 1147, 3.23, 2.67; 3.30, 3.70, 3.28, 3.69; 3.23, 3.67; 3.32, 3.75, cf. 6.60). Two of the smallest landowners received their inheritance in equal shares, although one declares his half of the 'saltus Tuppelius Volumnianus' at HS51,000, while the other is declared at HS50,000 (*oblig.* 7 and 29). Some inherited holdings remained intact in joint ownership (e.g. Veleia *oblig.* 4; Shaw (1982) Table 5 for Lamasba). But there would have been inherent difficulties in maintaining them intact for more than one generation. Sharing a property between two could mean that each owner took the income in alternate years (*D.* 19.2.35.1).   [31] *ERE²* 324.

[32] For the lure of vast estates, see Petronius *Sat.* 48; 53; 77; Seneca *de ben.* 7.10.5; Columella *de r. r.* 1.3.12.

Table 42. *Estate-sizes and component-valuations at Veleia*

	Average total	Average component	Average number of components
5 smallest (50,000–53,900)	HS51,050	42,542	1.2
7 intermediate (200,000–300,000)	HS251,032	42,931	5.8
5 largest (733,660–1,508,150)	HS1,098,076	69,498	15.8

One result of this fragmentation is that locally based lists cannot fully reflect the scale of the largest landholdings, which typically consisted of land in several districts. They will under-represent both the maximum and the mean size of holdings. But local lists can sometimes illustrate fragmentation as it affected landholdings concentrated in one neighbourhood.

In the most detailed land-register from Italy, the Trajanic inscription from Veleia, landholdings generally consist of a series of components whose valuation and position were specified individually. Their average value varies remarkably little, despite very large differences in aggregate value (Table 42).[33] Within these three classes, total variation in average component-value is only 1.6, compared with a variation in estate value of 21.5. These figures suggest that however large an estate became, the average size of its components normally remained small. On average, the holdings in the five largest private estates are each spread over as many as ten different *pagi* or parishes.[34]

6.2 Average property-size

Three pieces of evidence provide some direct information about average property-size.[35] Two come from Cicero's speeches against Verres and refer to Sicily in the first century BC. The third is a detailed land-register recording holdings in one of the four wards of an Egyptian town in the mid-fourth century AD.

According to Cicero, at Leontini in Sicily, 84 farmers had been registered in Verres' first year as governor (73 BC), but the number had fallen to 32 by the third year. The area under wheat in the third year was 30,000 *iugera* (Cicero *Verr.*

---

[33] Bormann lists the estate valuations and the component valuations on which loans were secured in *CIL* XI pp. 223–5.

[34] The estates are listed in *ERE*² 211. The average number of *pagi* represented in the five largest estates is 9.8; cf. Chilver (1941) 160–1. A similar pattern of dispersal of holdings within large estates can be seen at Hermopolis from analysis of the *pagi* mentioned there (Jones (1974) 252 and 249; Bowman (1985) Table 6).

[35] For further evidence about estate-sizes in Italy, see *ERE*² 323–6; for estate-sizes in the late Empire, see Jones (1964) 781–8.

2.3.113; 116; 120). since wheat was normally fallowed, the implied cultivable area is not less than 60,000 *iugera*; other crops would almost certainly have increased the total to not less than 70,000 *iugera* (176 km²). The mean average holding that this implies is 2,200 *iugera* (5.5 km²). Even on the artificial hypothesis that all land abandoned after year 1 was absorbed and declared by the remaining cultivators in year 3, the original average holding would still have been as high as 830 *iugera* (2.1 km).

Cicero says that 252 farmers were listed at Herbita, another Sicilian town, in Verres' first year. The corn tithe, apparently reasonable in this case, was sold for 18,000 modii (Cicero *Verr.* 2.3.75–80; 120). The tithe figure could imply that the total area of cultivable land was of the order of 14,000 *iugera* (35.2 km²), in which case the average holding at Herbita would be 56 *iugera* (14 hectares).[36] Though neither estimate can be more than an approximation, the Herbita average is clearly of a different magnitude from the average for Leontini in Verres' third year, apparently lower by a factor of 39. Herbita is more likely to be typical than Leontini, which was the prime wheat-growing region in Sicily according to Cicero.

The register of local land owned by residents of one of the four wards at Hermopolis in Egypt in the mid-fourth century AD (*PFlor* 71) provides fuller information. In the entries which survive complete, 238 owners are named; they own a visible total of 15,078.5 *arouras* (16,571 *iugera* or 41.7 km²).[37] The average holding is thus 69.6 *iugera* (17.5 hectares). This is broadly comparable with the average of 56 *iugera* deduced for Herbita in Sicily four centuries earlier.

Although useful as far as they go, none of these figures includes any land held outside the cities in question. Thus they certainly make the average territory per landowner too low. At Leontini the omissions are probably serious. Cicero singles out the fact (very curious in itself) that only one local family farmed any land at Leontini (*Verr.* 2.3.109). Cultivators almost all of whom came from other cities must frequently have held land at those cities as well. Highly developed capitalist agriculture of *latifundia* type is indicated in the large landholdings which Cicero's figures for Leontini imply. The revolts of the second century BC had already made Sicily notorious for its enormous work-force of slaves.

The Hermopolis list provides some indication of how large extra-territorial landholdings could be. Property at Hermopolis belonged to citizens of the

---

[36] If 18,000 modii represented a true tithe, the total wheat crop would be 180,000 modii. A gross yield of six-fold, a sowing quantity of five modii per *iugerum* and fallowing in alternate years (n.28) would imply a total wheat acreage of 12,000 *iugera*. Assuming as before that other crops would increase acreage by at least one sixth (see n.27 above), total area becomes 14,000 *iugera*, an average for 252 farmers of 55.6 *iugera*. Cicero indicates typical gross yield of wheat at Leontini, much the best wheat-growing area in Sicily (2.3.47; 2.3.109), as eight-fold, with ten-fold in better years (2.3.112). For later Sicilian grain-yields, see *ERE²* 377–8.

[37] See n.47 below. A detailed analysis and commentary is given in Jones (1974) 244–52.

neighbouring town of Antinoopolis is listed in full. A total of 7,576.75 *arouras* (8,327 *iugera* = 21 km^2) is owned by 203 landowners.[38] The average is thus 37 *iugera* (9.3 hectares), only half the average for the land there owned by Hermopolites (70 *iugera*). Although the extra-territorial holdings are predictably smaller, there was nothing to stop these owners from owning land in other cities as well.

Thus as evidence for personal landholdings, this material is still significantly less complete than statements about wealthy men such as Pliny, Cicero and Symmachus, which have some chance of showing the geographical extent or at least the diversity of the lands that they owned.

6.3 Differentiation of property-size

Evidence about the distribution of property between large and small landowners is more plentiful. Six registers can be considered. Each of these registers quantifies properties by a linear or broadly linear measure, either area, value, tax-potential or water-requirements. The main details are summarised in Table 43.

The first register refers to land at the small south Italian town of Ligures Baebiani at the start of the second century AD (*CIL* IX 1455). The list appears to be a cross-section of local properties of all sizes (9 out of 66 estate valuations are missing). The parallel register at Veleia omits estates below a certain size, and similar omissions from the Baebian list are almost certain. But any threshold at Ligures Baebiani was relatively low (the highest round figure possible would be HS10,000, the smallest estate being valued at HS14,000).[39] At the top of the scale 3.5% of the landowners own 21.3% of the land, and the wealthiest single individual owns 11.2% (see fig. 21). At the bottom, the poorest 14% own 3.6% of the land. The Gini coefficient of differentiation is 0.435.[40]

The contemporary register from Veleia in northern Italy (*CIL* XI 1147) lists the values of 47 estates, 46 of which are in private hands. Though much fuller than the Baebian register, estates worth less than HS50,000 were evidently

---

[38] Bowman (1985) Table 1(B).

[39] Estates listed in descending order of size in *ERE*² 211–15. The size of the loans assigned to the nine estates whose valuations are missing implies that they fell within the same range as the 57 estates whose valuations survive.

[40] The Gini coefficient is a product of the Lorenz curve. The Lorenz curve uses percentages to plot property against number of owners, from a distribution arranged in ascending order of property-size. If the position is one of perfect equality where all properties are the same size, the 'curve' will be a straight line. Otherwise, any deviation from equality creates a curve below the straight line. The Gini coefficient measures the area of the gap between this curve and the straight line, expressing it as a decimal fraction of the area of the triangle defined by the line of perfect equality (the area of the triangle being 1). The greater the inequality, the higher the Gini coefficient. Though widely used, the Gini coefficient is a crude measure which takes no account of the shape of the curve. In the present figures, histograms are used as the form of illustration because they reveal more details.

Table 43. *Land-registers illustrating differentiation of property-sizes*

Location	Date (AD)	Measure	Nature of measure	Total units	Maximum	Minimum	Mean
1. Ligures Baebiani	101	sesterces	value	57	501,000	14,000	78,442
2. Veleia	102/13	sesterces	value	46	1,508,150	50,000	264,328
3. Volcei	307	*M(illenae?)*	tax-potential	36	120	1	24.9
4. Lamasba	218/22	*K (?)*	water-entitlement	78	4,000	48.50	672.6
5. Magnesia	fourth century	*iuga* (tax)	tax-potential	67	75.15	0.01	5.2
6. Hermopolis		*arourae*	area	198	1,370	<2	70.1

Percentage I Number of units

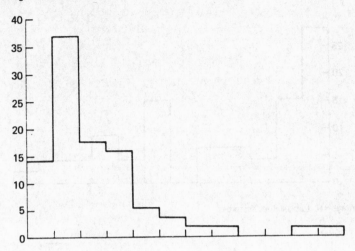

Percentage II Land-value (sesterces)

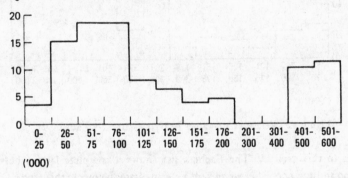

('000)

Figure 21. Ligures Baebiani: estate-values (N = 57)

excluded from the list at Veleia. The list is thus likely to be seriously incomplete in its representation of landed wealth. Yet, despite the high threshold, the range of differentiation is still greater than that shown at Ligures Baebiani. At the top of the scale, the biggest private estate accounts for 12.4% of the wealth, while at the bottom 23.9% of owners account for 5.1% of the land (see fig. 22). The Gini coefficient of differentiation is 0.526, nearly 21% higher than the Baebian figure.

A comparison of overlapping sections reveals more detailed differences (41 estates at Veleia fall within the range between HS50,000 and 510,000, while at Ligures Baebiani there are 36 estates in this range; see figs. 23–4). Although the Gini coefficients are now almost identical, at Ligures Baebiani 83% of the estates in this range are worth HS125,000 or less, whereas only 54% of Veleian estates

Percentage I Number of units

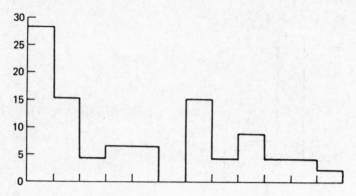

Percentage II Land-value (sesterces)

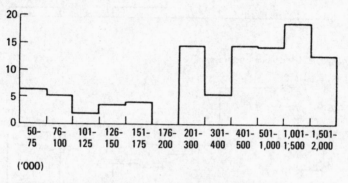

('000)

Figure 22. Veleia: estate-values (private estates) (N = 46)

belong to this group.[41] The Baebian list shows a complete lacuna between 201,000 and 400,000, whereas 22% of Veleian estates belong to this range. Of the Veleian estates 10% fall into the top sector, from 401,000–510,000, compared to only 6% at Ligures Baebiani. Thus the Veleian distribution is largely even throughout the range, whereas the Baebian estates are heavily concentrated at the bottom, and less heavily at the top, with a substantial gap in the middle. If non-random, the irregularities at Ligures Baebiani possibly reflect changes in the pattern of private landownership following the creation of nearby imperial estates.[42]

A third Italian land-register comes from Volcei in the south, in Lucania (*CIL* x 407). The register, dated to AD 307, two centuries later than those from Veleia and Ligures Baebiani, is connected with Diocletian's revisions of taxation. The surviving portion shows 36 farms. The unit of assessment is a measure

---

[41] For Ligures Baebiani the coefficient is now 0.348, while that for Veleia is 0.359.
[42] Out of 57 peripheral holdings at Ligures Baebiani 7 belong to imperial estates.

Percentage I Number of units

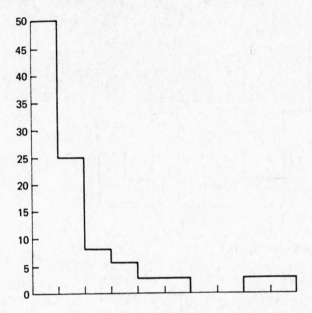

Percentage II Land-value (sesterces)

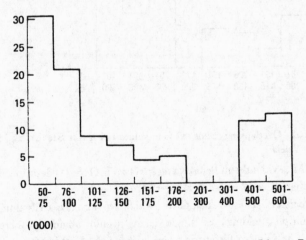

('000)

Figure 23. Overlapping sector of estate-values at Ligures Baebiani and Veleia: Ligures Baebiani

Percentage I Number of units

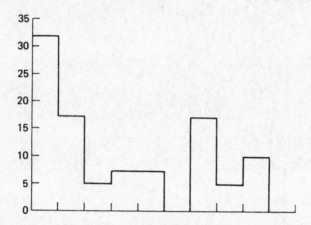

Percentage II Land-value (sesterces)

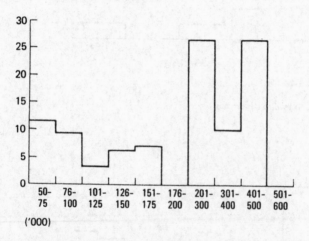

Figure 24. Overlapping sector of estate-values at Ligures Baebiani and Veleia: Veleia

abbreviated as 'M', evidently 'millena'. 50 *iugera* (12.6 hectares) is described as 4 'M', implying that the *millena* was 12½ *iugera*.[43]

The Volcei register lists individual farms, which are not necessarily units of ownership. Multiple holdings of single farms would obviously increase differentiation. The Gini coefficient is 0.394, 91% of the Baebian figure, and 75% of the figure at Veleia. The largest single unit accounts for 13.4% of the total area (see fig. 25). The equation 4 M = 50 *iugera* makes the average 312 *iugera*

---

[43] Déléage (1945) 221–3; see below, p. 202. Goffart (1974) 113–14 contests the reading 'M(illena)', but his alternative, the modius, is too small to match the area stated here (see chapter 13 at nn. 7–8).

Percentage I Number of units

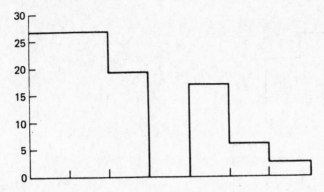

Percentage II Area (*m* (*illenae*?))

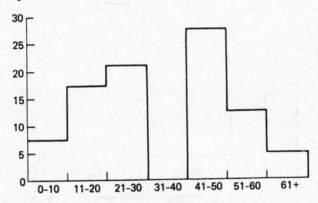

Figure 25. Volcei: farm-units (N = 36)

(78.5 hectares), and the largest unit 1,500 *iugera* (3.8 km²). These are relatively high figures, not nearly as high as the average from Leontini (2,200 *iugera*), but much above the level at Herbita (56 *iugera*).

A register from another part of the West, Lamasba, a small inland town in Numidia, shows the water-entitlement of a series of properties under a local irrigation scheme in AD 218/22. The list is compiled by locality, and the names of five owners occur twice. In the surviving section 78 owners are named. The unit of measurement is signified by the letter 'K'. This seems to be a linear measure, though its equivalent in watering-time varies somewhat according to the point in the irrigation cycle at which a given property received its water.[44] The Gini

[44] *CIL* VIII 18587 with de Pachtère (1908), who gives a commentary and incorporates further readings by Gsell. Shaw (1982) provides a valuable discussion and analysis, arguing that as much as 80% of the list is missing (97). But the area-equivalence of the unit 'K' remains intractable. The

Percentage I Number of estates

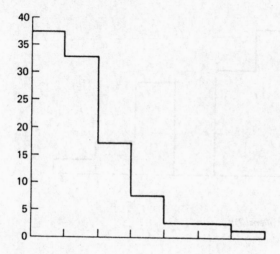

Percentage II Land-area (K)

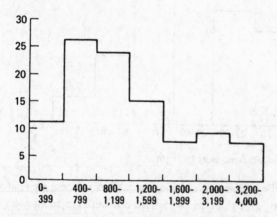

Figure 26. Lamasba: units of water-entitlement (N = 78)

coefficient is 0.447, only 3% higher than the value found at Ligures Baebiani, and 15% below that at Veleia (see fig. 26). The percentage of total assessment accounted for by the largest unit of ownership is only 7.6%. A complete list would almost certainly reveal more multiple holdings, thus increasing differentiation.

There is also evidence from the Greek East. An incomplete but originally very

two cases where numbers of olives are given instead of 'K' mean that olives were also an acceptable quantifying device, but not that they were equivalent to 'K'. Shaw's summary of the holdings includes seven restored figures which are not utilised here.

Percentage I Number of units

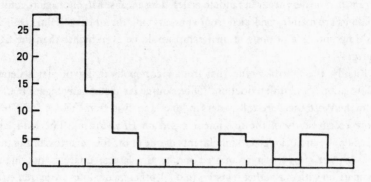

Percentage II Land-value (*iuga*)

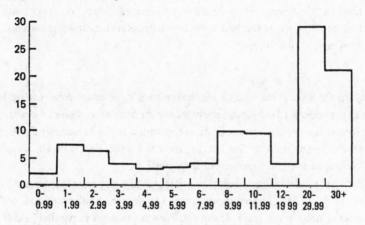

Figure 27. Magnesia: units of ownership (N = 67)

long list from Magnesia on the Maeander in Asia, evidently of the early fourth century, shows 81 farms of stated value, distributed among 67 owners.[45] The measure used is the *iugum*, a tax unit (see chapter 13). Differentiation is very marked (see fig. 27). The largest single estate accounts for 21.6% of the total assessment, and the wealthiest 7.5% owned 49.7% of the total. The Gini coefficient is 0.679, 56% higher than the level at Ligures Baebiani, and 29% higher than that at Veleia.

The alphabetical arrangement suggests that the surviving part of the list

[45] O. Kern *Inschriften von Magnesia am Maeander* (1900) 122. Jones (1974) 234–7 (cf. 229–31) provides a useful analysis and commentary (the figure reproduced on p.238, n.48 as 'iuga 4' should read 'iuga 6').

represents as little as 8% of the likely original length.[46] The listing by farm name means that owners occur in random order. This means that, once again, multiple holdings are mainly concealed from view, arguing that the true Gini coefficient for differentiation of units of ownership would be even higher than the figure shown.

Finally, the fourth-century list from Hermopolis in Egypt yields detailed information about differentiation.[47] The sample is substantially bigger than any from the West; there are 198 owners in Jones's analysis from *PFlor* 71 (238 in the more recent study of the document based on *PLandlisten*). The land lay at Hermopolis and belonged to inhabitants of one of the four districts of the town. Though the proportion accounted for by the largest estate is not high in comparison with most other registers (9.9%), other inequalities are extreme. The wealthiest 3.5% of owners have 53% of the area, while the poorest 47.5% have only 2.8% (see fig. 28). The Gini coefficient is very high (0.856 on Jones's figures, 0.815 from the *PLandlisten* reading). Nearly half the owners have holdings with an area less than 10 *arourae* (11 *iugera* or 2.8 hectares); Jones points out that a few of these smallholders in fact had urban occupations such as builder, potter, fuller, letter-writer or door-keeper.

7 Conclusions

Reading the broader implications of the registers involves a number of problems. Do all the registers describe differentiation within the same sector of wealth? Are the largest landowners always under-represented to the same extent? Does the greater differentiation in the late registers from the East indicate a regional difference, or is the difference chronological?

But closer examination mainly suggests that the contrasts thrown up by the Gini coefficient have limited significance. The degree of differentiation, and the number of units in the available samples turn out to move in parallel (Table 44). The Spearman correlation is 0.714 and r^2 (based on the product-moment correlation) is 0.718.

---

[46] Among 81 farms of known tax-value, 4 owners have three farms, 6 have two farms, and 57 have one. The alphabetical list contains at least 37 farms beginning with the letter beta. If we extrapolate from the ratio of beta to the rest of the alphabet in the place-name index in the *Corpus Inscriptionum Graecarum*, the projected total number of farms in the original list is about 1,066. It is worth noticing that in the Veleian list only 5% of the valuation units are also estate valuations (11 out of 226); all the rest belong to estates containing 2 or more such components.

[47] Jones (1974) 244–52 (retained as the source at this point for minor practical reasons). The further readings of *PFlor* 71 published in *PLandlisten* increase the total for complete holdings by Hermopolites from 13,883 to 15,078.5 *arouras*, making the Jones data a 92% sample of the one now available. This reduces the Gini coefficient by 5%, from 0.856 to 0.815, and lowers the average holding from 70.1 to 63.4 (Bowman (1985) Tables 1, 2 and 5). For a valuable discussion in detail of all the Hermopolis data in the light of the new readings (including corroborative and supplementary evidence from the earlier 'G' register), see Bowman (1985).

Percentage I Number of estates

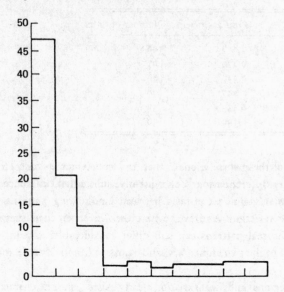

Percentage II Land-area (*arourae*)

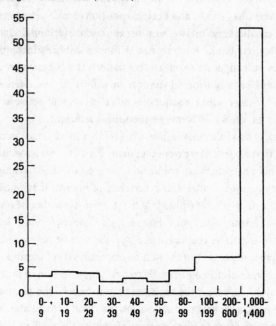

Figure 28. Hermopolis: estate-areas (N = 198)

Table 44. *Gini coefficient related to sample-size*

Sample	Gini coefficient	Number of units
Hermopolis	0.856	198
Magnesia	0.679	67
Veleia	0.526	46
Lamasba	0.447	78
Ligures Baebiani	0.435	57
Volcei	0.394	36

The implication of these correlations is that, to some extent at least, larger samples show greater differentiation. Consequently, substantial differences in sample-size mean that genuine contrasts between landholding patterns are obscured by sample-variation. And even where the Gini coefficient suggests close similarities, the real patterns can still differ considerably, as with the overlapping sections of the two alimentary land-registers from Italy (see above p.131).

Thus, although regional and local variation clearly existed, specific characteristics cannot readily be established by a single measure of this kind, because of non-linearity in the available evidence. On the other hand, interesting differences are on view in the histograms, which show the local position in each case in greater detail (figs. 21–8). The fullest regional delineation, the one at Hermopolis, shows very heavy differentiation of landholding by size. Although critically incomplete, the Magnesia register still suggests a comparable pattern at a big town in Asia. None of the western evidence considered seems to be sufficiently complete in its coverage to give a full picture, and consequently no valid contrast between East and West can readily be drawn in terms of the Gini coefficient.

It is also theoretically possible (although less likely) that local variation could undercut regional patterns to such an extent that many further samples would be needed before regional characteristics could be clearly established. Though it does not establish any regional contrast, it is certainly of interest that an earlier Egyptian land-register, from Philadelphia in AD 216, with a number of owners comparable to that at Hermopolis, again shows a high Gini coefficient, despite having a much smaller area. The coefficient is 0.737, the number of owners 186 and the total area 3,376 arouras, only 22% of the area recorded at Hermopolis.[48]

Almost all the registers point unequivocally to heavy aggregation of property in the hands of the rich. Although the registers vary so much, the proportion occupied by the largest single estate is almost always significant (Table 45). The proportion is 10% or more in five cases out of six. At the median level of

[48] Bowman (1985) 151, based on the full list from Philadelphia, *P Yale* III 145, not published at the time of writing.

Table 45. *Overall area and the largest estates*

Location	Largest estate as percentage of total
Magnesia	21.6
Volcei	13.4
Veleia	12.4
Ligures Baebiani	11.2
Hermopolis	9.9
Lamasba	7.6

12%, the largest estate at Leontini would occupy between 7,000 and 8,500 *iugera*, or 18–21 square kilometres. Granted that the largest landowners usually had properties in several districts, the implied total owned by a typical member of this class is very large indeed.

One illustration is provided by the immense wealth of Symmachus, a senator of the mid-fourth century, which was dispersed in landholdings all over Italy and parts of the provinces.[49] In some cases the large landholder could become completely dominant over a single area, and might own whole villages.[50] Single estates in Africa could engender settlements which became villages taking their name from the owner.[51] Land units on this scale could easily become little worlds on their own, often to the owner's advantage.[52]

The dominant trend seems to have been towards greater piling-up of territory in a few hands. Divided inheritance constituted an opposing but weaker tendency.[53] The main governmental constraint on private accumulation of land was not so much death-duty (whose standard rate of 5% was very low) as expropriation.[54] As well as inheritance within a propertied class in which childlessness was not uncommon, the mechanisms of accumulation probably included absorption of smaller landholders by larger ones, through processes of

---

[49] He owned 12 villas in different parts of Italy, and lands in Samnium, Apulia, Sicily and Mauretania; see Jones (1964) 554; 781–2.

[50] Cf. e.g. examples cited by MacMullen (1974) 159–60, nn.33–4.

[51] Cf. Vicus Annaeus, Vicus Haterianus, Vicus Phosphori (P. Salama *Les voies romaines de l'Afrique du Nord* (Paris, 1951) 139–40).

[52] Agennius Urbicus (Thulin 45). For the fundus Petrensis built up 'in modum urbis', see Ammianus Marcellinus 29.5.13. For the self-sufficiency of large estates cf. D. 33.7.12.5 (an estate may have its own bakers, barbers, masons and weavers) and in general *ERE²* 37–8.

[53] The custom of adopting an adult heir (cf. Syme (1988A) 4.159–73) could be seen in part as a provision against dividing the estate.

[54] A classic, though far from isolated, case is Nero's execution and expropriation of six men who owned 'half of Africa' (Pliny *NH* 18.35). Their lands re-emerge as imperial estates with names recalling their former owners (cf. chapter 4, section 1). Though it is impossible to say what percentage of large estates suffered in this way, many of those at risk politically in certain reigns were big landowners, and some big landowners were at risk because of their wealth; Millar (1977) 163–74.

coercion and rural debt. Accumulation of territory could readily be seen by the wealthy as desirable in itself.[55]

But although they show great inequality, the land-registers also clearly show big estates whose multitude of small cells tended to remain small, irrespective of aggregate estate-size (Table 42). The price of accumulation tended to be estates whose components were physically dispersed. This dislocation made direct exploitation with centralised management more difficult, and less cost-effective than in a compact domain. Obtaining adjacent land, 'pulchritudo iungendi' in Pliny's words, thus made economic sense, even if the reasons for desiring it were not always and not necessarily economic (cf. n.32). But geographical unity was difficult to achieve, and it did not usually become the dominant mode of landholding. However, where tenant-farms were more important than direct exploitation, the problems inherent in dispersal may have been reduced.

[55] Pliny *Ep.* 3.19; Petronius *Sat.* 48; *D.* 32.92. pr.

9
The price of wheat in Roman Egypt

1 Introduction

As the main source of bread, the staple foodstuff of antiquity, wheat has obvious interest for the economic historian. Its central importance has not always been fully recognised. The advertised menu at dinners of plebeian colleges in Italy under the Principate usually consisted of bread and wine.[1] In Egypt, small property-owners who made contracts with their heirs for their own maintenance, asked only for wheat and oil.[2] Apprenticeship and entertainment contracts in Egypt often show the same terms.[3]

The position was similar in the Mediterranean in more recent times. Labourers on a farm in Sicily in the late seventeenth century lived on bread and wine, with small amounts of cheese and oil. Paupers in eighteenth century Languedoc received bread and very small amounts of wine.[4] In Lucania under

---

*The present chapter adds 25 items to Johnson's list of wheat prices (Johnson (1936) 310–12). A few of his examples were discarded after examination. In the interests of simplicity, a version of the traditional division into Upper and Lower Egypt has been used here, Upper Egypt denoting the Thebaid. (For more precise divisions, see chapter 1, Table 3.)

Quantifying wheat-measures presents many difficulties (see briefly ERE^2 372). The tax-artaba used for synagoristic purchases contained 48 choenices (nos.49a and 58), and evidently equalled 4 1/2 Italic modii (Duncan-Jones (1976C); this article, together with Duncan-Jones (1979B), supersedes the brief metrological discussion in Duncan-Jones (1976B) Appendix 1). The size of the domestic artaba could vary (examined in detail in Duncan-Jones (1979B)). It cannot normally be reconstructed exactly for a given transaction, although leases often stipulated the use of a particular measuring-vessel, whose size (always much less than an artaba, for practical reasons) is often defined in choenices.

For discussion of a theory that Egyptian wheat prices were normally much lower than the levels shown by the direct evidence, see Duncan-Jones (1976B) Appendix 2.

[1] ERE^2 263 n.3; 364–5.
[2] For example *PMich* 321, AD 42; 322a, AD 46. The Egyptians were specifically said to be bread-eaters by Hecataeus (Athenaeus 418e). This presumably means that, unlike the Greeks who also ate meat when they could (Athenaeus 141b, 149e–f, 412e, 414f, 415b; Thuc. 4.16.1), the Egyptians actually preferred a cereal diet.
[3] E.g. *PMich* 355, first century AD; *POxy* 2721, AD 234, where wine is also provided. Music students at Alexandria supported by the emperor Julian received double rations of wheat, together with oil and wine (Julian 422a). See also papyri listed in Johnson (1936) 389–91; 299–300. Egyptian children were regularly reared on an even humbler vegetarian diet in place of bread (Diodorus Siculus 1.80.5–6).   [4] Aymard–Bresc (1975) 597–8; Vedel (1975) 486–9.

Mussolini the agricultural poor ate bread and little else.[5] Though a bread diet leads to malnutrition and greatly increases vulnerability to disease, the evidence for its prevalence through long periods of Mediterranean history is relatively clear-cut.[6]

Egyptian evidence is crucially important for the price of bread in the Roman world, though what it refers to (for reasons discussed in section 7) is usually wheat from which bread would be made.[7] Even Roman soldiers received rations in this form, and the warlike emperor Caracalla is said to have endeared himself to his troops by sharing their lot and baking his own bread while in camp.[8]

The Egyptian evidence for wheat prices falls into three categories. The largest is evidence from private transactions in Lower Egypt (nos.1–37). The same area provides official prices and valuations, which form the second category (nos.48–64). Finally, Upper Egypt contributes a few prices, mainly in the form of money-dues commuted for wheat (nos.38–47).

2 Regional price-variation

In the first century AD, when there is evidence from both areas, the median average wheat price in Upper Egypt is 3.5 drachmas per artaba. The corresponding figure for Lower Egypt is 8 drachmas. The prices from Upper Egypt (nos. 38–47) may refer to payments of taxes, which would probably involve a standard conversion-rate between money and wheat.

Provided that the Upper Egypt valuations were not kept artificially low, the extreme difference suggests that commodity prices there were well below those in Lower Egypt. The south was of course furthest from the capital and its mint, and overall liquidity might be lower there, notwithstanding any effects produced by garrison pay.

Prices from Alexandria, one of the biggest cities of the empire, are lacking. But they may easily have been higher than those in Lower Egypt, because of price pressure characteristic of large towns, and because of greater liquidity in the capital, where the mint was located.[9]

3 Seasonal variation

It is well known that wheat prices are usually volatile in agrarian societies with a high reliance on bread as a staple. Cicero singles out a fluctuation in Sicily of at least two-fold between what wheat cost just before the harvest, and what it cost

---

[5] C. Levi, *Christo si e fermato a Eboli* (1945) chapter 4. For a similar position in the Levant, see Jones (1964) 447.   [6] See n.4

[7] For milling at home see e.g. Athenaeus 263b and n.20 below. In a fourth-century work where the high cost of bread is discussed (Julian *Misopogon* 369d, 370a), all the prices refer to raw wheat (369b–c). Cato's 'free range' slaves received rations in the form of wheat, and only the chained slaves (who would be locked up when not working) were given bread (Cato 56–8).

[8] Herodian 4.7.5.   [9] For high prices in large towns, cf. *ERE*[2] Appendix 8.

just after the harvest. The earlier price was HS20 per modius, but the later price was so low that being forced to commute tax-wheat at HS12 per modius inflicted real hardship.[10]

Later evidence shows that fluctuations did not always follow a simple pattern. A 15-year price-series is known from San Sepolcro in Tuscany (1507–21). The figure at the beginning of August, when the harvest was beginning to affect prices, was below the level at the start of April, in 10 years out of 15.[11] On average, the early August price was only 9% below the April price in the fifteen years as a whole. But in some years prices could still double within a 12-month period (106% in 1507, 100% in 1508, 84% in 1509 and 86% in 1511). There were also years of relative stability (1518 with 20% variation between the extremes, and 1519 with 29% variation).

Only three Egyptian sources provide a series of prices within a 12-month span. They all show fluctuation. Wheat purchased for employees of the record-office at Tebtunis in AD 45 cost 4.4 drachmas per artaba on 7 September, rising on the 21st to 5.7 drachmas (nos.4–12). Three days later there was a sharp rise, with three purchases at 8 drachmas on the 24th. Prices fell very slightly to 7.3 and 7.6 drachmas on the 26th and after 1 October. But they had recovered to 8 drachmas soon afterwards. The total range of variation in this period of 3 weeks soon after the harvest was 93%.[12]

In the next series, sales of wheat by a producer at Hermopolis in AD 78 again begin in September. The price is 10 drachmas on the 10th, the 17th and on the 21st. In January the price had risen to 11 drachmas, and sales at this price took place on the 13th and 27th, and on the 3rd of February (nos.14–20). The range of variation here is only 10%.

A third series recording sales by a producer at Karanis in AD 191/2 shows much higher prices. These are partly inflationary, but their level may also reflect a time of shortage which affected Rome as well as Egypt (section 5). The prices rise from 18 to 20 drachmas in December, falling back to 18 in January/February, a variation of 11% (nos.26–8).

As a whole, this evidence gives the impression that month-to-month fluctuations in Egypt could sometimes be as great as the two-fold variation Cicero mentions, but that they did not always vary dramatically with the seasons. The fact that the state regularly paid a minimum of 8 drachmas per artaba probably argues that prices rarely went much below this level. If they did, it would have been more advantageous to buy in the open market.

---

[10] *Verr.* 2.3.214–15.

[11] Fanfani (1940) 81–111. The averages (for the first-week of the month) are April: 77.8; and August: 70.75.

[12] Leases of the Roman period often specify payment of the wheat rent in Pauni (26 May–24 June), presumably the earliest date at which it was available (e.g. *PSI* 315; *POxy* 910; 2188; 2351; *SP* v 119, VII).

Evidence from Egypt in the Middle Ages shows some tendency for the price to rise sharply in winter or spring, before the main harvest. Thus in January 1300, the Cairo price was 10–13 dirhams per irdabb (69.9 kg), but in the spring it had more than doubled to 27 dirhams. In the summer after the harvest it fell to 20 dirhams, and fell further to 15 in the autumn. At the beginning of 1328, the price in Cairo rose from 13 to 20 dirhams. The price rose in February 1336 from 15 to 50, and efforts to impose a controlled price only led to black market dealings at 60–70 dirhams. The price in 1375 fell back after the harvest from 130 to 60, and then to 30 dirhams.[13]

Prices like these from a big city were probably more volatile than prices in the countryside. Their pattern of violent seasonal change, however, may in some degree model the pattern in ancient Alexandria, about which direct evidence is lacking.

4 Fluctuation from year to year

In the absence of market prices from successive harvests, year-to-year fluctuations are largely invisible. The figure of 1.9 drachmas per artaba in 5 BC, which is completely isolated, is so low as to be dubious, and it probably depends on an uncertain reading (no.2). But a clear variation in official prices in AD 99, when the rate doubled to 16 drachmas, belongs to a time of famine, and must reflect underlying change in market prices (nos.48A, 49 and note).

Comparable fluctuations can be found in the later evidence from Tuscany. At San Sepolcro, the average price in 1505 was 4.6 times greater than the price in 1525; and it was 4.3 times greater in 1540 than in 1538.[14] Fluctuations of this kind in Egypt obviously cannot be ruled out, but probably, as in Tuscany, year-to-year variations of 100% or more were the exception rather than the rule.

5 Long-term price movements

Divided into three periods, the prices from private transactions in Lower Egypt give a consistent impression of increase over the long term.

Table 46. *Wheat prices by century (private transactions in lower Egypt)*

	pre–AD 100 (sample in brackets)	AD 101–200	AD 201–300
Median	8 (19)	12 (10)	16 (7)
Maximum	11	20	200
Minimum	(?)	10	7

[13] Ashtor (1969) 284–6.   [14] Fanfani (1940) 68.

Inflation during the third century is seen much more clearly in the official wheat prices. The compensation price was still 8 drachmas under Antoninus Pius (no.59, cf. no.60), but had risen three-fold to 24 drachmas by 246 (no.61a). By the 290s, the price had risen a further 10-fold, to 220–300 drachmas (nos.63–64). The figures for private transactions are too incomplete to spell things out so clearly, but they include a price of 200 (?) drachmas at Karanis in AD 276 (no.36).

These very large price rises in the later third century are incontestable, but the details of earlier change are less easy to discern. The three short-term price-series (section 3) show median averages as follows:

AD
45/6   7.8
78/9   10.5
191/2   18.0

The last figure belongs to a time of famine which affected Rome as well as Egypt, and may be high for this reason.[15] Nevertheless, there are indications of the same price-levels in other evidence of approximately this period (18 and 19.4 drachmas, nos.31, *c.* 180/220; 30, before AD 200).

If Egyptian wheat prices by the end of the second century were about twice those of a century earlier, this would roughly mirror evidence from Ephesus, where bread prices show a similar increase between the early second and the early third centuries.[16]

6 Official wheat prices

The system of official wheat prices in one of Rome's provinces is explained in Cicero's Verrines. Cicero shows that there was a regular three-tier system of compulsory purchase in Sicily, over and above the 10% tithe for which the taxpayer received no payment.

As the first tier, a second tithe (*frumentum emptum*) was levied, with a refund of HS3 per modius. As the second tier, a further amount of wheat was levied proportionately on all the cities (*frumentum imperatum*). The refund was at the higher rate of HS3½ per modius. As the third tier, yet more wheat was requisitioned, in theory for the governor's use (*frumentum in cellam*). Cicero maintains that governors could enrich themselves by selling or commuting what they did not need, without blemish to their reputations. Verres, like his two immediate predecessors, commuted his personal wheat at the high rate of HS12 per modius which they had adopted (but culpably prolonged the arrangement for the whole of his three years as governor).[17]

---

[15] The sources report the famine as being due to manipulations at Rome, not to harvest failure (Herodian 1.12.3–4). Cf. Whittaker (1964) 348–69. There is no apparent basis for Johnson's view (435–6) that all 3 price-series were exceptional.

[16] See Broughton in Frank vol. 4 (1936) 879–80.   [17] *Verr.* 2.3.163; 188; 217; 214–15.

By comparison with this blueprint from Sicily, the evidence from Egypt is very incomplete. If the prefect requisitioned wheat for his own use, as he is almost bound to have done (or if he chose to commute it for money), this was probably a charge on the nearby Delta region, from which few records survive. The available papyri do not appear to differentiate between *frumentum emptum* (tier 1 in Sicily), and *frumentum imperatum* (tier 2). What they do show is frequent payments for 'synagoristic' or requisitioned wheat (nos.48–64). The payment is generally at a rate of 8 drachmas per artaba in a series of records extending up to 154, briefly doubling in the crisis year of 99 (no.49 and note); but it emerges later as 24 drachmas in 246, and as 220–300 drachmas in sales to the *annona* in 293/4.

The price of 8 drachmas occurs in five separate records, spanning the period AD 79–154. It seems likely that the rate only changed under strong market pressure. Such pressures had certainly been felt by AD 246, by which time the price had tripled. But the evidence is so incomplete that it leaves room for a prior change, perhaps from 8 to 16 drachmas, at some point in the intervening period.

Cicero represents the system of compensation in Sicily as being at least fair to the taxpayer. Official compensation ranged from HS3 to HS4 per modius, whereas the usual market price in Sicily was HS2, HS2½, or at most HS3 per modius.[18] The fact that under Verres Sicilian farmers rarely received the stipulated rates of compensation was apparently no fault of the system.

In Egypt, however, the rate of compensation appears to have sagged below the market price. The standard price of 8 drachmas for synagoristic purchases approximately equalled the median price in the series from Tebtunis of AD 45/6. But it is well below the average of the seven prices from Hermopolis of AD 78/9 (10/12 drachmas). If all artabas here are identical, the compensation would be about a quarter less than the median market price.

Thus government practice in Egypt was possibly less favourable to the farmer than the system in Sicily as described by Cicero. If Augustan, the synagoristic rate of 8 drachmas may have been more favourable at the outset than it was to become with the slow inflation of the first two centuries.

7 Wheat marketing

In the evidence from Lower Egypt, three-quarters of the prices from private transactions dated by month belong to the five months from September to January. Clearly this reflects the fact that farmers tended to sell most of their crop soon after the harvest. The seasonal price-fluctuations, sometimes of consider-

---

[18] Official compensation: *Verr.* 2.3.163; 188. Market prices: HS2: 2.3.174; 189; HS2½: 84; 90; 173; 175; cf. 72; HS2–3: 189; 194.

able size, again reflect this practice, which made wheat abundant and cheap soon after a harvest, but scarce and dear later on (section 3).

If the wheat had been mainly sold to dealers who would market it throughout the year, this could have acted as a smoothing mechanism which would restrain price-fluctuation. But there is little here to suggest that wheat was normally sold to intermediaries. The two first-century price-series, from Tebtunis and Hermopolis, represent on the one hand purchases by a consumer, and on the other sales by a producer (nos.4–12, 14–20). The average price achieved by the producer in this case is actually above that paid by the consumer in question, as a result of casual differences between the two series, which are three decades apart. But the discrepancy would have to be very big before there was any margin for a middleman's profit.

Similarly, in Cicero's long account of wheat-taxes and wheat sales in Sicily, there is no hint of the presence of corn–dealers. Cicero claims to be able to show from the accounts of the richest farmers that wheat never changed hands at more than HS2½ in a particular year. Cicero here implies that a producer's records of 'farm-gate' prices would be enough to show the highest levels at which wheat was selling.[19]

Probably the consumer who was not also a producer often bought his grain in bulk from a farmer, at a time of year when prices were most favourable, using it up over an extended period as required. Pliny wrote that Rome had no bakers before 171 BC, bread being baked by the women of the household, as it still was in many countries in his own day.[20] Nevertheless, corn-dealers certainly existed in Egypt (they were one of the categories liable to a special poll-tax), and there were also professional bakers in big towns.[21] How prevalent these trades were, and what role they fulfilled in the overall pattern of exchange are questions which would benefit from further investigation.

8 Conclusions

Egyptian wheat prices fall into three categories which must be considered separately: market prices and valuations from Lower Egypt, official valuations from Lower Egypt, and official or quasi-official valuations from Upper Egypt. The prices from the two areas show a clear regional contrast, those from Upper Egypt being substantially below those from Lower Egypt. Official valuations in lower Egypt are stereotyped at a level which appears to be somewhat below that of typical free market prices. But they could be adjusted in years of harvest crisis,

---

[19] *Verr.* 2.3.173.   [20] Pliny *NH* 18.107.

[21] Wallace (1938) 211; Johnson (1936) 369ff. The one reference to corn–dealers in the present evidence occurs in no.9, a purchase from 'corn–dealers in the grain-stores (thesauroi)'.

and they were eventually raised by a very large factor when 'hyper-inflation' took hold in the last decades of the third century.

The market prices fluctuate seasonally by as much as a factor of 2. Average prices rose by roughly half between the first and the second centuries. A typical level by the end of the second century seems to have been 18 drachmas per artaba, approximately twice the normal level of the first century. Prices seem to have risen at least a further 50% by mid-century, and were roughly thirty times the first-century level by the 290s.

Comparisons with wheat prices elsewhere in the empire are hampered by shortage of evidence. At Antioch in Pisidia, the normal price per modius was HS2$\frac{1}{4}$ at the end of the first century AD, or in Egyptian terms, about 10 drachmas per tax-artaba.[22] Prices in Africa in the late second century may have been about HS2$\frac{1}{2}$ per modius (roughly 11$\frac{1}{4}$ drachmas per tax-artaba), apparently lower than contemporary market prices in Lower Egypt. Prices in Italy at the start of the second century of HS4 per modius (roughly 17 drachmas per tax-artaba) were noticeably higher than contemporary Egyptian levels.[23]

It is not obvious that wheat was much cheaper in Egypt than in other Mediterranean provinces, although cheapness might have been expected in one of the primary producing areas. At a simplistic level, that could argue that tax took away so much of the crop that what was left fetched a relatively high market price. But Egypt also had a closed monetary system, and its liquidity-level did not necessarily match that in other provinces closely.[24] This obstructs comparison with other wheat prices, and would do so even if external evidence were less incomplete.

The Egyptian evidence nevertheless provides the one prime dossier showing price-levels and price movements in wheat under the Principate. The lack of contemporary parallels makes its typicality difficult to assess, but increases its practical importance for the economic historian.

---

[22] *AE* 1925, 126b.   [23] *ERE²* 50–1.   [24] For Egyptian currency, cf. chapter 2, n.45.

PRICES

Entries numbered in italics are the subject of notes on pp.154–6 below.

I Prices and valuations from private transactions in Lower Egypt

No.	Price (drachmas per artaba)	Quantity (artabas)	Place	Date	Reference
1.	*c.* 9.3	60	Euhemeria	*c.* 18 BC	*PFay* 101
2.	1.9(?)	77.7	?	27 Nov.–26 Dec. 5 BC	*PTeb* 459
3.	9		Tebtunis	26 May/24 June AD 16	*PSI* IX 1028
4.	4.4	1.83	Tebtunis	7 Sept. 45/6	*PMich* 127
5.	5.7	3.5	Tebtunis	21 Sept. 45/6	*PMich* 127
6.	8	2	Tebtunis	24 Sept. 45/6	*PMich* 127
7.–					
8.	8	1	Tebtunis	24 Sept. 45/6	*PMich* 127
9.	8	3	Tebtunis	24 Sept. 45/6	*PMich* 127
10.	7.3	1.1	Tebtunis	26 Sept. 45/6	*PMich* 127
11.	7.6	2.1	Tebtunis	after 1 Oct. 45/6	*PMich* 127
12.	8	1.5	Tebtunis	after 1 Oct. 45/6	*PMich* 127
13.	8.7	1.83	Tebtunis	15 Dec. 47	*PMich* 123 verso XI, 26–7
14.	10	6	Hermopolis	10 Sept. 78	*PLond* 131
15.	10	14	Hermopolis	17 Sept. 78	*PLond* 131
16.	10	4	Hermopolis	21 Sept. 78	*PLond* 131
17.	11	5	Hermopolis	13 Jan. 79	*PLond* 131
18.	11	5	Hermopolis	(?) Jan. 79	*PLond* 131
19.	11	2	Hermopolis	27 Jan. 79	*PLond* 131
20.	11	4	Hermopolis	3 Feb. 79	*PLond* 131
21.	12		Oxyrhynchus	7 Oct. 112	*POxy* 2351
22.	9	5.5	Hermopolis	30 Mar.–25 April 124	*PSarap* 60
23.	7		Hermopolis	100/135	*PSarap* 92
24.	12	7.8	Hermopolis	27 Nov./26 Dec. 100/135	*PSarap* 79b
25.	6		Heracleopolis	Sept./June 138/161	*PBaden* 79
26.	18	1.3	Karanis	27 Nov./26 Dec. (191)	*PCair Goodsp* 30, col. 13
27.	20	1	Karanis	27 Nov./26 Dec. (191)	*PCair Goodsp* 30, col. 15
28.	18	2	Karanis	26 Jan./24 Feb. (192)	*PCair Goodsp* 30, col. 20

Table (cont.)

No.	Price (drachmas per artaba)	Quantity (artabas)	Place	Date	Reference
29.	8	17	Socnopaiou Nesos	100/200	*SP* XXII 110
30.	19.4	0.5	(Fayum)	21 March 100/200	*PGrenf* I 51
31.	18	50	—	(*c.* 180/220)	*PIand* 94
32.	12	13	Theadelphia	29 Aug/27 Sept. 254 (?)	*PLond* III 1226
33.	16	100	(Memphis)	25 July/17 Aug. 255	*BGU* I 14
34.	(12)	13	Theadelphia	25 Feb./26 March 250/260	*PFlor* 321
34a.	16 (internal valuation)	-	Oxyrhynchus	*c.* 259/60	S.A. Stephens *ZPE* (1978) 147
35.	24	1	Oxyrhynchus	(*c.* Aug.?) 269	*PErl* 23 (101)
36.	200?	2	Karanis	276	*OMich* I 157 with H.C. Youtie, *TAPhA* 76 (1945) 144–6
37.	20	1	Philadelphia	100/300	*BGU* VII 1717

II Wheat prices from Upper Egypt

The sources for wheat prices from Upper Egypt (ostraka instead of papyri) are short and inexplicit. Most take the form of receipts for money taxes or dues paid in wheat at a rate which may or may not have been officially determined. They do not show consistent patterning such as can be seen in the government assessments of wheat prices in Lower Egypt (nos.48ff.).

No.	Price (drachmas per artaba)	Quantity (artabas)	Place	Date	Reference
38.	4	—	Thebes	15 Sept. 13 BC	*OStrassb* 46
39.	2.5	1.25	Thebes	10 BC	*OStrassb* 48
40.	2.5	20.5	Thebes	31 July 9 BC	*OStrassb* 51
41.	3.5	2	Coptos	25 Jan. 4 BC	*OPetr* 97
42.	3.5	1	Coptos	25 Jan. 4 BC	*OPetr* 199
43.	3.51	2.12	Coptos	25 Jan. 4 BC	*OPetr* 201
44.	5	1/6	Thebes	24 Feb. AD 56	*OWilck* 1558
45.	2.2	11.5	Coptos	1 March 65	*OBod* 210
46.	24?	1/24	Thebes	153	*OWilck* 1587
47.	9	2	—		*OAsh* 91

III *Official wheat prices and valuations from Lower Egypt*
The artaba in use here is likely to be one of 48 choenices.

No.	Price (drachmas per artaba)	Quantity (artabas)	Place	Date	Reference
48.	8 (sale to *annona*)	1	Hermopolis	Feb. 79	*PLond* 1 131
48A.	16 (synagoristic)		Oxyrhynchus	99/100	*POxy* 3355
49.	16 (synagoristic purchase)	12	Oxyrhynchus	2 Dec. 99	*POxy* 2958
49a.	8 (synagoristic)	25.8	Oxyrhynchus	23 Jan. 100	*POxy* 2960
50.	(8) (customs valuation)	990	Nile shipment	before 200	*POxy* 1650 Wallace (1938) 465 n.41
51.	8 (synagoristic)		Hermopolis	128	*PSarap* 79e
52.	8 (synagoristic)	217.4;3	Oxyrhynchus	137	*PSI* 1262
53.	7(8) (synagoristic)	8.25	Tebtunis & Kerkeosiris	23 March 149	*PTeb* 394
54.	8 (synagoristic)		Themistes division	100/150	*PIand* 138
55.	(8) (customs valuation)	5	Umm el Atl	152	*PFay* 76a, cf. pp. 199–200
56.	8 (synagoristic)	5.4	Oxyrhynchus	28 Feb. 154	*POxy* 2961–63
57.	8 (synagoristic)	10	Oxyrhynchus	15 Feb. 154	*POxy* 2964–66
58.	8 (synagoristic)	$9\frac{5}{6}$	Oxyrhynchus	3–7 March 154	*POxy* 2967
59.	8 (commutation of wheat due to donkey-drivers)		Theadelphia	155	*PCol* 14; *P. Berl. Frisk* 1
60.	(8) (customs valuation)	12	Socnopaiou Nesos	162	*PRyl* 11 197 with *PFay* pp.199–200
61.	8 (commutation of prosthema)	1		100/200?	*SB* 12088
61a.	24 (compulsory purchase)	—	Oxyrhynchus	17/18 March 246	*POxy* 3048

Table (cont.)

No.	Price (drachmas per artaba)	Quantity (artabas)	Place	Date	Reference
62.	40 (tax-payment)	33;2	S. Fayum	*c.* 260/290	*PStras* 295
63.	300 (sale to *annona*)	67	Oxyrhynchus	293	*POxy* 2142
64.	220 (as no.59)		(Oxyrhynchus)	294	*PHarris* Appendix pp.109–10

NOTES

1 The papyrus indicates that $34\frac{1}{3}$ artabas of cummin, 50 artabas of cnecus and $15\frac{14}{15}$ artabas of lentils equal 60 artabas of wheat in value. The price of cummin is stated as 7 drachmas per artaba, and that of cnecus as 4 drachmas per artaba. If lentils:wheat stood at 15:19 (as in *PCol* I recto 6), then 47.42 artabas of wheat cost $440\frac{1}{3}$ drachmas, and the wheat price per artaba is 9.29 drachmas. (Johnson's price of 3 drachmas, 2 obols is based on a misreading.)

2 The transaction, reported to a correspondent in Tebtunis, took place at another location which is not identified. The extraordinarily low price appears to be uncertain.

3 The figure refers to a cash payment to which the borrower becomes liable should he fail to repay an interest-free grain loan in kind after the harvest.

4 Nos.4–12 refer to purchase of wheat on the open market by Kronion, one of the operators of the *grapheion* at Tebtunis.

13 The $1\frac{2}{3}$ artaba of wheat was used to pay for beer, but its money valuation (16 drachmas) is stated. Like nos.4–12, the purchase was made by one of the employees of the *grapheion* at Tebtunis.

14 Nos.14–20 and no.48 are all sales by a producer whose detailed accounts survive. For a general commentary on these accounts, see Swiderek (1960).

21 Under the terms of a 4-year lease, the half of 24 arouras that was planted with chickling was to pay a rent of 2 artabas of wheat or 24 silver drachmas per aroura. The money equivalent may have been set high to allow for any possible future fluctuation during the 4-year period.

23 Eutychides reported in a letter to his father Sarapion that the price of wheat was no more than 7 drachmas (per artaba) at the time of writing. Since from what he also says in the letter Eutychides had sold the young barley, but not (evidently) the wheat, the letter may have been written soon after the harvest.

24 Though 12 drachmas per artaba is apparently high for the early second century, it should be noted that this is still a selling price by a producer (see section 7 above).

26 Nos.26–8 all come from the same detailed set of accounts and apparently refer to selling prices by a producer. For discussion of their level, see p.145.

29 The commodity is not stated but is probably wheat. The small fragment does not identify the nature of the transaction, which may even be synagoristic (cf. p.148), since 8 drachmas was the standard price for synagoristic wheat.

30 Since the price for oil mentioned in the same accounts (1.3 drachmas per cotyle) is as low as first- and second-century prices (Johnson (1936) 316–7), the date is probably not later than 200, as suggested by Johnson (1936) 317 (in contrast to Johnson (1936) 311).

31 This is a selling price by a producer, part of whose proceeds a brother of the vendor, apparently writing from the country, remits to a third brother to be used for specified purchases, presumably in a town.

32 Like no.34, this is one of the monthly accounts submitted to Aurelius Appianus, former exegete of Alexandria, by his steward Heroninos, who ran Appianus' estate in Theadelphia. The 'sale' of wheat here was purely an accounting device representing the notional value of wheat consumed by casual employees and others. That is why its value in September is the same as in March of what may well be a different year (no.34). See Bingen (1951) 381.

33 Since it comes from a similar contemporary synopsis of estate-accounts, the wheat price may represent an internal valuation, as in nos.32 and 34, not a free market exchange. The attribution to Memphis comes from Johnson (1936) 311.

34 See note on no.32.

37 This is the value of wheat received by an indentured labourer from his employer, and not strictly a market price.

44 Johnson (1936) 311 extrapolates the price of 5 obols for $\frac{1}{8}$ artaba as 4 drachmas 2 obols, using the 7-obol drachma. But the 6-obol drachma more usual in official transactions would make the price 5 drachmas (cf. Schuman (1952) 214–18).

49 That AD 99 was a year of famine in Egypt is indicated by Pliny *Pan.* 31. See p.148.

49a See note on no.58.

50 Dues of 44 drachmas on 550 artabas and 43 drachmas on 540 artabas evidently represent a 1% tax levied on a notional value of 8 drachmas per artaba, rounded to the nearest drachma.

53 This transaction seems to represent payment of the 8 drachmas due on an artaba of 48 choenices scaled down proportionally to take account of payment in an actual local artaba of 42 choenices (see Duncan-Jones (1979B) 369, no.57 and note).

58 The figures show that a 48-choenix artaba was in use (see Duncan-Jones (1979B) 370, nos.68–9 and note).

60 Three drachmas were paid on freight of 12 artabas as the 3% duty, strictly pointing to a notional price of 8.33 drachmas per artaba. But the correct tax if the notional value were exactly 8 drachmas would be 2 drachmas 5.28 obols, for which suitable denominations did not exist. This probably means that 3 drachmas were only paid as a convenient rounding-up tax calculated on the standard valuation of 8 drachmas.

PART IV

THE WORLD OF CITIES

10

The social cost of urbanisation

1 Introduction

The spread of cities on the Roman model, within at least the western Mediterranean, can be seen as one of the great successes of Roman rule.[1] This was not merely a question of institutions and procedures imposed under compulsion, even though Rome did often provide local constitutions and the strongest single impetus came from veteran settlement.[2] Urbanisation on the Roman model also rapidly became a movement sustained by positive forces at the local level.

First, there was some direct eagerness to imitate the city of Rome and the existing cities of Roman type, both in their institutions and in their physical appearance. Roman practices tended to spread even where Roman institutions did not exist. The introduction of magistracies and priesthoods soon fuelled the social ambitions of local aristocracies. And the newly invented position of Augustalis provided a surrogate office for wealthy former slaves, excluded by Augustus from the town council.[3] Provincial cities competed with each other for titles and other marks of status.[4] The rites of urban life meant ceremonies, shows, handouts and new public buildings. Ulpian defined domicile as the place where a man makes his purchases, sales and contracts, and where he goes to the forum, the baths and the shows.[5]

Many of these features had obvious popular appeal and reinforced the involvement of ordinary people in town life. Under standard Roman constitutions, towns appointed magistrates by popular election, giving the electorate democratic rights of choice between candidates, even though access to office depended on financial thresholds.[6] Cicero describes what happened when Verres sold the office of censor in each town in Sicily to the highest bidder, instead of allowing the people to elect the censors.[7] The results were catastrophic. The

---

[1] Cf. in general Jones (1971A). For the nature of Roman towns, cf. *ERE*[2] 259-60.

[2] Tac. *Ann.* 14-31; Hyginus 176-78L.   [3] Duthoy (1978).

[4] Aristides 23; 27.44; *Syll.*[3] 849. Dio Chrys. *Or.* 34.47-8; 40; *D.* 50.10.3.pr.   [5] *D.* 50.1.27.1.

[6] *ILS* 6089, 52. See Jacques (1984); Willems (1887); Castrén (1976). For financial charges and thresholds, see *ERE*[2] 82-8; 147-55. At Concordia in N. Italy, decurions made as many as four payments for their office (Fronto 2.7, 192 N).

[7] *Verr.* 2.2.131. Cicero states that Sicily had 130 censors, two for each town.

censors who bought their way in drew up rating-schedules which consistently favoured the rich at the expense of the poor.[8] Local reactions were so violent that the new governor had to fall back on earlier schedules. The episode implies that effective popular constraints were normally exercised through the electoral process. Even if evidence for democracy at work is usually less explicit, it also includes a host of inscriptions which show expressions of popular will, and popular pressure being exerted on office-holders in Roman towns.[9]

But the urban system also contained restrictive forces. The financial obligations of local office, formal and customary, could weigh heavily on the individual. Town finance was essentially 'liturgical', with much or most cash revenue coming from a narrow tax-base of well-to-do office-holders. Even outside the context of local office, the customary expenditures expected of the local aristocracy could be substantial. Cash-handouts, effectively to all comers, at weddings and family events of the wealthy were already a recognised feature of provincial life under Trajan.[10] In the mid-second century, Apuleius admitted to having held his wedding outside the town specifically to avoid the townspeople of Oea, who would have expected another cash-handout like the large one that his wife's family had already given them.[11]

The town's income in money was supplemented by *munera*, direct physical obligations on its inhabitants to furnish services. These had an impact on a wider section of the town's inhabitants, in some cases women as well as men. *Munera personalia* (or *munera civilia*) took many forms, such as care of buildings, heating public baths or even (in the charter of Urso) providing five days' labour to work on the town walls, on the pattern of the five-day dyke-corvée in Egypt. The numerous *munera patrimonii* could include transport corvées, providing billets, supplying recruits for the army, and even, for the very rich, holding the priesthood of the province.[12]

The descriptions in the Digest partly belong to later periods, but a letter of Hadrian to an eastern province outlines the more important *munera* in his time. He writes that philosophers, rhetoricians, schoolteachers and doctors are to be free from responsibility for the gymnasium and for the market-place, free from

---

[8] The 'tributum' here, which Cicero says was paid by every Sicilian, can only be a local tax, since seven towns in Sicily were free from direct taxation by Rome (2.3.13). Cf. Neesen (1980) 34. For capricious tax terminology in Roman authors, see chapter 12, section 7.

[9] Cf. Plut. *praec. ger. reip.* 29. For example, a 'duovir suffragiis populi creatus' is seen in Narbonensis (*CIL* XII 1121). Popular demands are expressed at the shows in *ILS* 5054: 'cum et populus in spectaculis adsidue bigas statui postulasset et splendidissim(us) ordo merito decreviss(et)' (S. Italy). Further evidence in Liebenam (1900) 248, and Jacques (1984) 410–17.

[10] Pliny *Ep.* 10.116.

[11] *Apol.* 87. The Aemilii had already given HS50,000 in this way, enough to pay for a small public building.

[12] Cf. Liebenam (1900) 417–30; Langhammer (1973) 237–62. Urso: *ILS* 6087, 98. Dyke-corvée: Sijpestein (1964).

priesthoods, from providing billets, from charge of the supply of corn and oil, free from jury-service, from going on embassies, from compulsory provision of army recruits, free from any obligation to the province and from any local compulsory service.[13]

2 Exemption and evasion

This makes it clear that the amenities of urban life were not provided without a direct social cost. Heavy financial demands upon the few could lead to evasion of responsibility, or excessive pressures on those who were eligible. The law ruled that if a town did not have enough men with the wealth needed to hold office, then existing office-holders must go on repeating their tenures of office. Repetition of office became governed by formal rules. Holding a magistracy gave five years' respite from holding the same post, but only three years' immunity from holding some other office. Going on an embassy for the town gave only two years' worth of immunity.[14]

As already seen, certain categories were specifically exempted.[15] But these concessions to philosophers, rhetoricians, doctors and school teachers, were made in the teeth of a system which was primarily concerned to maximise the number of suitable office-holders available. As a result, the quotas were quite small and were rigidly enforced. The scale of immunities laid down by Antoninus Pius writing to the province of Asia allowed each of the grandest cities (meaning *metropoleis*, in Modestinus's view) immunity for 10 doctors, 5 rhetoricians and 5 schoolteachers. Cities in the next grade (thought to mean the assize-towns) were allowed corresponding quotas of 7, 4 and 4, while the lowest grade (all other cities) had quotas of 5, 3 and 3.[16] Caracalla, replying to an army doctor who asked about his position after discharge, was careful to point out that he would keep his immunity only if he fell within the medical quota for his town.[17]

Army veterans had immunity for five years after discharge under Marcus Aurelius, but by the late Severan period they had indefinite immunity if they had served a full twenty years.[18] And Severus Alexander ruled that an army veteran who had agreed to be a town councillor had sacrificed his immunity once and for all by doing so, unless he had sworn a public oath of limitation beforehand.[19] By contrast, social categories specifically denied immunity included poets, primary-school teachers and *calculatores*.[20] Pursuing legal studies as a student at Beirut gave immunity, but only up the age of twenty-five.[21] Moving to another town in

---

[13] *D.* 27.1.6.8, Modestinus. [14] *D.* 50.4.14.6; *CJ* 10.41.2.

[15] See n.13; cf. *Vat. fr.* 149. For immunities, see also Jacques (1984) 618–47, and Neesen (1981).

[16] *D.* 27.1.6.2, Modestinus. [17] *CJ* 10.53.1.

[18] *SP* 285, AD 172; *D.* 27.1.8.3, Modestinus; *CJ* 5.65.1. Cf. Jacques (1984) 618–25.

[19] *CJ* 10.44.1.

[20] *CJ* 10.53.3, Philip; *D.* 50.4.11.4, Caracalla; *CJ* 10.53.4, Pius. [21] *CJ* 10.50.1, Diocletian.

order to study did not change domicile and the obligations attached to it, unless the stay lasted over ten years.[22]

In principle, shipping grain to Rome brought immunity from local obligations. This was also recognised as an attractive tax loophole. Repeated imperial edicts limited the concession to *bona fide* shippers, to those primarily engaged in shipping, and to those whose ships were above a certain size. Oil-shippers and oil-retailers were entitled to local immunity for five years between stints.[23]

The grandees of Roman society, men belonging to the Senate, though few of them now came from Rome, prove to have been very selective in dealings with their native cities. This may show something about the way in which the city was regarded. Senators and their descendants were free from legal ties with their place of origin, and retained domicile in Rome even when allowed to leave the capital. Senators nevertheless sometimes made public gifts and held local office in towns in Italy and in towns in the eastern provinces, where apparently it helped their prestige to do so.[24] But in the west outside Italy, senators very rarely played any role in cities beyond that of patron, which might be purely titular.[25]

3 Residence and local obligations

Towns obviously absorbed resources as well as money. Agennius Urbicus, a land-surveyor of the second century writes of cities in Africa as tiresome neighbours for owners of large estates. They make disputes over territory, claiming that part of an estate owes civic *munera*, trying to obtain military recruits from the estate village, and trying to levy transport animals or supplies from land which they say is theirs.[26]

The potential harshness at work here is seen even more clearly in documents from Egypt. These show for example complaints by a doctor who is a Roman citizen that he has been made to serve for four years as supervisor of sequestrated property at Bacchias in the Arsinoite nome, despite professional immunity; he says that he is quite impoverished.[27] In another petition, an army veteran at Karanis says that he is serving a liturgy only two years after discharge, despite the five year immunity of veterans at that time.[28] In a third case, a small cultivator complains that he is being conscripted as a donkey-driver outside his own district.[29] At a grander level, a man tries to refuse the local magistracy of *cosmetes*;

---

[22] *CJ* 10.40.2, Hadrian.
[23] Shippers: *D.* 50.5.3, Scaevola; 50.6.6.3–6, Callistratus. Oil-dealers: 50.4.5, Scaevola.
[24] *D.* 50.1.22.5, Paulus; ibid., 6 ('urbs'). Senators were immune from *munera*, but eligible for *honores*. Prestige and involvement in cities: Duncan-Jones (1972) 15, n.26.
[25] Lists of senators active in towns in Eck (1980). Towns and colleges collected patrons in considerable numbers, cf. *ILS* 6121; 6174; 6175.
[26] Thulin 45 (Agennius Urbicus, probably using Frontinus, cf. Thulin 20).
[27] *SP* 283, *c.* AD 140.   [28] *SP* 285, AD 172. See above n.18.   [29] *SP* 290, AD 207.

the minutes of a hearing show him being urged on by the townspeople, as well as by his own colleagues, and his reluctance is overruled.[30]

The passage from Agennius Urbicus also shows the importance of territorial definitions. By Hadrian's time at least, those who lived on a city's territory were in principle liable to its *munera*.[31] That held good whether or not the person who lived there was a local citizen. If domiciled in the city or on its territory, that normally gave him the status of *incola*; and *incolae* were fully liable to *munera*.[32]

Though *incolae* might have to hold *munera* at home, as well as in their domicile, a man was protected from being magistrate in more than one place. Women who married someone from another town were obliged to perform *munera* in their husband's town. But if not legitimately married, they performed *munera* in their home town.[33]

4 Decline or steady state?

In the first century AD, evidence for difficulties in assigning *honores* and *munera* is scarce. But during the second and third centuries, difficulties become increasingly obvious. A natural inference suggests that the cities were in decline, and that their problems were progressive.[34]

The position is not so clear-cut in reality. Before trying to assess it, a brief assessment of the chronological evidence is needed. The areas considered are legal decisions by the emperors, together with evidence from western epigraphy and from scattered literary sources.

Reflections of the oppressiveness of *munera* are present even in the tiny amount of juristic evidence referring to the Flavian period. Vespasian ruled that certain occupational categories (apparently law-teachers free from civil *munera*, together with schoolteachers, rhetoricians, doctors and philosophers) should be immune from billeting and from exactions of money, on pain of a fine.[35]

The earliest mention of shortage of candidates belongs to the charter from Malaca in Spain from Domitian's reign, late in the first century. One of the clauses of the town's charter sets out the procedure to follow if there are too few

[30] *SP* 241, AD 192.

[31] *D.* 50.1.37. pr., Callistratus. There could be specific local exemptions, cf. *SP* 288. But the sense of Paulus *D.* 50.1.20 is that *incolae* are liable to *munera*.

[32] The Severan jurist Modestinus reproduces a ruling in Greek that a man who lives in the country, and uses no urban facilities, is not an *incola* (a single sentence whose context is missing), *D.* 50.1.35. Under the Flavian municipal law in Spain, *incolae* with Roman citizenship or Latin rights could vote in elections, but were restricted to a single one of the voting *curiae*, which meant one-eleventh of the total voting-strength (Gonzalez (1986) chapter 53).

[33] See n.63 below. *D.* 50.1.17.4, Papinian. 50.1.37.2, Callistratus; 50.1.38.3, Papirius Justus.

[34] For perceptive discussion of modern works which argue municipal decline, see Jacques (1984) v–xvii and xxix–xxxiv.

[35] *D.* 50.4.18.30, Arcadius Charisius; *FIRA* 1.73. Bowersock (1969) 32–3 argues that as philosophers are missing from this inscription, Charisius inserted them in error. But Pliny *Ep.* 10.58 can be read as an indication that philosophers already had some claim to immunity by Trajan's time.

candidates to fill the town's magistracies. The person in charge of the election is to nominate candidates himself in order to make up the numbers.[36]

There are several pointers under Trajan. One is Pliny's reference to town councillors who hold their positions unwillingly.[37] Another is the concession obtained from Trajan for the town of Aquileia by a senior procurator, whereby *incolae* would be liable to the *munera* of the town.[38] This meant that the town could now distribute burdens among all its free inhabitants, including those not its citizens (probably a significant number in such a big town with its substantial commercial activity).[39] About the same time, the Fanestres further south in Italy had obtained a similar concession from the emperor. Some towns, however, had this facility from the start, like Tuder, where it was built into the charter.[40]

Trajan also allowed expansion in the number of town councillors at Prusa, and almost certainly at other cities in Asia Minor.[41] Clearly this was regarded as a benefit by cities which needed more revenue. But there was some ambivalence in a concession which allowed cities, regardless of the preferences of the individual, to tap sources of wealth which had been there all the time.

Under Hadrian there are rescripts mentioning compulsion. Magistrates are to be forced to serve again if there are not enough suitable new candidates, ambassadors must serve again in similar circumstances, and *incolae* are again said to be liable to *munera*. Hadrian also ruled against men trying to claim shippers' immunity without having made the necessary investment in shipping.[42]

Antoninus Pius took up this theme of men who used shipping as a tax umbrella, and enacted that all shippers must be scrutinised to see that they had not gone into the business in order to obtain immunity. He also excluded the very old and the very young from the colleges of craftsmen whose members were immune, and stipulated that the rich in general should not shelter behind immunities conferred on the colleges of the poor.[43] Two inscriptions from Italy show pressures of office in cities under Pius. At Tergeste (Trieste) a senator was honoured for obtaining an important concession from the emperor. This allowed the city to draw on the Carni and Catali (tribes 'attributed' to Tergeste by Augustus) for new supplies of magistrates and town councillors, even though

---

[36] *ILS* 6089, 51. Cf. Gonzalez (1986) 214.

[37] *Ep.* 10.113; see *ERE²* 310, n.7. At about this date, Dio Chrysostom found himself nominated for the second time as archon at Prusa (and declined, or tried to do so), *Or.* 49.

[38] *ILS* 1374. One of Claudius's concessions to the war-damaged town of Volubilis, a Roman outpost in Mauretania, is described simply as 'incolas' (there were also specifically fiscal benefits, including ten years' immunity from tribute). The main way in which measures concerning *incolae* could benefit a town appears to have been by making them liable to the local *munera*. If that applied here, it should be added to other early examples (see n.40; *FIRA* 1.70).

[39] For Aquileia, cf. p.33.   [40] See n.26 (the concession to the Fanestres was recent).

[41] See *ERE²* 84.   [42] *D.* 50.4.14.6; 50.7.5.5; 50.1.37.pr.; 50.6.6.8.   [43] *D.* 50.6.6.9; 50.6.6.12.

they did not possess Roman citizenship.[44] And in a much more modest context, a benefactor at Petelia in southern Italy presented a vineyard to the local Augustales, in the explicit hope that by reducing entertainment costs, he could make things easier for those compelled to hold this office in future.[45]

Another feature of the mid-second century is the adlection of men from another town as local citizens so that they could hold office in their new town (a version of what had been granted at Tergeste). One man from a small town was adlected to the colony of Caesaraugusta (Saragossa) by concession of Hadrian. He then held all the magistracies at Saragossa, in addition to those of his native town.[46] In another case, a wealthy citizen of Rome, given the *equus publicus* by Hadrian, was adlected citizen at Carthago Nova, where he held the aedileship.[47] In a third example, a man was 'transferred by the late Emperor Antoninus Pius from the municipium of Saetabis to the colony of Tarraco', where he held the chief magistracy.[48] And at Saldae in Mauretania in AD 152, two men adlected citizens of the town put up a statue of the emperor in gratitude.[49]

In these examples of transferred citizenship, there is nothing to indicate office-holding as anything but voluntary. But in a further case, a man from Magellum was adlected to the larger town of Italica, 'but was excused from the adlection by the late Emperor Antoninus Pius'.[50] This, like the inscription from Tergeste, and the earlier evidence from Bithynia, shows that the towns were actively seeking new recruits for local office, and that their wishes did not necessarily reflect those of the individual.

The reign of Marcus Aurelius brings further revealing evidence from Spain. In the 160s, a retired centurion and local magistrate bequeathed money to Barcino (Barcelona) for boxing matches and hand-outs. But he made his gift on the condition that none of his freedmen, and none of his freedmen's freedmen, should ever have to be *magister* of the Augustales.[51] The office was clearly seen as irksome. Later in Marcus's reign, the abolition of the state tax on gladiators was

---

[44] *ILS* 6680. It was also under Antoninus Pius that Aelius Aristides's heroic struggle to avoid local duties took place. The posts that he managed to escape, partly by invoking the help of the emperor, were: a priesthood of Asklepios at Smyrna; the priesthood of Asia (as nominee of Smyrna); tax-collector and *prytanis* at Smyrna; and chief of police (*irenarch*) nominated by Hadrianoutherae, his native town. Bowersock (1969) 36–40; for the chronology, see also Syme (1988A) 4.325–46.

[45] *ILS* 6469. For this donor's gifts, see *ERE*² 269, 284–5 and Bossu (1982).

[46] *ILS* 6933.

[47] *ILS* 6953–4. He was also a citizen of towns in Greece; his very wide contacts presumably had some commercial or territorial basis.   [48] *ILS* 6943.   [49] *ILS* 6875.

[50] *ILS* 6934. This inscription appears to belong to the present context; but Gagé uses it when interpreting the obscure reference to 'Italica allectione' in *HA* Marc. 11.7 in terms of military recruitment (Gagé (1969) and Le Roux (1983) 287–8). The passage is corrupt, but the adjacent sentences are not concerned with military affairs. The post of 'decurialis' in the inscription seems to be separate from the adlection, as shown in Dessau's punctuation, not part of the same event as assumed by Mackie (1983) 81 and n.12. *AE* 1964, 276 shows an 'adlectus Italicensis' at Merobriga.

[51] *ILS* 6957.

hailed by a speaker in the Senate as providing economic safety for future priests of the province in Gaul who would otherwise face ruin.[52]

The known rulings of Marcus and Verus about municipal affairs are numerous (more so than those from any other single period before the Severi).[53] The 'divi fratres' laid down for example that immunities could be overridden if there were no candidates with enough money to support the burdens of office. They also prescribed that decurions must serve as magistrates as often as they could afford to do so.[54] And in a third ruling, they stipulated that magistrates serving under compulsion required financial sureties as much as those holding office voluntarily. Bastards could be made town councillors if there were not enough men of legitimate birth.[55]

Pertinax returned to the crux about bogus shippers, by overriding the immunity of any man adlected to the shipping corporations if he had already become a decurion.[56] In a similar vein, Septimius Severus ruled on the immunity of craftsmen's colleges. In a letter known from an inscription, he told the governor of Noricum that wealthy members of the college of clothes-dealers at Solva should perform civic *munera*, as should those who do not carry on any trade that rightly qualified them for membership.[57] Septimius and Caracalla also extended town income from *summae honorariae*, something that Trajan had done: they imposed the charge on holders of the priesthood at Lanuvium, as a means of funding the restoration of the town baths.[58] They also extended the field for recruiting magistrates to members of the Jewish faith.[59] Though Antoninus Pius had apparently ruled differently, Severus and Caracalla laid down that a man practising or teaching rhetoric outside his native town was still liable to *munera* at home, unless working in Rome. On the other hand they allowed a sophist who had held office as *strategos* at Smyrna despite occupational immunity, to remain immune in respect of all other offices.[60] In a concession rare in this context, Severus excused fathers of five sons from serving as priest of the province (a financial Everest); and this benefit conferred on Asia was extended to other provinces. But he laid down that in lesser contexts, five children were not enough to bring exemption, though Pertinax did allow exemption to a father of sixteen who had written to the emperor from the east.[61] In Egypt, Severus, who gave municipal recognition to the larger communities of this under-privileged province, provided that villagers from other communities should not have to shoulder burdens belonging to the towns.[62]

[52] *ILS* 5163, 9340. The tax was 25–30%; see Oliver–Palmer (1955) and *ERE*[2] 245.
[53] Mainly shown in Gualandi (1963). They come in particular from a collection by Papirius Justus.
[54] *D.* 50.4.11.2; 50.4.6.pr.   [55] *D.* 50.1.38.6; 50.2.3.2.   [56] *D.* 50.6.6.13.
[57] *FIRA* 1.87. Alföldi (1966); Weber (1968); Jacques (1984) 639–46.   [58] *ILS* 5686.
[59] *D.* 50.2.3.3.   [60] *D.* 27.1.6.9–11, Modestinus, cf. Nutton (1971) 53; *Syll.*[3] 414.
[61] *D.* 50.5.8.pr.; 50.6.6.2.   [62] *SB* 7696. For the municipal concessions, see Bowman (1971).

After Severus, the third-century evidence for municipal rulings mainly comes from the private rescripts in the *Codex Iustinianus*. These are generally on a smaller scale, but they still reflect some of the same local problems. Caracalla as sole emperor ruled that a native of Byblos who lived at Beirut must hold *munera* in both places, re-enunciating established doctrine. He also laid down that those who received a dishonourable discharge from the army could not hold *honores*, but must hold *munera*.[63] Those who owed the city money could not hold *honores* until their debts were paid off. But those banned from local office for a specified period could nonetheless hold office again once the period had expired.[64]

Severus Alexander was appealed to in a case where a man's father had obtained a priesthood for him by promising that he (the father) would pay for a gladiatorial show. The emperor ruled that the governor would have to take account of this promise and divide the cost of the show among all the father's heirs. The episode casually reveals some of the mechanics of obtaining high local office. In a second case, Alexander ruled that a man unjustly assigned *munera civilia* because of personal enmities should have the assignment annulled.[65]

Gordian ruled that having five healthy sons gave immunity from the *munera personalia*. Valerian and Gallienus were later to give fathers of three healthy sons immunity from going on embassies.[66] Gordian also provided a summary of the terms under which performing an office carried immunity for a limited term. Gordian enacted that a decurion exiled for a specific misdemeanour could not hold new *honores* unless he waited for a period equal to the period of exile. A man who was totally blind would be exempt from the *munera personalia*.[67]

Philip laid down that sons whose parents came from different towns should fulfil their local obligations in their father's town unless living in their mother's town. A woman could be compelled to hold any *honores* or *munera* for which she was eligible in the town where her husband lived as an *incola*, Philip and many of his predecessors ruled. She was also liable to *munera patrimonii* in any town where she owned property. But in another ruling by Philip, local lands carrying a rent-charge could not be withdrawn from tenants unwillingly.[68]

5 Problems of diachronic interpretation

In essentials, the emperors seem to have been encountering similar local problems, offering similar solutions, and applying similar rulings throughout the period considered. Perhaps the content of their rulings reflects an underlying deterioration in the cities, but this is difficult to establish.

---

[63] *CJ* 10.39.1, cf. *D.* 50.1.29, Gaius; *CJ* 10.55.1, cf. 12.35.3.
[64] *CJ* 11.33.1; *D.* 50.2.3.1.   [65] *CJ* 10.63.1; 10.68.1.
[66] *CJ* 10.69.1; 10.65.1.   [67] *CJ* 10.41.2; 10.61.2; 10.51.1.   [68] *CJ* 10.39.3; 10.64.1; 11.31.1.

A series of themes start to emerge very early in the available evidence, beginning with the Flavians. For example, shortage of candidates, leading to compulsion and to repetition of office is seen in one form or another under Domitian, Trajan, Hadrian, Antoninus Pius and Marcus Aurelius.[69] Attempted evasion of local obligations is apparent from Hadrian onwards.[70] Widening of the contributing class is seen under Trajan, Antoninus Pius, Marcus and Severus. Liberalisation of the rules of eligibility takes place under Marcus and Severus.[71]

Any argument to the effect that what is seen here did not exist in earlier periods must take into account serious limitations in the chronological evidence. In particular, shortage of first-century imperial rulings about municipal problems is a reflection of limits in the surviving corpus of juristic citations. It does not in itself show anything about the volume of judicial activity by first-century emperors, nor about the nature of the problems which faced them. The later compilers on whom our knowledge of Roman law depends drew heavily upon Severan sources, but progressively less on previous reigns. No doubt this was partly because it was in the nature of later rulings to replace earlier ones, and in the nature of earlier rulings to survive in smaller numbers. The pattern of the evidence (preserved mainly by the Digest) is very skewed. It shows a strong peak under Severus with a steady diminution in the amount preserved the further reigns are from his (Table 47).

After Severus's death, the quotients rapidly decline, because much of the juristic evidence in the Digest belongs to the early and mid-Severan period. However, the independent figures for private rescripts from the *Codex Justinianus*, which show further high peaks both under Severus Alexander and under Gordian III, argue that judicial activity by third-century emperors did not start to fall off in reality before the middle of the century.[72] Apart from obvious limitations in the representation of emperors who received *damnatio memoriae* (Nero, Domitian, Commodus and Caligula, who is missing altogether), the pattern is relatively clear-cut, with a steeply rising curve of frequency (see fig. 29).[73]

---

[69] See nn.36, 37, 42, 45, 54, 55. See also Jacques (1984) 369–70.

[70] See n.23.   [71] See nn.55, 59.

[72] Honoré (1981) Tables 1 and 2. The peaks of mean annual activity implied by Honoré's totals are: Caracalla 39, S. Alexander 33, Gordian 38, Diocletian 57. In the deep trough between AD 250 and 283, this quotient falls to 3 rescripts per year.

[73] Honoré (1981) 14 sees the shortage of citations of Commodus (whose memory was condemned, then restored) as a sign of a lazy emperor; but the quotient for Commodus conforms to those for Nero and Domitian (who were not rehabilitated), and lethargy is not altogether borne out by epigraphic evidence from Commodus's reign, which later generations were not able to censor so fully. Furthermore, it is unlikely that the annual output of legal decisions really fell by three-quarters in the part of Marcus's reign when Commodus was sharing the throne (Table 47); manipulation, and juristic prejudice against any tainted source, are suggested by this low figure also.

Table 47. *Number of surviving legal citations per reign*

Emperor	Number	Per year
Tiberius	6	0.3
Claudius	15	1.1
Nero	4	0.3
Vespasian	7	0.7
Titus	4	1.8
Domitian	4	0.3
Nerva	6	3.5
Trajan	45	2.3
Hadrian	198	9.7
Antoninus Pius	254	11.0
Marcus and Verus	125	16.2
Marcus	137	19.6
Marcus and Commodus	22	4.4
Commodus	7	0.5
Pertinax	5	24.0
Severus	136	27.2
Severus and Caracalla	239	18.9
Caracalla	68	11.0
S. Alexander	4	0.3

Source: Digest evidence set out by Gualandi (1963).

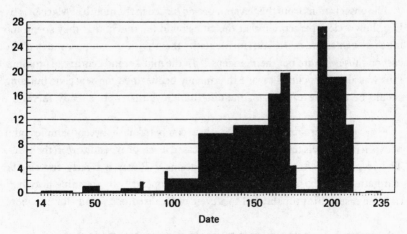

Source: Digest and other data from Gualandi (1963).

Figure 29. Rulings by emperors in extant legal sources: average number per reign-year

The chronology of western inscriptions, though not affected by any agent of transmission, is subject to similar distortions. Explicit inscriptions happen to be more numerous in the second century than the first. Consequently, the lack of direct indications of strain in the municipal system from this source in the first century means little in itself.

Chronological emphases in documentary papyri are likewise an uncertain guide, since papyri are much more numerous in the second century than the first.[74]

If arguments for major secular change must remain uncertain it is still possible to identify some changes and contrasts.

5.1 There are underlying indications of an increase in government intervention, or at any rate, government involvement in municipal affairs. The *curator rei publicae* was an official from outside the town to whom new expenditures had to be referred. Curators spread throughout large parts of the Roman world during the second and third centuries, and had become a more or less universal feature by the fourth.[75] Pliny's commission as a special overseer of the cities in Bithynia revealed seriously slack financial administration in some of the biggest cities in the east, as early as the reign of Trajan. The piecemeal introduction of curators seems to reflect a greater awareness by the government of the actual financial weakness of the cities.[76] Similarly, the second-century introduction of *iuridici* for the different districts of Italy came from a realisation that for some purposes local affairs in Italy needed the attention of Roman magistrates as much as those in the provinces.[77]

The observations from the Severan period placed in the mouth of Maecenas by Dio show a clear perception that the cities build too much; that they spend too much on games and races; and (incidentally) that they like to impose much of the cost on those who are not their citizens.[78] In the mid-second century, Antoninus Pius was already inclined to rule that money bequeathed for new civic building should be used instead for maintaining buildings that were already there.[79]

5.2 There is little doubt that competition between families and between individuals tended to lead to increased levels of expenditure in the cities. The results are often implied in inscriptions.[80] Plutarch clearly reveals the temptations that existed for magistrates to win popularity by spending heavily.[81] In some cases, this probably led to a cycle of localised boom and slump, where

---

[74] See chapter 4. For citations of documentary papyri, see nn.27–30 and 62 above.
[75] See Eck (1979) 190–246; Jacques (1984).   [76] *Ep.* 10.37; 39; 43.
[77] Eck (1979) 247–66.   [78] Dio 52.30.3–8; cf. *ERE*[2] 137.
[79] *D.* 50.10.7.pr.; 50.8.7.   [80] Cf. *ERE*[2] 87–8; Duncan-Jones (1963) 160–2.
[81] *Praec. ger. reip.* 29; Dio Chrys *Or* 34.29–30.

heavy overspending in one generation might be followed by acute cash shortages in the next. Such a cycle did not necessarily destroy the underlying real assets of the families concerned. But it would use up available cash surpluses which might then take a very long time to re-accumulate from available revenue.

5.3 The constitutional features of a Roman town were bound to fit some communities better than others. A liturgical system bore heavily on the economic elite, and the minimum outgoings were relatively high. The cash demands of a Roman constitution, with its 100 or so town councillors who paid for their office, and another half-dozen fee-paying magistrates and priests every year, cannot always have been an easy target to meet.[82]

The degree of wealth and the degree of monetisation varied from one community to another. Geography gave some towns ready access to trading and cash, while leaving others much more deprived (Ephesus and Massilia for example had substantial revenues from tolls).[83] In all probability, shortage of candidates was more or less endemic in some towns, and part of the evidence for difficulties is likely to refer to these places. There was some proportioning of burdens to means, in the form of smaller town councils, and variation from town to town and from office to office in the size of the payments demanded. But the amount of flexibility was limited.[84] It was inherent in the steepness of the wealth-curve that those at the top could afford to outstrip local demands by a handsome margin, and gain prestige by doing so; while some of those lower down, but still within the scope of local demands, would have great difficulty in meeting the minimum obligations.

5.4 The great linguistic and cultural divide which separated the empire has some bearing on how the juristic evidence should be interpreted. In the Greek East, cities were generally older, less Roman, and run by a more articulate ruling class than those in the West; and they may have generated a disproportionate number of surviving legal rulings.[85] Moreover, town constitutions which did not have a Roman origin, like some of those in the East, were an obvious potential source of variation or difficulty. In one case, an emperor referring to practice in the East rules that the age-limits for town councillors shall be determined by local custom.[86]

---

[82] In large Greek cities the town council might number several hundreds (Liebenam (1900) 229 and n.5; for a total of 80 decurions ordained by Antoninus Pius, see *ERE*² 83, n.6). For western councils of 100, and occasionally fewer, see *ERE*² 283–4. For payments by decurions and magistrates, see 82–7 and 147–53.   [83] Strabo 4.1.8 (Marius); 14.1.26.   [84] See n.82.

[85] For the overwhelming preponderance of eastern material in the epigraphic evidence for exchanges between emperors and cities, see Millar (1977) 418–20. A rough tally of Gualandi's tabulation of Digest rulings by the emperor also indicates that out of 35 sent to identified provinces, three-fifths went to the Greek East, and two-fifths to the West (Gualandi (1963)).

[86] *D.* 50.2.11. But this is also seen in Africa, 50.6.6.1.

5.5 Against the view that any major secular change or decline took place is the fact that the rules for office-holding were maintained. Relatively little attempt was apparently made to bring in new categories of office-holder. The continuing major exclusions, and in particular the disbarment of freedmen from the *ordo*, seem to have been much more important than the social concessions that did take place.[87]

6 Conclusions

Few would dispute that there were radical differences between the world of Hadrian and Antoninus Pius and the world of Diocletian and his successors. The towns had changed markedly, town councils in the West apparently being larger than before, and direct compulsion had now become a much more widespread tool of government policy.[88] Yet even during the Principate, compulsion and the need for compulsion in the municipal context are already clearly visible, and it is important to realise that they emerge almost as soon as explicit municipal evidence becomes available.

Prolonged political and military instability, the loss of one of Rome's Danube provinces, the onset of virulent plagues, an unprecedented spurt in inflation, and the cessation or near cessation of some central legal processes, all suggest that the Roman world passed through a crisis of very great magnitude in the third quarter of the third century.[89] An important part of what now changed was the degree of government intervention, much more powerful centralised control being imposed in an attempt to preserve a structure which was threatening to disintegrate. Any shifts as fundamental as these were bound to have their impact on municipal affairs, as they did on almost all areas of Roman life. But it is much more difficult to show that any generic or qualitative change took place in the functioning of the municipal system before the later third century. Furthermore, even in the fourth century, there were important parts of the empire where municipal life was still relatively flourishing.[90]

Distortion in the evidence prevents explicit comparison between municipal conditions in the first century and those later on. But although early emperors,

---

[87] See nn.55 and 59 above. Callistratus, a jurist of the Severan period, also reports that those liable to flogging by the aediles, i.e. shopkeepers, could be admitted to the town council if there were acute shortages of suitable candidates (*D*. 50.2.12.). The section of Paulus which excludes non-decurions from the *honores* may be a later interpolation (*D*. 50.2.7.2; Jacques (1984) 592–4).

[88] Cf. Jones (1964). For the size of the western *ordo*, Chastagnol (1978).

[89] Loss of Dacia, *HA* Aurelian 39.7; Eutropius 9.15; plagues, Orosius 7.21.4; Zos. 1.26; Zonaras 12.21; Cyprian *de mortal*. 14.16 (Boak (1955) 136–7); inflation, Callu (1969); legal rulings, n.72 above.

[90] Lepelley (1979–81). For continuity in municipal life under the Principate, see Jacques (1984) 663–765.

with fewer administrators at their disposal, may have been less preoccupied with local issues, to conclude that there was ever a point when cities failed to throw up problems over tenure of offices and liturgies is almost certainly unrealistic. The difficulties were to some extent inherent in the municipal system. And however attractive local offices and displays could be for wealthier members of the municipal class, the general obligation to hold and to pay for offices and liturgies also represented a drain on local resources which was bound to intensify the drain caused by government taxation.

I I
Who paid for public building?

The aim here is to ask how the civic burdens discussed in the previous chapter were distributed, and to look at the dividing-line between what came from town funds and what was directly paid for by the individual. Two African towns, Thugga and Thamugadi, are taken as test cases (Thugga is considered from a different perspective in chapter 4). Evidence from other towns in Africa is considered in a short further analysis (Table 48).

1 Direct labour

Cicero writes of the ancient Capitol at Rome as having been built for nothing, because it was built with forced labour. Livy says that the Capitol was built with a mixture of forced labour and public funds.[1] Forced labour on public works continues to figure to some extent in Rome's later history, where there is better documentation. One of the more severe legal punishments was *damnatio ad opus publicum*, being condemned to labour on public works.[2] When the younger Pliny was governing Bithynia under Trajan, he found that the largest cities contained many men who had been condemned *ad opus publicum*, but who had managed to escape. Instead of working on buildings, they had found alternative employment in the city as public slaves. When told of this, Trajan ruled that they must go back to their original punishment, unless condemned more than ten years previously. Trajan laid down that they must work on servicing public baths, cleaning sewers and building roads and streets. This is a valuable definition of what *ad opus publicum* meant, and it clearly does include working on major building projects.[3]

The supply of criminals was not necessarily sufficient. The town-charter at Urso in Spain provided for conscripting citizens and other inhabitants of the town for local building works. In itself this apparently placed the free citizen on a level with the serious criminal. But the amount of time that any citizen had to

---

*The discussion concentrates on the distinction between publicly and privately financed buildings. Variants existed, in the form of subscription-financing, and part-financing by private gift (*ERE²* 90, no.16 and note; Duncan-Jones (1974) 84, n.52).

[1] *Verr.* 2.5.48; Livy 1.56.1–2.   [2] Cf. Berger (1953) 610.

[3] Pliny *Ep.* 10.31–2; for corvée in the Digest, cf. Brunt (1980) 82, n.5. See now Millar (1984).

contribute was insignificant. The stint was five days per year, with exemption for anyone aged over 60 or under 14. The owners of teams of oxen had to contribute these also, the stint for ox-teams being three days per year.[4] In Egypt there was a similar standing requirement of five days' labour per year, to be spent in cleaning out the irrigation channels on which Egypt depended.[5]

In the nature of things, compulsory labour or corvée is very rarely mentioned in building inscriptions. The magistrate who had access to criminal labour or the labour of ordinary townsfolk was unlikely to mention this in the inscription. But there are a few exceptions. The colony of Auzia in Mauretania built a covered market in the year AD 230; the inscription says it was provided from the *sportulae* of the decurions, but also by the *operae*, the labour contributions, of the people of the town.[6] At Tiddis, one of the *castella* of Cirta in central Numidia, big rainwater cisterns were constructed to feed the town baths in the 250s. The work included pulling down the ruins of previous buildings and levelling the site. It was carried out 'per populum', by the labour of the citizens.[7] Building labour provided by the citizens is again referred to in Mauretanian inscriptions of the early or mid-third century.[8] Direct labour, when specifically mentioned in the inscriptions, appears to be always the labour of free citizens. When the emperor is recorded as a major builder, the labour, unless explicitly provided by the army, may have included criminal labour. An enormous project like Claudius's attempt to drain the Fucine lake, which occupied 30,000 men for eleven years, is likely to have depended on criminal labour; and when Nero tried to cut a canal through the isthmus of Corinth, he is said to have had criminals, apparently sent from all over the empire, to work on it.[9]

2 Town cash-resources

Though forced labour may have been crucial to some imperial building projects, public buildings in secondary towns were normally paid for in money. Using the citizens as workers on a large scale, as at Tiddis, was a sign that money was lacking. This may be why the few epigraphic references to direct labour come from communities which were either very small or very remote. The typical building inscription, in contrast, tells us that the building was paid for with town funds or by a private individual. That does not necessarily mean that the labour was free. The contractors who put up a building for cash may still have employed a mainly servile work-force. At the end of the Republic Crassus had a big labour-force of slaves engaged in building redevelopment in Rome.[10]

---

[4] *ILS* 6087, 98. For the amphitheatre at Tibur, a donor gave, besides money, 200 *operae* or man-days of building labour (ILS 5630).   [5] Sijpestein (1964).
[6] *ILS* 5590.   [7] *ILAlg* 2.1.3596.   [8] *ILS* 6887–9.
[9] Suetonius *Claud*. 20.2; ps-Lucian *Nero* 3; cf. Dio 62.16.2. But imperial road-building could also result from cash expenditure (*ILS* 5875; cf. *ERE*[2] 157, no.454).
[10] Plut. *Crassus* 2.4; for free building labour in the city of Rome, see Brunt (1980).

In theory a Roman town should have been capable of putting up buildings from its own funds, and a great many buildings actually were financed in this way. To see what this implies we need to look briefly at the sources of town funds. One source was taxes on trade and money-changing. These could include local tolls, sales taxes, shop-rents and licences to trade.[11] It might seem that Roman towns should have been able to make good any deficit by levying new taxes or increasing old ones. But the central government actively restrained provincial cities from bringing in new taxes and from beginning large spending-projects.[12] There seems to have been a simple underlying reason. If local communities were allowed to tax and spend as much as they liked, that could affect their ability to pay taxes to the central government. Consequently local taxation was not flexible enough to be the answer to every financial problem that a city might have.

A second source of revenue was land or urban property belonging to the town. Haphazard survivals show that some public lands and urban property were bringing in 12,847 sesterces a year at Pompeii in the middle of the first century A.D.[13] The scale of town lands was sometimes much more impressive. Augustus gave Capua land in Crete worth 1.2 million sesterces.[14] In Trajan's time the town of Luca in northern Italy owned an estate worth 1.6 million sesterces, bequeathed by a private owner.[15] At the Flavian veteran settlement of Arausio in Narbonensis, about 20% of the very large cultivated territory seems to have belonged to the town.[16] Clearly town land was a sizeable source of income in these cases. But its extent is bound to have varied greatly, and some towns may have owned no land.

A third and probably crucial source of income was payments for office by the town magistrates. In many cases this may well have been the most important single source. The *summa honoraria* or payment for office, is sometimes mentioned as though it could make all the difference to a town's ability to put up buildings. Cities in Bithynia were petitioning the emperor in Trajan's time for permission to elect more town councillors, apparently so as to increase their income. Pliny mentions that the *summae honorariae* of new councillors at one town, Claudiopolis, were immediately put to use in building new town baths.[17] He writes as if this was not what the payments were intended for. Nevertheless, *summae honorariae* often were put towards monumental building.[18] We find at least one other instance where they were used *en masse* to finance a major building

[11] Cf. Broughton in Frank vol.4 (1938) 566 (tolls); 800 (market taxes). For the sale of the right to trade, see the money-changing monopoly at Mylasa (ibid, 896) and the annual sale of the right to sell oil at Heracleia (*PAmherst* 91–2, no.lvi). The determined opposition to a market on a senator's estate in northern Italy by a neighbouring town suggests that towns also derived income from taxes on retailing in the west (Pliny *Ep*. 5.4).   [12] Brunt (1981) 161.

[13] Frank (1940) 103; *CIL* IV 3340, cxxxviii–cxl, cxli–cxliv, cxlv–cxlvii, cxli.

[14] Velleius, 2.81.

[15] *CIL* XI 1147, obligatio 43   [16] Chapter 8, section 3.   [17] *ERE*[2] 84.   [18] *ERE*[2] 86, n.2.

work. The town of Lanuvium records that public baths were enlarged and renewed using the *summae honorariae* which Septimius Severus had just allowed the town to levy on holders of priesthoods.[19]

3 Town budgets

There is enough information about *summae honorariae* in African cities to allow an estimate of income from this source. At Thubursicu Numidarum in central Numidia we know the *summae honorariae* for three offices in the early third century. The payment for the position of town councillor and for the duovirate was 4,000 sesterces. The office of flamen, the priesthood which represented the supreme office in almost all African towns, cost 6,000 sesterces. The aedileship probably cost 4,000 sesterces like the first two offices. These figures suggest that the town's annual income from fees for office was roughly 35,000 sesterces.[20] The figure is quite impressive, though it is much lower than that implied for the leading African cities, such as Carthage, Lepcis or the Cirtan colonies.

Building was not of course the only expense that towns had to face. There was also the cost of municipal employees. At Urso in Spain these cost about 17,000 sesterces per year, which is half the amount estimated for *summa honoraria* income at Thubursicu.[21] But there were other sources of income, such as public lands and sales taxes, as we have seen. Perhaps at a guess something like half the *summa honoraria* income, or its equivalent, would have been available for building purposes.

We can compare this very rough estimate of about 17,000 sesterces per year with the cost of building in Africa. A medium-sized temple cost 60–70,000 sesterces in the second century.[22] A small paved forum with porticoes could cost 200,000 sesterces.[23] A theatre could easily cost three times as much, 600,000 sesterces, or more if it was at all large.[24]

If we translate these figures into the number of years' building income estimated for Thubursicu, a temple works out at about four years' income, a forum at about eleven, and a theatre at 33 years or more. Public baths, if at all

---

[19] *ILS* 5686.

[20] *ERE*[2] 72. This envisages that the town council, presumably of 100 men (*ERE*[2] 283–4), was replaced on average every 30 years, assuming entry at age 25, and assuming a demographic regime similar to the one implied for office-holders at Canusium (chapter 6). The calculation of annual revenue is:

flamen	(x 1)	6,000
duovir	(x 2)	8,000
aedile	(x 2)	(8,000)
town councillor	(x 100/33)	12,500
Total		34,500 sesterces

[21] *ILS* 6087, 62.   [22] *ERE*[2] 90, nos.8, 9, 10a, 11.

[23] *ERE*[2] 92, no.42.   [24] *ERE*[2] 77–8.

extensive, would be another very large item, perhaps comparable with the cost of a theatre.[25] It was quite common for African towns to have two or more sets of baths. Thus, if a representative town had four average temples or their equivalent, a set of baths, a theatre, a market, and at least one square with a portico, the construction cost would potentially be enough to absorb over 90 years' building income. The further cost of paving the streets, and building drains, walls, gates and an aqueduct would probably add a third or a half to the total. From this estimate it would take something of the order of 120–140 years' building income to cover the cost of providing essential buildings for a town. Towns in practice varied greatly in their level of income and thus in the speed with which they could carry out a building programme based on public revenue.

4 A town built by benefactors

African inscriptions give the impression that the construction of public buildings was generally spread over a long span running into many decades, and even centuries. The first main example, though not a town where building depended on public funds, still offers a case in point.

The hill-town of Thugga on a remote site in northern Tunisia is extraordinarily well preserved.[26] Here we can see in detail what buildings were put up at what dates in the first three centuries of the Empire. Thugga has several peculiarities. The town only received proper Roman status at the start of the third century. For most of the period it was not a full Roman community. In fact it had two separate halves, one a *pagus* of Roman citizens, the other a native *civitas*. The *civitas* went back hundreds of years further, but in terms of inscriptions and the events they record, the *pagus* was the dominant partner. By the late second century the two communities each had their own town councils. But there were no proper magistrates in the Roman sense, save a flamen or priest of the imperial cult. Under Septimius Severus, Thugga became a *municipium* and all this must have changed: the two communities were welded into one, magistracies were created, and *summae honorariae* were introduced. Thugga's other main peculiarity was that it lay in the *pertica* of Carthage. The *pertica Carthaginiensis* was a zone of tax-free cities spreading across northern Tunisia whose land was deemed in some sense to belong to the territory of Carthage.[27] As a result there were wealthy

---

[25] *ERE*[2] 91, nos. 29–30.

[26] Broughton (1929) 213–16; Poinssot (1958); (1962); (1969). For Thugga see also chapter 4, section 1.2. For office-holding and local families, see Jacques (1984) 758–60.

[27] The important inscription found at Thugga in 1961 honouring a defender of the 'immunitas perticae Carthaginiensium' (*AE* 1963, 94) implies that immunity from direct government taxes was inherent in the territory on which Thugga lay (cf. Broughton (1969)). This immunity is evidently reflected likewise in the dedication to Severus Alexander as 'conservator libertatis' in 232, in the dedication honouring the procurator A. Vitellius Honoratus for his embassy 'pro libertate publica' in the time of Gallienus, and in the fact that Thugga, unlike most African cities

men and women who held office at Carthage, but who also had associations with Thugga and were prepared to benefit this small town with their wealth.

The dated inscriptions from Thugga start extraordinarily early for an African city.[28] They show a first wave of building activity under the Julio-Claudian emperors. Thugga already had a *templum Caesaris* by the late years of Tiberius. In AD 36/7 a private benefactor, Postumius Chius, who was patron of the *pagus*, gave three buildings. These were a forum and square in front of the temple of the emperor, a small shrine of Saturn and an arch.[29] At about the same date a freedman patron, Licinius Tyrannus, restored a temple and its statues. He also built a temple of Ceres, consisting of a shrine with stone columns.[30] His wife, not to be outdone, gave the town a temple of Concordia.[31] These monuments are all likely to have been small, to judge from the size of the inscriptions. A few years afterwards, probably under Caligula, another benefactor, Caesetius Perpetuus, built an arch. This was dedicated in the reign of Claudius, but the emperor's name has been restored over that of Caligula. Probably also under Claudius a small shrine of Jupiter was built by another patron.[32] Then in the middle of Claudius's reign, in AD 48, a local office-holder from the native part of the town, Iulius Venustus son of Thinoba, put up a statue of Augustus. Six years later, at about the end of Claudius's reign, a further private donor gave a market. The benefactor, M. Licinius Rufus, was an equestrian, prefect of an *ala* of cavalry in Syria, but also patron of the *pagus* of Thugga. Besides the market he gave another small temple.[33]

This brief list shows about a dozen monuments put up in the twenty years between the 30s and the death of Claudius. Though the monuments were modest, we can see an intense burst of competitive spending in this brief period. There is no sign in these inscriptions that the community itself had the financial capacity to put up monuments. This may show that there were as yet no sources of revenue of significant size.

whose titles are known, was a 'municipium liberum' (*ILS* 6796, 9018; *CIL* VIII 26539). Other *municipia libera* of Severus were Aulodes, probably Thibursicum Bure, and Thysdrus (*ILS* 6792, 1430, 2911; for titles of African cities, see Galsterer-Kröll (1972)). The suggestion that Thugga's 'libertas' was notional appears untenable (Gascou (1972) 180). Even if there were no inscription mentioning immunity, a 'libertas' which was merely notional could hardly cause a procurator to carry out an embassy in its defence.

Carthage, Utica and Lepcis received *ius Italicum* from Severus, probably at the time of the emperor's visit to Africa in 202/3 (cf. Birley (1971) 216; the Lepcitanes had become 'Septimiani' by 202, *IRT*, p.81; cf. nos.292, 606). The first explicit mention of Thugga as a *municipium* dates from 205 (*CIL* VIII 26539), but this is only a *terminus ante quem*. The grant to Thugga may even have been contemporary with the grant to Carthage.

[28] For early building development at another African secondary town, compare Zitha in Tripolitania, whose forum was begun under Claudius (*CIL* VIII 11002; cf. *BCTH* 1886 (1887), 54–65). [29] *ILAf* 558. [30] *AE* 1969–70, 651; 648.

[31] *AE* 1969–70, 650; it is not Hadrianic, as stated in the commentary on no.193.

[32] *ILAf* 520; *CIL* VIII 26475. [33] *ILS* 6797. *AE* 1969–70, 652; 649.

It is striking that the evidence for public buildings at Thugga comes to a virtual halt for half a century or more. Though there were one or two minor benefactors, the Flavian period does not yield clear evidence for building.[34] We next have evidence in the reign of Hadrian. Two temples of Concord, which are clearly dated to the reign, cost over 50,000 sesterces and were given by a family named Gabinius.[35] The benefactors appear to have been the sons of a *conductor* or chief tenant of the imperial estates which surrounded Thugga. Another patron and his daughter, who held the office of flamen, gave a temple of Fortuna costing over 70,000 sesterces.[36] Probably at about this date, or a little earlier, a third benefactor gave a temple of Pietas. This was a small temple in the shape of an apse given by bequest by Pompeius Rogatus.[37]

From this point on, a new building-boom had evidently begun, and we find several buildings being erected in every major reign for the next century (cf. chapter 4.1). Under Antoninus Pius members of the Gabinius family gave the portico surrounding the forum. A women benefactor, Iulia Paula Laenatiana, also gave a temple of Minerva.[38] The building is of substantial size. Under Marcus Aurelius, Thugga received some improvement in status. The emperor granted the *pagus* the right to receive legacies. Some grant was probably made also to the native community, the *civitas*, which appears shortly afterwards with the epithet Aurelia.[39] These political benefits were celebrated by the building of a Capitol. True to local tradition, this was paid for by a private benefactor. The donor, Marcius Simplex, had been created a iudex in the jury courts at Rome by Antoninus Pius.[40] He was one of three brothers who received this honour from the emperor. Another brother, Marcius Quadratus, gave Thugga its theatre at almost the same date.[41] A third donor, whose name is unfortunately missing, gave Thugga a substantial temple, also in the reign of Marcus. It cost 150,000 sesterces.[42]

Building activity remained intense during the reign of Commodus. The centre of the town was further adorned with a square and portico by the forum. A temple of Mercury was put up next to the Capitol.[43] Both buildings came from private benefactors. Another shrine was given by L. Octavius Victor Roscianus. Most important, the town built an aqueduct seven miles long, which was dedicated in the mid-180s by Antonius Zeno, proconsul of Africa.[44] The main purpose of aqueducts was to feed public baths. This one was evidently linked to the large baths to the south of the town, which have not been excavated, but are presumably contemporary with the aqueduct. Under Severus, a large temple of

[34] Poinssot (1969) 230–1, nos.9–10.   [35] *CIL* VIII 26467–70 = *ERE²* 90, no.12.
[36] *CIL* VIII 26471 = *ERE²* no.8.   [37] *CIL* VIII 26493 = *ERE²* no.15.
[38] *ILAf* 521; 518, 522; *CIL* VIII 26525.   [39] *ILS* 9399. *CIL* VIII 26534.
[40] *CIL* VIII 26609; Duncan-Jones (1967) 173, no.103.
[41] *ILS* 9364; Duncan-Jones (1967) 173, no.102.   [42] *CIL* VIII 26527.
[43] *ILAf* 516; *CIL* VIII 26482.   [44] *CIL* VIII 26500; Poinssot (1966) 772–4.

Saturn was built by Octavius Victor Roscianus, at a cost of over 100,000 sesterces.[45] Severus at last made Thugga a *municipium* (see n.27), and this was celebrated by the building of a triumphal arch dedicated to the emperors.[46]

The short reign of Caracalla saw the building of another temple; the donor, Gabinia Hermione, gave 100,000 sesterces to pay for it.[47] Under Severus Alexander a big circus or race-track was built by a number of different benefactors; public funds may also have been spent on it.[48] A private donor, yet another member of the Gabinius dynasty, gave a large semi-circular temple of Caelestis. The town built another triumphal arch, honouring the emperor for his help in preserving Thugga's 'libertas', or tax-privileges.[49] The reign also saw the erection of another privately given building, donated by Vitellius Privatus, and the restoration of the temple of Fortuna by the city.[50]

The main building development of Thugga was now complete, after two or more centuries. From this point on, following the serious upheavals in Africa in the late 230s, there was much less building in African cities. But a revival took place under Gallienus, and at least three more buildings were erected. One was a second set of baths, the Licinian baths. The dedication does not survive and we do not know how they were paid for. This impressive building was no doubt put up to celebrate the colonial status Thugga received from Gallienus.[51] We know that private generosity continued in the mid-third century. A women donor, Botria Fortunata, paid for a temple of Tellus. An equestrian benefactor gave a portico and a large cash sum to the city a few years later in 264.[52] The inscriptions then appear to be silent for another two or three decades, after which we find building activity starting once more under Diocletian. A temple of the Genius Patriae was adorned with private money, and the city itself built a portico of the temple of Mater Deum.[53]

This sketch of Thugga's building history shows a number of things. Firstly, Thugga started acquiring public buildings very early, and was still receiving new ones even under Diocletian; the overall span approaches three centuries. Secondly, the source of financing was overwhelmingly the pockets of private benefactors, not the coffers of the community. Thugga lacked proper municipal institutions for most of the period, and payments by magistrates for office-holding were not being made on the large scale that occurred in African cities with fully Roman institutions. Even after the grant of municipal status at the start of the third century, Thugga went on acquiring buildings paid for by private generosity. Perhaps by this date private generosity had become so deeply engrained that there was little question of leaving the building programme in the

---

[45] *CIL* VIII 26498.   [46] *CIL* VIII 26539.   [47] *ERE*[2] 90, no.6a.
[48] *CIL* VIII 26552.   [49] *CIL* VIII 26549–50; 26460.
[50] *CIL* VIII 26547; *ILAf* 528; *CIL* VIII 26548.   [51] *ILTun* 1500. *ILS* 9018.
[52] *ILAf* 530; *CIL* VIII 26559; *ILTun* 1416.   [53] *CIL* VIII 26472; *ILAf* 531.

hands of the city. Perhaps also public funds remained too small to give it buildings of much note. The wealthy classes who lived in the splendid villas in the town's best residential district may have wanted something better than the buildings the town could have afforded. The building history of Thugga certainly demonstrates to a remarkable degree the powers of a small community to attract wealthy benefactors.

5 A town built from public funds

Thugga only illustrates one type of African town. Some others offer a quite different picture. At Thamugadi in Numidia, now eastern Algeria, a cross-section of buildings in the period up to the Severi shows a clear majority being paid for by the city from its own funds, not by private benefactors.[54]

There are conspicuous differences between Thamugadi and Thugga. Thamugadi was the larger of the two. For example, whereas Thugga had two sets of public baths, Thamugadi had four. Another difference is that Thamugadi was a full Roman community from the start. Founded by Trajan in AD 100, it was a Roman colony of veterans from *legio III Augusta*. As a civil community it was a Roman town with a flamen, duoviri, aediles and quaestors.[55] There was a system of *summae honorariae* for offices. The flamen paid 10,000 sesterces, quite a large amount, for his office, while a duovir paid 2,000. Income from this source must have given a firm basis to the town's finances. Since Thamugadi was founded as a new colony, there was almost certainly also an endowment of town land which would have been a further source of revenue.[56]

Thamugadi was able to put up monuments considerably grander than most of those at Thugga, usually without resorting to private benefactors. The Capitol for example was much larger than the one at Thugga, having twenty-two columns compared with only six at Thugga.[57] Of the dated buildings at Thamugadi listed by Romanelli in the period up to Caracalla, almost all were paid for by the town (see n.54). Nevertheless, there were some rich benefactors here also. A market was given in the late Severan period by the *eques* M. Plotius Faustus, and a library was given in the mid-third century by a senator, at a cost of 400,000 sesterces.[58]

[54] Using dated material from Romanelli (1959), and omitting statues, the ratio at Thamugadi in the period Trajan to Caracalla is: public 17, private 2. Public: Hadrian: *CIL* VIII 17844, 17845; Pius: *CIL* VIII 17852–3; *AE* 1940, 19; *CIL* VIII 17854, 17857–8, 17849; *BCTH* (1921) cli; *AE* 1899, 3; Marcus: *BCTH* (1915), 238; Boeswillwald (1905) 290; *CIL* VIII 17869; Commodus: *AE* 1934, 40; Severus-Caracalla: *CIL* VIII 17940, 17872, 2369–70; *AE* 1948, 111. Private: Marcus: *AE* 1968, 647; Commodus: *CIL* VIII 2699.

[55] Duncan-Jones (1974) 81, n.19. *ILS* 6841. The fullest account of local offices is the celebrated Album of the fourth century (*ILS* 6122; Chastagnol (1978)).

[56] *ERE*² 110, no.366a; 109, no.356. Cuicul, a veteran colony in Numidia founded at almost the same date as Thamugadi, employed a slave bailiff, 'Onesimus vilicus Cuiculitanorum', to run the town's estates (*BCTH* (1917) 346 no.76).   [57] Boeswillwald (1905) 178, 161.

[58] Boeswillwald (1905) 183, 297; *ILS* 9362 = *ERE*² 91, no.38 and note; Duncan-Jones (1967) 170, no.62.

These gifts show that Thamugadi did not lack a ruling class rich enough to make major benefactions. Nevertheless, the town was able to put up a very large complement of public buildings mainly from its own official sources of income. This pattern probably obtained in other veteran colonies, and possibly in other African towns of pre-Roman origin where Roman institutions had been introduced by the grant of municipal or colonial status.

Many African towns, however, did not have proper Roman status and were either *civitates* or *pagi* without full municipal rights. It might be tempting to think that these would have belonged to the same category as Thugga. But the fact that a community lacked a Roman constitution did not automatically mean that it would have had citizens wealthy and generous enough to pay for a large building programme themselves. Thugga, perhaps because of its connection with Carthage and its tax-free status, may have been exceptionally lucky in its number of benefactors.

6 The relative importance of public and private financing

Probably there was no such thing as a normal African city, but a small spectrum of different types. Each would have its characteristic financial structure and the pattern of building development that this structure dictated. The average seems to lie between the extremes represented by Thugga and Thamugadi. An analysis of the buildings dated between Trajan and Caracalla in Romanelli's lists (excluding material from Thugga and Thamugadi) shows publicly financed buildings as 42% of the whole and privately financed as 58% (Table 48).[59] This is closer to the Thugga pattern than to that of Thamugadi. But the sample of 115 buildings is not very large, and in broad terms it suggests that public and private financing had roughly equal importance.

However, a definite chronological shift takes place. Evidence from the start of the second century shows only one-fifth of the building as being paid for by the

[59] The dated building inscriptions from Romanelli (1959) have been classified in terms of financing; Romanelli's sample has not been added to significantly. Statues, building by the army, and buildings whose financing is uncertain, are deliberately omitted. The dated evidence from Thugga and Thamugadi has already been considered separately (see section 4 above and n.54). Trajan: public: *CIL* VIII 621 = 11798; *ILAlg* 1.1230–2; private: *IRT* 352; *ILAlg* 1.1026; *AE* 1938, 43; *ILAf* 384. Hadrian: public: *CIL* VIII 21514; *ILAlg* 1.1028; private: *IRT* 357–9; *CIL* VIII 98, 6047, 23955, 23861, 20076, 15381, 16441; *ILAlg* 1.2082. Pius: public: *CIL* VIII 18509, 228, 11193; *IRT* 372; *AE* 1930, 40; private: *CIL* VIII 14851, 25852, 26178, 14301, 16368, 17679, 26245; *AE* 1925, 23–4; *AE* 1949, 40; *IRT* 370–1, 374–5; *ILTun* 102; *ILAf* 238. Marcus: public: *CIL* VIII 18510, 4209, 801, 587, 23696, 22691, 23022, 11799, 17958; *ILTun* 699 = *ILAf* 244, 495, 126; *AE* 1914, 39; private: *CIL* VIII 26121–2, 15576, 22710, 12361, 955, 14378; *IRT* 232; *AE* 1909, 126; *ILAlg* 1.863; *ILAf* 125. Commodus: public: *CIL* VIII 12014, 27769; *AE* 1935, 45; private: *CIL* VIII 23862, 16417, 14811–2, 23983, 1402, 26125, 14362; *IRT* 230, 29, 396; *ILAlg* 1. 3032. Severus: public: *CIL* VIII 8321, 306, 14395, 1798, 12274. Caracalla: Public: *CIL* VIII 8375, 20135, 307, 4364–5, 21628, 12366, 2194, 11194, 12331; *IRT* 398; *ILAlg* 1.3037; *ILAf* 608, 267, 195, 268; *AE* 1911, 106; *ILTun* 1206, 585; private: *CIL* VIII 12094, 14690, 14465, 23107, 25515, 25484, 25500, 12031, 12364, 12141, 12142, 12349, 10569, 9030, 12006–7, 709, 2670, 26259; *ILAlg* 1.1255, 1256; *AE* 1904, 75.

Table 48. *Financing of dated town buildings in Africa*

AD	Public	Percentage	Private	Percentage	Total
98–138	4	24	13	76	17
138–161	5	29	12	71	17
161–192	16	43	21	57	37
193–217	23	52	21	48	44
Total	48	42	67	58	115

Source: n.59 (material from Thugga and Thamugadi is excluded).

city. A century later the proportion has risen to a half (Table 48). This very marked increase seems to reflect the spread of Roman civic institutions, bringing as it did more widespread payment of the *summa honoraria*.[60]

The distinction between public and private financing can be pressed too far. When a municipal building was paid for with public money, a large part probably still came from the pockets of the propertied class through the *summa honoraria*. Where it existed, this system made the distribution of burdens more even, though it did not draw on the resources of those outside the ranks of the town council. In Africa and other Mediterranean regions of the empire, rich individuals were willing in significant numbers to finance large town projects themselves. Although there was no direct institutional constraint to do so, whether these acts were always as spontaneous as their inscriptions might suggest is less certain, granted the known social pressures and the competition that existed between office-holding families (chapter 10).

Larger-scale private munificence was much rarer in northern provinces, from what we can see of the building record. But pressures to spend on municipal purposes were still there. Tacitus speaks of Britons who had to pour out their whole fortunes while serving as priests of the colony of Camulodunum.[61] Even if exaggerated, his remark vividly reflects the way that institutions could work in a Roman town, and it suggests that in essence the system may have functioned in the north much as it did in the Mediterranean heartland of the empire.

[60] Useful statistics for later periods are provided by Lepelley (1979) 67, 74–5. The proportion of public building work in Africa paid for by the city had risen to approximately 80% by the late Empire (Diocletian to Valentinian III). The work was mostly restoration of existing buildings; new buildings were only a sixth of the total (52 out of 332 examples). Of the 198 buildings whose type is known, 21% were baths, 19% temples or altars, 14% porticoes, 11% aqueducts or water installations, 9% theatres, etc. and 8% arches (ibid, 295–6).

[61] *Ann.* 16.31. For the exorbitant cost of provincial priesthoods, see *ILS* 5163, 16–18, and chapter 10 at nn.52 and 61. For pressures on private individuals to spend their money on city purposes, see chapter 10, section 5.2, and Duncan-Jones (1974), 85 n.55, 83 n.37.

PART V

TAX-PAYMENT AND TAX-ASSESSMENT

12
Taxation in money and taxation in kind

1 Introduction

Despite prevalent assumptions that its character is well known, the surviving details of provincial taxation under the Principate are remarkably incomplete. Under Augustus some systematisation evidently took place, with the introduction of provincial censuses. The epigraphic evidence does not in itself suggest that these were regular (the surviving references per province are very few save those for Gallia Comata), or that they were introduced in all provinces (the evidence is concentrated overwhelmingly in the 'imperial' provinces).[1] Censuses involved, or could involve, surveys of land and property as well as of population. Their occurrence implies that tax was being proportioned in some way to assets, instead of being levied as a fixed amount, which might be arbitrary.

But census-taking was made necessary by poll-tax, if nothing else. Though poll-taxes were levied in money, the occurrence of a census does not in itself indicate that land in the province was taxed in money. The evidence about the way in which the main tax of a province was paid reveals diversity, not consistency.

1.1 The evidence of Hyginus

The closest that any ancient source comes to a general description of Roman tax-regimes is in a passage from the second-century land-surveyor Hyginus (205L). Soon after distinguishing between tax-free land (*ager immunis*) and land liable to tax (*ager vectigalis*), Hyginus gives a brief description of the way in which direct taxes are assessed. His words can be understood as follows: 'In some provinces they pay a part of the crop, some (provinces) paying one-fifth, others one-seventh, while other (provinces instead) pay in money, based on assessment of area. Land (-types) are valued at set amounts, as in Pannonia, where the categories are: first- and second-class arable; meadow-land; first- and second-class woodland; fruit-bearing trees; and pasture. A tax-charge [*vectigal*, or

---

*This chapter can be read either as a self-contained discussion, or in conjunction with chapter 2, which is concerned with the economic and monetary impact of taxation.
[1] Cf. Unger (1887); Jacques (1977); Pflaum (1960) vol. 3.

money-payment] of so much per *iugerum* is levied on each of these according to its productiveness. Estimates of area need to be made by careful measurement, in order to avoid (under-assessment through) dishonest declarations (of area). For in Phrygia and in the whole of Asia, disputes arising from this source are as frequent as they are in Pannonia.'

There is perennial dispute over what kind of land Hyginus is writing about.[2] But the fact that he generalises about whole provinces, and describes a complex tax-structure like that seen in provincial taxation elsewhere, not the simpler regime seen on imperial estates, clearly implies that provincial taxation is in question.[3]

Hyginus's description shows several things:

(1) Some provinces paid land-tax in kind, others in money. Though he is writing long after the time of Augustus, Hyginus gives first place to payment in kind, specifying rates amounting to 20% and 14% of the crop.

(2) Some provinces had a more elaborate structure under which tax was proportionate to area, not to the size of the crop, but was levied at different rates on different grades and types of land.

(3) Provinces which paid tax according to land-type, and which suffered accordingly from disputes about the size of taxable areas, included Pannonia, Phrygia and Asia. Although Hyginus seems to indicate that Pannonia paid in money, that is apparently not true of Phrygia. Evidence cited below shows that in Phrygia modules of area were in use in direct taxation under the Principate, but that taxation was nevertheless taking place in kind.

2 Direct taxation in money

2.1 According to Cicero, **Spain** and most of **Africa** ('plerique Poenorum') paid a fixed sum in taxes ('certum stipendium') at the time of the Verrine speeches in the 70s BC (Sicily by contrast paid a tax in grain whose total varied with the harvest).[4] It is usually assumed that because the amount was fixed, payment of direct taxes in Spain and Africa was in money and continued to be so under the Principate. (For Africa, see 4.3).

Spain was celebrated in antiquity as a land rich in precious metal, and money-taxes were being levied there from an early date.[5] Metellus collected tribute of over HS14 million from the Celtiberians, whom Strabo called 'rich in money'. Caesar similarly shows that the taxes in Spain imposed by Metellus and removed by himself as quaestor were in money. But Baetica was sending tax-grain to the army in Mauretania under Claudius.[6]

---

[2] Cf. Neesen (1980) 45, n.6; Lo Cascio (1986) 46–7.
[3] For some analogies, see the schedule from the Syro-Roman Lawbook (chapter 13, section 3.4), and Ulpian's schema for tax declarations *D.* 50.15.4 For imperial estates, see *FIRA* 3.100–3; Kehoe (1987) 55–63.   [4] *Verr.* 2.3.12.   [5] Cf. Strabo 3.2.8; 14.
[6] Strabo 3.4.13. *Bell. Hisp.* 42. Dio 60.24.5.

2.2 Appian states that **Syria and Cilicia** pay a tax (*phoros*) which is 1/100 of the assessment (*timema*).[7] Appian introduces this as a gloss on the specially high poll-tax imposed on the Jews by Pompey. To be directly relevant, the statement should also be about poll-tax, but it is difficult to see what the 1% charge can plausibly refer to if that is so. These taxes were presumably in money (see 2.3).

2.3 The tax-decree of Julius Caesar for **Judaea** as reported by Josephus indicates double taxation in kind at annual rates equivalent to 10.7% in one case and 8.6% in the other (25% per biennium, and 10% per year, with a suspension in every seventh year in both cases). The total of 19.3% approximates the one-fifth reported by Hyginus for some provinces (Hyginus 205L). The census of Syria and Judaea by P. Sulpicius Quirinus in AD 6 required the inhabitants to declare their property in money.[8] The new money-taxes were presumably no lower than the taxes that they replaced. (If the 20% tithe of Caesar's day and the 1% tax on assets reported for Syria by Appian were more or less equivalent, that would imply an envisaged return on assets of 5% ($0.01/0.20 = 0.05$)).

A tax-rate of 20% in a pre-modern society is high, and under ancient conditions, taxes in money were probably more onerous than taxes in kind. In fact in this case, the difficulties that resulted meant that only a decade after the census Syria and Judaea appealed to Rome for a reduction in their tribute.[9]

2.4 In Roman **Messene** a tax of 8 obols was being levied at an uncertain date. This apparently meant 8 obols in the mina, about 1.3% of capital. The rate is high, but the circumstances, possibly a special levy, remain very obscure.[10]

3 Direct taxation in kind

3.1 Egypt was mainly taxed in kind under the Empire, grain-land paying a tax of one artaba of wheat per *aroura*, or more, if it fell into one of a number of special categories. Vines and fruit-trees were taxed in money.[11]

3.2 Cicero's Verrines show that **Sicily** was being taxed in wheat in the late Republic. The view that the system changed to tax in money under the Principate seems to be based only on the belief, going back at least to Rostovtzeff, that a 'stipendiary' city was one that paid its taxes in money.[12] This inference is

---

[7] *Syr.* 50.   [8] *AJ* 14.202–6; 18.3, cf. 26.   [9] Tac. *Ann.* 2.42, AD 17.
[10] *IG* 5.1.1433, cf. Lo Cascio (1986) 50.
[11] *PBouriant* 42, with Bagnall (1985) 292. Wallace (1938). For censuses in Egypt, see chapter 4, section 2.   [12] Rostovtzeff (1957) 208, citing Pliny *NH* 3.88–91. Brunt (1981) 162.

rightly disputed by Brunt (see also 7.0 below). In Cicero's day, the tithe-corn from Sicily's taxes was handled by 'mancipes'; under Trajan, a 'promag(ister) portuum provinc(iae) Siciliáe item frumenti mancipalis' is seen in several inscriptions. It is not obvious from this that any essential change had taken place.[13] Strabo, writing under Augustus or Tiberius, was able to say that Sicily sends all its fruits to Rome. And in the second century AD, Aelius Aristides placed Sicily between Egypt and Africa in his list of provinces which supplied Rome with grain.[14]

3.3 **Sardinia** paid a decuma or 10% tax, which Caesar increased to $12\frac{1}{2}\%$ on a community which had opposed him.[15]

3.4 **Asia** paid a tithe or proportion of the crop after becoming a Roman province in the second century BC.[16] Whether this situation changed under the Principate is uncertain (see 4.2 below).

3.5 **Phrygia** was at first left untaxed by the Romans (Appian, *Mith.* 57, describing a speech by Sulla). For a few years in the first century BC, including the period of Cicero's governorship, Phrygia belonged to the province of Cilicia. Afterwards it was grouped with Asia, though some separation apparently continued, since Phrygia occurs in its own right in the titles of administrative posts under the Principate.[17] An inscription of the reign of Claudius shows an adjustment in the module of grain-taxation in use at Cibyra, one of the chief Phrygian cities. The concession was made to redress extortion by an imperial procurator, making it clear that this tax was imperial, not local.[18] Some years earlier, in AD 25, Cibyra had suffered a severe earthquake, and been given a remission of taxes for three years; though evidently paid in kind, from the Claudian evidence, these were described as 'tributum' by Tacitus.[19]

3.6 Cities in **Thrace** were paying tax in grain under Septimius Severus.[20] **Cyrene** paid tax in silphium under the late Republic.[21] A tribe in **Pontus**, the gens Sannorum, paid tribute in wax. A tithe or tax in kind of 10% was being paid at the start of the second century at Nicomedia in Pontus–Bithynia.[22] The **Frisii** because of their restricted circumstances, 'angustia rerum', paid tribute in hides (the implicit contrast is with payment in grain or

13 *Verr.* 2.3.172; *ILS* 7193–5. For fuller discussion, see Cimma (1981) 115ff.; collection of tribute by tax-farmers continued, Ulpian *D.* 39.4.1.1.

14 Strabo 6.27; *Roman Oration* 12. See also Seneca *Ep. mor.* 114.26. Cf. also Garnsey (1988) 232.

15 *Bell. Af.* 98.   16 Appian *BC* 5.4.17; *pro lege Man.* 15.   17 Pflaum (1960) 3.1073–4.

18 See chapter 13, section 2.   19 *Ann.* 4.13; cf. below 4.2.   20 *Syll*³ 932.   21 *NH* 19.40.

22 *NH* 21.77; Dio Chrys. *Or.* 38.26, following Brunt (1981); if this were the local tax suggested by Jones (1971B) 161 and others, the rate would seem high.

money, not merely with payment in money).[23] The **Batavi** provided army recruits in place of tax.[24]

4 Mixed payment and ambiguous evidence

4.1 Mauretania paid tax in grain *or* in money under Caracalla. Caracalla's letter about recent failures to pay taxes, after making a concession to provincials who have fallen behind with their taxes, refers to their future payments · as 'annual payments whether in grain or in money' ('annuas pensitationes sive in frumento seu in pecunia').[25] The alternatives probably denote payments some of which were in grain (e.g. land-tax) and others in money (e.g. tolls, and tax on slave-sales). A duality of this kind is seen in Mithridates' taxation of regions which soon afterwards became Roman territory: the Chersonese and the Asiatic districts round Sindice paid taxes of 180,000 medimni of grain and 200 talents (of silver), HS 4.8 million.[26] Even Egypt of course paid part of its land-tax in money (see 3.1).

4.2 According to Dio Cassius, Caesar in 46 BC made a levy of money from **Asia** (*eklogē chrēmatōn*), abolished tax-farming, and (in a sentence whose exact implications are disputed) introduced a combined payment to replace existing taxes. Plutarch states that Caesar reduced taxes in Asia by one-third. According to Appian, whose account is the most coherent, Rome at first collected the taxes as a proportion of the crop, through tax-farmers. Caesar remitted one third of the amounts then being collected, and transferred collection from the tax-farmers to the cities.[27] Appian, though a former procurator and expert in these matters, does not state that Caesar changed the levying of taxes in kind to levying taxes in money. The phrase that he uses to describe the tax after Caesar's time, 'the *phoros* which is collected from the *georgoi* (farmers)', would be equally congruent with taxing in kind.

Whether Dio actually provides evidence for a change to taxing in money, as has been widely thought, depends on whether *synteleia* necessarily means payment in money.[28] When Dio wishes to make clear a monetary contribution, he specifies *synteleia chrēmatōn*. *Synteleia* could also be used in non-monetary contexts such as *tirōnōn synteleia* meaning 'collatio iuniorum'.[29] If Caesar did introduce regular payment of taxes in money, it is not clear why Dio nevertheless identifies Caesar's levying of money on Asia as a separate action. Caesar made himself notorious for

---

[23] Tac. *Ann.* 4.72.   [24] Tac. *Hist.* 5.25.
[25] *AE* 1948, 190 = *Insc. Ant. Maroc* 100; Corbier (1977) 211.   [26] Strabo 7.4.6.
[27] Dio 42.6.3; Plut. *Caes.* 48; cf. Jones (1971B) 59–60; Appian *BC* 5.4.17–19.
[28] Cf. Appian *BC* 5 (E. Gabba (ed.) 1970) *ad loc.* For differing views of this crux, see also Magie (1950) 2.1260.   [29] Dio 47.30.7. Rostovtzeff (1918).

his ad hoc levies of money wherever he went.[30] It is likely that his cash levy on Asia belongs to this context, and not to the context of tax-reform.

That Asia paid some direct taxes in money under the Principate is implied by an inscription from Nakrasa in Lydia of the late first century A D.[31] This reference to a will shows tax in money being due (at a rate which appears remarkably high) on a small portion of vineyard. But vineyards were taxed in money even in Egypt, whose main land-tax was paid in grain.[32] Consequently, this evidence does not demonstrate the dominance of money-taxation in Asia. Other regions in Asia Minor, Bithynia and Phrygia, evidently continued to pay taxes in kind (see above).

4.3 Despite evidence for payment of a fixed 'stipendium' by 'most of Africa' in Cicero's day (see 2.1 above), and Appian's evidence for the early introduction of a poll-tax on both sexes, there is also clear evidence for payment of tax in kind. Notwithstanding Cicero's remark, Broughton takes it that 'the tax-payment (in Africa) must necessarily have been made in kind'. It is worth noticing in this context that a tax whose amount was fixed could in fact be paid in grain; a levy of 20,675 modii per year was paid by Sidon under Caesar's legislation.[33]

4.3.1 Africa was one of the main suppliers of grain to Rome. In the second or early third century, a benefactor at Rusicade in Numidia put up a statue of 'Annona sacrae Urbis', clearly implying that Numidian grain for Rome was a feature of life at this port.[34] Inscriptions in the third century show a 'procurator ad fusa frumenti et res populi Numidiae'. The 'curator frumenti comparandi in annonam Urbis' who functioned under Trajan, apparently in Numidia, probably anticipates this post.[35]

In Tacitus, *Hist.* 3.8, Egypt is said to hold the 'claustra annonae'. A host of scholars have accepted Josephus's parenthetical remark that Africa was more important than Egypt for Rome's corn-supply.[36] But Tacitus's statement here, and the fact that the setting-up of an African grain-fleet could be delayed till the end of the second century A D, make that uncertain. Aelius Aristides later put Africa third after Egypt and Sicily in his list of the provinces that supply Rome with grain.[37]

4.3.2 There is evidence under the Principate for officials concerned with *frumenta mancipalia* (i.e. tax-grain) in Africa.[38]

---

[30] Dio 42.49–50; 42.9.1; 42.34.1; cf. 43.18.2. Levy on Asia: 42.6.3.
[31] *Sitz. Öst. Ak. Phil.-hist. Kl.* 265 (1969) 7.   [32] Neesen (1980) 234.
[33] Broughton (1929) 65. Josephus *AJ* 14.206.   [34] Tac. *Hist.* 3.48; 4.38. *ILS* 5077.
[35] Pflaum (1978) 1.113–16. Cf. Pflaum (1960) 1.228; *ILS* 1435.
[36] Cf. e.g. Rickman (1980) 67; 112; see also Duncan-Jones *JRS* 68 (1978) 197.
[37] *Roman Oration* 12.   [38] *AE* 1952, 225.

4.3.3 Surviving regulations for the imperial estates in northern Proconsularis all show payment in kind at a basic rate of 33%.[39] A 'conductor quintarum' or 'farmer of the 20% tax' is found at Timgad under Trajan. He may be associated with imperial estates, but the 'quinta' appears to be more general in later Numidian evidence.[40]

4.3.4 African land elsewhere is described in one of the inscriptions as 'ager octonarius', possibly denoting land paying one eighth as a tithe.[41]

4.3.5 Caesar levied fines of HS200 million on 'the 300 of Utica', a senate of Roman merchants and money-lenders, and a further HS13 million on Thapsus and Hadrumetum. This shows an abundance of money in Africa at this time, but one largely concentrated in the hands of a small Roman business community. By contrast, Caesar's fine on Leptis was in oil, 3 million pounds per year, and the fine on Thysdrus was in grain.[42]

5 The utilisation of taxes in kind

Despite the government's need for cash with which to pay the army, it is clear that a number of the wealthier 'civilian' provinces paid substantial taxes in kind, among them Egypt, Africa, Sicily and Asia; and it is relatively unclear how much of Rome's tribute was actually paid in money (see preceding sections). How did the government benefit from this? Though some tax-wheat went to feed the 'plebs frumentaria', such figures as we have strongly suggest that not all can have done so (see below). Some tax-wheat almost certainly went to the armies. But because of distance, it is generally doubtful whether transfers from 'civilian' to 'military' provinces took place on a scale sufficiently large to absorb all available tax-grain.

When Tacitus, the prime narrative source for the early Principate, describes food shortage at Rome, he writes in terms of the price of grain, and of a populace dependent on the grain that it buys from day to day.[43] He does not mention the free grain distribution. The amount of grain needed to feed the number who benefited from that distribution is at most half the amount that Rome seems to have been drawing in revenue from Egypt and Africa.[44] Presumably that shows that tax-grain found its way on to the commercial market. One of the few western documents for the grain-trade shows a large holding of Alexandrian grain being used as loan-security by a private owner at Puteoli in the late first century AD.[45]

In this case the government was probably converting some of its revenues in

---

[39] Kehoe (1987).   [40] *ILS* 6841; *NVal* 13.2, AD 445.

[41] *FIRA* 1.100, 2.19; Brunt (1981); disputed by Lo Cascio (1986) n.58.

[42] Plut. *Cat. Min.* 59.2; *Bell. Af.* 90; 97; cf. Plut. *Caes.* 55.1. For discussion of oil production at Lepcis Magna (which assumes that Caesar's reference is to Lep(t) is/Lepcis in Tripolitania, not to Leptis Minor, which is much closer to the other cities referred to), see Mattingly (1988) 37.

[43] *Ann.* 2.87; 15.39; *Hist.* 4.38. Cf. *ERE²* 346.   [44] Duncan-Jones *JRS* 68 (1978) 197.

[45] Cf. Casson (1980).

kind into revenues in cash.[46] If that possibility existed, it becomes much easier to understand how so much taxation in kind could take place. The main regions of agricultural production were not prima facie likely to be highly monetised. By taking taxes in kind and converting part of them into cash, presumably in urban locations where cash was plentiful, the government would have been able to steer round regional disparities in liquidity, and collect the revenue that it needed without aggravating existing differences.

Assuming even a modest degree of economic rationalism in the behaviour of ancient governments is not necessarily correct. But unless the amounts of tax-grain not consumed by the free issue in Rome (which appear to have been very large) all went to the army, there must be a presumption that revenues in kind were sometimes turned into revenues in cash.

6 Indirect taxes

Indirect taxes were an important part of Roman fiscal strategy, and one which evidently provided a substantial part of overall tax-revenue. They were levied on areas of the economy which were essentially monetised, on traders, travellers and ultimately on the property-owning classes who could pay for imported goods. The proceeds, collected in money, must have contributed a significant part of government revenue in cash. Cicero singles out the customs-payment from Asia as one of Rome's leading sources of revenue.[47]

The main indirect taxes, in approximate order of importance, can be briefly summarised as follows:

6.1 *Portoria*, meaning customs dues and tolls. These were levied at rates within the empire most often ranging between 2% and 5%, for example 2% in Spain, $2\frac{1}{2}$% in Asia and Gaul and 5% in Sicily. But the rates were not always as low: the tariff at the eastern frontier may have been as much as 25%; and the 24 sesterces per amphora said to have been levied on wine leaving the empire from Gallia Narbonensis can hardly have been much less than this.[48] Dues on goods entering Egypt were very high under the Ptolemies (25–50%), and may have been maintained at these levels by Rome. Pliny's remarks about the way that the price of eastern goods increased a hundred-fold on their way to Rome seems to imply high tolls as well as high mark-up by traders.[49] Strabo refers to the large profits Rome gained from her tolls on British trade before the conquest, also suggesting a high frontier-tariff (in this case at the Gallic ports).[50]

---

[46] The fate of tax-grain usually remains hidden. But Cicero claims that governors could make substantial *legitimate* profits by disposing of grain from their personal allowance (*Verr.* 2.3.217).

[47] *de leg. ag.* 2.80.

[48] De Laet (1949) 242; 307–8, 335, Cic. *pro Fonteio* 19; for wine prices, cf. *ERE²* 46–7.

[49] De Laet (1949) 299, n.4; *NH* 6.101.   [50] Strabo 4.5.3 (Madvig).

Portoria were levied very widely, and undoubtedly had a heavy impact on everyday life. Because resented so much, they were briefly abolished in Italy in 60 BC, only to reappear shortly afterwards in Caesar's tax on foreign imports. The taxes were levied at a great many different points. Goods travelling any distance within the empire could expect to pay duty several times on the way. Eastern goods travelling west paid duty twice in Egypt, on entry and on departure.[51] The fact that two provinces shared a land frontier still meant that duty was levied at the common border.[52] There were internal customs barriers within provinces as well.[53] Unsold commercial goods which were carried from port to port would potentially pay duty each time that they were landed.[54]

The existence of a special exemption for soldiers shows that most travellers had to pay duty on what they took through a customs point; and even soldiers were liable to pay duty on any goods that they intended to sell.[55] The unending complaints imply that the tax-farmers who administered the *portoria* frequently took too much; honesty on their part was worth immortalising.[56]

6.2 The inheritance tax of 5% levied on Roman citizens was introduced by Augustus in AD 6 in order to fund the cost of paying discharge bonuses to the troops.

The considerable fiscal potential of this tax is reflected in the fact that Caracalla chose to double the inheritance tax and extend its application as a means of easing his serious financial difficulties.[57]

6.3 There was a 4% tax on buying slaves, which Nero transferred from purchaser to seller.[58] The sums of 10 and 12 denarii levied on slave-sales at Palmyra in AD 137 may show this tax in operation. The implied slave-valuation of HS1,000–1,200 is relatively plausible. Though the Palmyra tariff is often said to be municipal, its text incorporates at least three interventions by Roman authorities.[59]

6.4 The 5% tax on freeing slaves, the *vicesima libertatis*. This tax went back to the relatively early days of the Republic, and had already produced substantial receipts by the end of the Republic.[60]

6.5 A 1% sales tax existed under Augustus and Tiberius. Though this

---

[51] Suet. *Caes.* 43. Strabo 17.1.13.   [52] *CIL* VIII 4508.
[53] Cic. *pro Fonteio* 19, cf. De Laet (1949) 324.   [54] Cic. *ad Att.* 2.16.   [55] Tac. *Ann.* 13.51.
[56] Strabo 4.6.7; Tac. *Ann.* 13.50; cf. De Laet (1949) 437–46; Suet. *Vesp.* 1.2.
[57] Marquardt (1885) 2.281. Dio 77.9.4.   [58] Tac. *Ann.* 13.31.
[59] Cf. Matthews (1984) at 175–6; Jones (1971B) 459; for slave prices, cf. *ERE*² 348–50, and Straus (1973).   [60] Cf. *ESAR* 5.50, n.40.

was apparently abolished by Gaius, some tax on sales continued into the later Principate.[61]

7 Problems of terminology

The vocabulary of Latin references to provincial taxation offers surprisingly little guidance to forms of taxation. In one of the few conscious attempts at definition in surviving texts, the second-century jurist Gaius tells us that 'stipendium' was the tax levied from the provinces of the Roman people, and 'tributum' the tax levied from the provinces of the emperor. But other writers show little awareness of such a difference: Pliny for example violates it by referring to the taxes paid by Cyrene, one of the 'public' provinces, as 'tributum'.[62] The taxes that Pliny refers to here were paid in kind, and if 'tributum' had a technical meaning, it would be inconsequential for Pliny to remark elsewhere that the Romans always demanded payment of 'tributum' in silver, not in gold.[63]

There is little sign of any technical meaning underlying the terms by which provincial taxation is referred to. 'Tributum' is again used to mean payment in kind when Tacitus describes the tax paid in hides by the Frisii. And in the Verrines 'tributa' are what is paid by Sicily, a province taxed in grain.[64] But elsewhere in the same speech, 'tributum' is the special levy in money that Verres imposes on an individual town.[65]

In a similar way, in Velleius Paterculus, 'stipendiarius' and 'tributarius' are merely stylistic alternatives. 'Stipendiarius' is used first of tax-payment by all the provinces, and then of tax-payment by Spain; for his third reference, to tax-payment by Macedonia, Velleius uses 'tributarius'.[66] Cicero makes Sicily pay 'stipendium' in *pro Balbo* 24, whereas in a passage in the Verrines, as we have seen, Sicily pays 'tributum'.

The connotations of 'vectigal' are equally changeable. In *Verr.* 2.3.12 and 2.3.20 it simply means a charge or payment, which Cicero then attaches to the context of provincial taxation by using the phrase 'vectigal stipendiarius'. In *de imp. Cn. Pomp.* 6, 'vectigalia' mean 'provincial revenues', as does the Greek equivalent *telai* in Plutarch *Pomp.* 45.[67] In legal usage 'ager vectigalis' can have the specific technical meaning of land subject to a rent-charge.[68]

Despite this obvious imprecision, Neesen nevertheless suggests that 'vectigal' means tax in kind, and that when Pliny writing under the Principate calls Sicilian cities 'stipendiary', that means that they were now being taxed in money.[69] Jones identifies 'stipendium' as an arbitrarily assessed sum of money used in provincial

---

[61] Marquardt (1885) 2.228.   [62] Gaius *Inst.* 2.21. Pliny *NH* 21.71.
[63] *NH* 33.5. This remark further contrasts with Polybius 21.32, where the Aetolians are allowed to pay up to 1/3 of their reparations in gold.   [64] *Ann.* 4.72. *Verr.* 2.2.131; 2.3.20.   [65] 2.3.100.
[66] 2.38.1; 4; 5.   [67] Marquardt (1885) 2.297, n.1.   [68] Bove (1960) 61ff.
[69] Neesen (1980) 29, 204; but see Brunt (1981) 162.

taxation of the Republic, and 'tributum' as the *pro rata* land-tax (by implication in money) substituted for it by Augustus.[70] This likewise seems to impose a technical meaning on terminology which most ancient writers treated as fluid.[71]

8 Conclusions

The contention that a general change to levying taxes in money took place in the time of Caesar and Augustus can be seen to rest on very little. Evidence for payment of taxes in kind continues under the Principate, both in Egypt and in other provinces. The case most often cited as showing a transition from tithe to money-tax (Asia) is in fact surrounded by uncertainties (see 4.2 above). Jones's interpretation suggested that a full-scale systematisation of taxation took place in the Augustan period, through the introduction of censuses and the abolition of tax-farming, with the corollary that taxes were now collected in money. But none of these moves seems to have been total. The evidence for post-Augustan censuses is sporadic and intermittent; tax-farming continued, even for direct taxes; and taxes went on being levied in kind.[72] Though there was a move towards systematising the tax-base and extracting a bigger revenue, there is little to show a general or uniform change.

From Hirschfeld onwards, evidence for payment of taxes in kind under the Principate has been associated with land outside private ownership, usually with *ager publicus*.[73] Payments for occupying land on imperial estates like those in Africa were certainly in kind. But where the taxing of 'public' land can be seen alongside that of privately owned land, as in Egypt, we find that the taxes differed only in amount.[74] Thus, seeking to classify taxes as coming from 'public' land where they were paid in kind is quite unconvincing.

We can locate a few cases in which provinces appear to have paid tax in money, a few in which they were paid in kind, and one case where the two forms appear together. But we cannot fill in the many blanks by generalising from particular examples, or by appealing to a supposed uniformity of practice imposed by Augustus.

As Brunt has argued, there were probably sharp limits to Rome's ability to extract payment of tax in money, and payment in kind may have taken its place in practice, even where money-payment was apparently stipulated (Brunt points out the seeming contradiction between the tribute of HS40 million imposed on Gallia Comata, and the extreme paucity of Roman coinage in first-century finds from Gaul).[75] What may be signs of fluidity over whether a tax obligation was met in kind or in money can sometimes be seen, as in Mauretania. The provincial governor of the Republic could apparently ask for his 'personal' entitlement to

---

[70] Jones (1971A) 540, cf. 528.   [71] Marquardt (1885) 2.184. n.5.
[72] See n.74. For tax-farming, see Cimma (1981) 99ff.   [73] Cf. e.g. Rickman (1980) 84.
[74] See n.11.   [75] Brunt (1981) 162.

grain to be commuted for money – and his powers were easily sufficient to make the demand binding.[76]

As already seen, taxes which by their nature were levied in money (indirect taxes) fell on monetised sections of the economy. The imposition of money poll-taxes nevertheless shows a desire to extract money revenue from all free taxpayers in a province, and a willingness to do so without obvious regard for the amount of liquidity available. The difficulties that this could create seem to have been felt especially in some Mediterranean islands.[77]

But poll-taxes of the Principate were, from what we can see, generally low.[78] Where there is any evidence, the land-tax visibly remained a tax in kind in a number of the provinces. This apparently recognised the limited extent to which money could be extracted from an agricultural population in which ownership of money was sporadic. Cicero's comments on attempts to exact money from the Sicilian farmer are worth recalling: he says that for a farmer to hand over something which he could not grow would mean selling off his equipment ('Nummos vero ut det arator, quos non exarat, quos non aratro ac manu quaerit, boves et aratrum ipsum atque omne instrumentum vendat necesse est').[79]

[76] Cf. Cic. *in Pisonem* 83; *Verr.* 2.3.191–2.   [77] Cf. Duncan-Jones (1964B).
[78] Ibid. and Wallace (1938) chapter 8.   [79] *Verr.* 2.3.199.

13
Land, taxes and labour: implications of the iugum

1 Introduction

As seen in the previous chapter, our knowledge of the tax-system of the Principate is very indistinct. Tax inscriptions are very few, and surviving legal sources, almost all selected at a much later date, throw very little light on taxation in this period.[1] With the late Empire, the position changes. Legal texts bearing on taxation become relatively abundant, and a series of detailed census inscriptions survives, together with some relevant literary evidence.

This extreme imbalance between what is known at different dates greatly restricts comparisons. It seems obvious in itself that important features of the Diocletianic tax-system, if not explicitly encountered in earlier sources, should represent innovations. But there are almost no detailed general descriptions of what preceded it. Where evidence will allow, it is worth trying to assess how new Diocletian's system was. The present chapter examines the main Diocletianic land tax-unit, and its implications both for the tax-system, and for the level of agriculture manpower.

Our knowledge of land-taxation of course remains very imperfect even in the late Empire. It is limited both by the increasing insistence of imperial draftsmen on literary elegance at the expense of exactness (adding to the problems of terminology in literary sources of the Principate seen in the previous chapter), and by the fact that isolated fragments of information are spread over a long period. Though the constitutions are dated, they are generally too few to allow effective inferences about long-term change.

---

[1] For brief discussion, see chapter 12. The case of Egypt is different, but the relevance of its tax evidence to the rest of the Empire is uncertain. The often fragmented and localised Egyptian material now needs a fresh synthesis (cf. Wallace (1938)). Apart from Egypt, the only province where any detailed autopsy of pre-Diocletianic taxation can be carried out is Sicily, and this relies on Cicero's Verrines, a source from the late Republic. This chapter is not a general examination of taxation under Diocletian, although an effective up-to-date study, which would inevitably be much longer, is still needed. Déléage (1945) remains the basic outline, with Jones's chapter on *iugatio* and *capitatio* (though this does not always allow enough for ambiguity in the use of the words *caput* and *capitatio*); Jones (1974) 280–92. The discussion by Segré (1945) is wide-ranging but erratic.

2 Precursors of the Diocletianic system

The tax-unit at the heart of Diocletian's system was the *iugum*. In surviving legal sources of the Principate, this literally means a yoke of oxen.[2] But *iugum* already had a transferred meaning, as the area that a single yoke of oxen could plough. This usage is seen early in the Principate in the agricultural writers. Columella implies its area as 50 *iugera*, while Pliny gives a *iugum* as 40 *iugera* or 30 if the soil is difficult.[3]

In the late Republic, the *iugum* had an official meaning as a land-measure in one part of the Roman world. In Spain at Caesar's colony of Urso, the fine for usurping town-land was 100 sesterces per *iugum* per year. Varro confirms that the *iugum* existed as a land-measure in Hispania Ulterior.[4]

In the terminology of the Diocletianic system, the Greek equivalent of the Latin *iugum* was *zugon*. Here too Diocletian's usage was anticipated by several centuries. At Amorgos as early as the fourth century BC, rent was being charged on arable at 3 drachmas per *zugon*.[5] And in the early Roman period, under Claudius, one of the concessions obtained for Cibyra, a leading town of Phrygia, in the wake of a tax-scandal involving a government procurator, was the agreement that the 'praxin' of grain should take place in the town market-place according to a *zeugos* of 75 modii ('kata zeugos modion hebdomekonta pente'), from all the territory of the town.

Though the benefit is extremely obscure at first sight, Magie convincingly identified it as a tax-transaction by reading *praxin* (exaction) in place of *prasin* or sale.[6] The passage can be understood more effectively by bearing in mind the different ways in which land could be quantified. There were four main methods:

1. by area
2. by sowing quantity
3. by ploughing capacity
4. by productive capacity

In the Cibyra text, what we seem to be dealing with is type 3 defined in terms of type 2, quantification by sowing quantity. The use of sowing quantity is very

---

[2] *Vocab. Iurisp. Rom.*, s.v. iugum.

[3] The 100-*iugera* ploughing module cited for Italy by Déléage (1945) 220 does not allow for fallow: see in general *ERE²* 329–30.   [4] *ILS* 6087, 82; *MSR* 2.51–2.   [5] *Syll³* 963.

[6] *IGRR* 4.914; Magie (1951), with L. Robert *Bull. ép* 1953, no.171. Magie took it that the figure represented the amount of grain to be collected (cf. Nollé (1982)). But the phrasing 'assessment according to a zeugos of 75 modii' indicates that the total in modii qualifies 'zeugos' and not 'assessment'. 'Zeugos' comes from the same root as 'zugon', which is the usual term for *iugum* in Greek tax inscriptions of the fourth century. The words, both potentially or actually meaning 'yoke', were readily interchanged or confused; one legal source, referring unmistakeably to the Diocletianic tax-measures, uses 'zeugos' and 'zeugokephalon' for 'zugon' and 'zugokephalon' (*CJ* 10.27.2.8; cf. *LSJ* s.v., where *zeugos* in this passage is mistranslated as 'iugerum').

familiar both from Columella and from metrological writers.[7] The sowing quantity for wheat, the most standard crop, is usually given as 5 modii per *iugum*.[8] Thus one possibility is that the Cibyra inscription is quantifying the *zeugos* by sowing capacity, and implying its size as 15 *iugera* (75/5).

The practices of the Diocletianic tax-system make this more intelligible. That gave different sizes for the *iugum* or *zeugos*, depending on land-quality. The concession obtained at Cibyra seems to have given the *iugum* a larger rather than a smaller land-area, and the inscription states that it did so for the whole city-territory. As the details belong to a list of benefits, the tax-reform must be a benefit also. The reform would be beneficial if, as in the Diocletianic system, tax-obligations were set at so much per *iugum*, in other words, tax would be less if the *iugum* was larger. Since by this date, the *iugum* had already entered customary and official use as a measure of area in parts of the Roman world, its utilisation for tax-purposes is not an obvious anomaly.

The use of variable land-quality in the Diocletianic system was quite clearly taken over from earlier practice. Hyginus writing in the Trajanic period shows that in Pannonia there were two grades of arable land for tax-purposes.[9] Thus the Cibyra inscription strongly suggests that Diocletian's system was being anticipated in important respects in tax-practices in Phrygia of the mid-first century A D. It will be seen that comparisons between the module at Cibyra and the Diocletianic *iugum* reinforce this conclusion.

3 The *iugum* of the Diocletianic era

Probably the most important single source is one not usually cited in this context. Epiphanius, bishop of Constantia in Cyprus at the end of the fourth century, wrote amongst other surviving works a treatise on measure. In it he defined the size of the *iugum* (see Appendix 6 below).

3.1 The *iugum* first-class in Epiphanius's definitions equals $12\frac{1}{2}$ *iugera*. His definitions of the *iugum* second-class are less consistent. But the first and most clear-cut definition implies it as 15 *iugera* (one-fifth more than the *iugum* first-class; Appendix 6).

Although much later, this information potentially throws light on the benefit at Cibyra: land exclusively assessed in the larger of Epiphanius's units, second-class *iuga* of 15 *iugera* (the size inferred at Cibyra), must contain fewer *iuga*. It will

---

[7] Columella *de r. r.* 2.12; Isidore *MSR* 2.136.1–8. For quantification by ploughing capacity, see n.3 above. Productive capacity was used in the system of the Principate in Pannonia (Hyginus 205L), and in the Diocletianic system itself; see also Siculus Flaccus 156.15L; *Lib. col.* 216.11; 222.11; 224.12L.   [8] Varro *r. r.* 1.44.1; Columella *de r. r.* 2.9.1; Pliny *NH* 18.198.

[9] 205L. Reconstructions of the *iugum* below are inevitably approximate, since no allowance for different modules based on first- and second-class land is normally possible.

thus benefit by paying less tax, in a system which attaches tax-liabilities to the *iugum*.

3.2 Epiphanius's *iugum* first-class is the same size as a tax-unit in an early fourth-century land-register from southern Italy. That register identifies 4 'M' as 50 *iugera* ($\frac{50}{4} = 12\frac{1}{2}$).[10] Southern Italy had a tax-unit called the *millena* in a sixth-century source. And in the fifth century taxes were being assigned according to *iuga* or *millenae*.[11]

These facts make it likely that southern Italy had a tax-unit of $12\frac{1}{2}$ *iugera* called the *millena*, equal to, and in practice equated with, the *iugum* first-class.[12]

3.3 According to its bishop, the town of Cyrrhus in Syria in the mid-fifth century had a territory measuring 40 by 40 miles, much of which consisted of mountain and trees which bore no fruit. For tax-purposes, the territory contained 60,000 *iuga*.[13]

The largest figure with these dimensions, a perfect square with sides of 40 Roman miles, would contain 1,388,889 *iugera* giving the average *iugum* at Cyrrhus a maximum size of 23.14 *iugera*.

A square whose *diagonals* measured 40 miles would have exactly half that area, and the average *iugum* could not exceed 11.6 *iugera*. Theodoret is probably reporting maximum dimensions, in other words the diagonal or its closest approximation. This makes the second figure the more plausible. If the territory approximated a rectangle, not a perfect square, that would make the average *iugum* still smaller.

3.4 These co-ordinates from Cyrrhus are not precise enough to provide any positive definition of the size of the *iugum* in their own right. They do, however, impose limits on its size, and these limits tend to conflict with the definitions of the *iugum* in Syria that are given in the much-quoted passage from the Syro-Roman Lawbook.

The Syro-Roman Lawbook defines the *iugum* as 20 *iugera* of arable first-class, 40 *iugera* second-class and 60 third-class. In terms of vines, the *iugum* represents 5 *iugera*, and in terms of olives, 225 trees first-class or 450 second-class. The area of olives first-class thus implied (using Columella's co-ordinates from Italy)

[10] *CIL* x 407.1.11, AD 323, Volcei.

[11] Justinian *Prag. Sanct.* 7.26, AD 552; *NMaj* 7.16, AD 458.

[12] See also Déléage (1945) 223. The security in land asked for Trajan's alimentary loans as shown by the Table of Veleia was almost exactly $12\frac{1}{2}$ times the amount of the loan (*ERE*[2] 311, n.2: the target was 12.42:1). Possibly the reckoning was 1 *iugerum per millena*.

[13] Theodoret *ep.* 42, AD 447. His account shows 60,000 as the total *iugatio*, the 2,500 *iuga* about which there was dispute being part of this total.

would be between 5 *iugera* (25-foot spacing) and 28 *iugera* (60-foot spacing).[14]

These co-ordinates do not appear consistent with the Cyrrhus evidence. If the average size of the *iugum* at Cyrrhus was about 11 *iugera* (3.3), reconciling it with the Lawbook tariff would only be possible if almost half its terrritory was under olives or vines, even if the arable was all assessed as first-class, notwithstanding the mountainous territory whose inclusion Theodoret emphasises. The Lawbook says that mountainous territory counted as third-class land. Even if all the arable was nevertheless rated as first-class, arboriculture does not usually occupy such a large share of the land as this in traditional Mediterranean agriculture.[15]

Thus the Lawbook co-ordinates seem to conflict with the only test case from the same province. But the tariff presumably has a historical basis, and it is conceivable that a metrological error in the text may underlie some of these difficulties.[15A]

4 Farms, farm-labour and tax-revenue

A crucial census inscription from Thera in Asiana allows us a glimpse of what the Diocletianic system of assessment looked like on the ground. Readings of the inscription by Déléage and Jones made the *iugum* implied there remarkably large. Both took the view that totals in *iuga* must be a complete account of the totals by area, despite the fact that *iugum*-totals are not consistently aligned with total farm-holdings.[16] A more straightforward approach is to take the lineation as it stands, accepting the text as a description of a number of farms, of which some possess corresponding totals in *iuga*. Most lines have no totals in *iuga*, and

---

[14] E. Sachau *Syrische Rechtsbücher* 1 (1907) 134. Ferrini's Latin translation in *FIRA* 2.795–6, followed in Jones (1974) 228–9 and reluctantly in *ERE*² 36 n.5, erroneously makes the unit of assessment for olives the perch or *pertica* (Syriac 'qnyn'), instead of trunk or root ('knyn'). (I am grateful to Dr S.P. Brock for identifying the Syriac alternatives.) Apart from the fact that this reading reduces the *iugum*-equivalent in olives to an almost negligible size, the census inscriptions directly show that olives were assessed by the number of trees, not by area (*IG* 12.3.343–9).

[15] For example, the estates summarised by Jones (1974) 233–4 show 1,472.5 *iugera* of arable, 303 of vineland and 2,500 olives at Thera, and 1,420 *iugera* of arable, 109 of vines and 5,200 olives at Lesbos. If olives were planted at a density of 50 per *iugerum* as reported for present-day Lesbos by Paton (*IG* 12.2.80 n.), arboriculture would account for only 19% of the area at Thera, and 13% at Lesbos.   [15A] See Addendum p.210.

[16] *IG* 12.3.343. Jones (1974) 229–30. Déléage (1945) 182 read 116.5 *iugera* of arable, 5.08 *iugera* of vines and 97 olive-trees as equalling 2.11 *iuga*. Jones noticed a third *iugum*-total overlooked by Déléage (1945) (cf. *Syll*³ 3, p.75), but likewise assumed that the *iugum*-totals must represent whole declarations. He derived the equation 1 *iugum* = 100 *iugera* of arable = 24 *iugera* of vineland = 480 olive-trèes. Jones's interpretation, like the one here, involved one substantial emendation. The present interpretation is more straightforward in not assuming that any *iugum*-totals are wrongly placed in the inscription (the exigencies of space that Jones cites do not explain every eccentricity of placing that his reading involves).

contemporary parallels show that it was quite possible for inscriptions listing *iugatio* to remain incomplete.[17]

The results are then as follows:

	Arable (*iugera*)	Vines (*iugera*)	Olive-trees	*Iuga*
Farm A	30	—	—	1.8551
Farm B	18	—	27	0.2367
Farm C	60	50	143	8.0222

The figures for farm A give an equivalence for arable of 1 *iugum* for 16 *iugera* (literally 16.17). If that is right, the figures for farm B must contain a serious mistake, since the total for arable alone would be more than 1 *iugum*. If the figure 1 is restored here, making the total for B 1.2367 *iuga*, the co-ordinates for A and B no longer conflict. The equivalence for olives resulting from B is 1 *iugum* = 240 trees (literally 241.7). In the Syro-Roman Lawbook, olive-trees are 225 per *iugum* first-class, and 450 second-class. Farm C implies an equivalence for vines, from the ratios so far, of 1 *iugum* = 13.60 *iugera*, perhaps an approximation to 14 *iugera*.

The most important result, the equivalence for arable of 16 *iugera*, is in keeping with other evidence, since it is close to the Epiphanius figure for the *iugum* of $12\frac{1}{2}$–15 *iugera*. The figure for olives, as already seen, finds some support in the Syro-Roman Lawbook. The figure for vines is mysteriously high. Possibly it is meant to refer to low-density vines intercultivated with grain, called in Italy 'arbustum' (n.25 below). These area-based equivalences are also both within the order of magnitude suggested by the Cyrrhus evidence (3.3 above).

4.1 Further tests
There are several ways in which the plausibility of the new interpretation of the Thera inscription can be assessed. One is by using the census inscriptions to compare average farm-sizes for farms quantified in *iuga*, with averages for farms of known area. Another is by comparing ratios of farm-population to area based on the Thera *iugum*-equivalences, with manning-ratios in the agricultural writers. A third method is to compare tax-yields per *iugum* with tax-yields based on area.

4.2 Comparisons based on farm-size
A résumé of 43 farms on Thera from Jones's account has a total area of 1,776 *iugera* of arable and vines (olives cannot be quantified exactly by area, but are clearly no more than a small additional component). This gives an average area per farm of 41.3 *iugera* of arable and vines.[18]

---

[17] Chios census inscription reproduced in Déléage (1945) 183–4.
[18] Totalling figures summarised by Jones (1974) 233.

Similar inscriptions from Lesbos show a total of 27 farms whose figures appear complete, with a total area in arable and vines of 1,802 *iugera*. Their average size is 66.7 *iugera* per farm (excluding olives as before, and in this case excluding additional pasture, whose value in terms of *iuga* was, as Jones suggested, probably very low).[19]

A long inscription from Magnesia on the Maeander (on the mainland of Asia, but in Asiana, like Thera and Lesbos) shows 67 farms with a combined assessment totalling 347.62 *iuga*. The resulting average is 5.19 *iuga* per farm.[20]

If mean farm-sizes did not vary drastically within Asiana, the averages of 5.19 *iuga* and 41–67 *iugera* should roughly coincide. The Thera equivalences suggest a typical mean *iugum*-size of roughly 14 *iugera*, assuming that the lesser area probably occupied by a *iugum* of olives offset the fact that arable at 16 *iugera* was more plentiful than vineland at 14 (see n.15).

5.19 *iuga* of 14 *iugera* would total 72.7 *iugera*. Since this figure is very close to the observed range of 44–67 *iugera* per farm, it is consistent with the equivalences for the *iugum* deduced at Thera.

4.3 Comparisons based on manpower

Two of the census inscriptions provide parallel statistics for tax-assessment of persons and tax-assessment of land. On a big estate at Astypalaea, the *capitatio* totals 13.66, and the *iugatio* 10.248. The ratio of *capita* to *iuga* is thus 1.33:1. At Magnesia, five adjacent declarations show in aggregate *capitatio* of 21.71, and *iugatio* of 17.215.[21] The ratio is 1.26:1, almost the same as at Astypalaea. Jones's totalling of figures for 29 farms containing declarations for *capita* in the same Magnesia list gave a ratio of 212:183 or 1.16:1.[22]

The narrow range seen here runs from 1.33:1 to 1.16:1. It implies that one *iugum* of land had associated with it roughly one and a quarter *capita*. The *caput* probably represented $1\frac{1}{3}$ adults, and assuming that half the population was male, there would thus be 1 male worker for every $1\frac{1}{2}$ *capita*.[23] If as inferred above, the typical *iugum* underlying these inscriptions contained some 14 *iugera*, that would argue approximately 1 male adult worker per 12 *iugera* (or slightly less if the *capitatio* included children in their early teens).[24]

The manning-ratios in the western agricultural writers (excluding women where mentioned) are shown in Table 49.[25] Detailed comparisons with the census manning-figures are impractical, since the agrarian writers are chiefly illustrating types of monoculture, whereas the census inscriptions refer to a real world where mixed cultivation was the norm. But the median figure in their seven

[19] Paton *IG* 12.2, p.37.
[20] O. Kern *Inschriften von Magnesia am Maeander* Berlin (1900), no.122.
[21] Déléage (1945) 193; 194–5.   [22] Jones (1974) 238.
[23] Jones (1974) 231. 1.33/2.0 = 0.67; 1.0/0.67 = 1.5.
[24] 1.25 × 0.67 × 14 = 11.7.   [25] *ERE*² 327–8.

Table 49. *Manning-ratios in Roman
agricultural writers*

Type of cultivation	Area per man (*iugera*)	Source
Arable	25	Columella
Olives	20	Cato
Vines	6.67	Cato
Vines	10	Pliny
Vines	7	Columella
Vines	8	Saserna
Arbustum	18.2	Saserna

statistics is 10 *iugera* per man. That figure is directly comparable with the 12 *iugera* deduced from the census inscriptions, using the Thera equivalences. This test therefore supports those equivalences.

4.4 Tax-yields per *iugum*

Limited comparisons of tax-rates also support the lower reading of the *iugum*. A letter from the emperors about the rebuilding of city-walls in Asia in AD 370–1 refers to former civic lands totalling 6,736½ fertile *iuga* which yield [9],000 solidi, a revenue of 1⅓ solidi per *iugum*.[26]

Interpreted in terms of the Jones *iugum* for Asiana, the revenue per *iugerum* would be roughly one solidus from every 61 *iugera* (reckoning the mean Jones *iugum* (n.16) as 81 *iugera*, on the basis of a notional 75% arable and 25% vineland).[27] The revenue on the present interpretation is 1 solidus from every 10.5 *iugera*.[28]

Other extraction-rates in the late Empire look much higher. One detailed example is the tax paid by the town of Antaeopolis in Egypt in the sixth century, whose total specifically includes all fees and supplements. It shows a payment per *iugerum* of 1.086 artabas of wheat and 0.1818 solidi.[29] Converting the wheat at a rate of 10 artabas per solidus, the total tax paid is 1 solidus for 3.44 *iugera*.[30]

The figure for lands in Asia represents net revenue, and if fees and overheads could be restored, they might increase it substantially. By AD 451, fees and supplements were being consolidated at a rate of 2½ solidi per *iugum*, almost twice

---

[26] *FIRA* 1.108 (not cited in Jones's discussion of tax-rates (1964) 462–4), following Mitteis in reading 'VI MILIA' as the base figure for income, to which the supplement is 3,000.

[27] The likely area of vineland is deliberately overestimated (cf. n.15) in order to compensate for the fact that no precise area-based calculation can be made for olives.

[28] Taking the mean *iugum* as 14 *iugera*; see above p.205.

[29] The *aroura* is reckoned as 1.099 *iugera* (*ERE*² 371); 51,655 *arouras* paid tax of 61,674 artabas and 10,322 solidi (PCair 67059: see Jones (1964) 464).

[30] For the wheat price, Jones (1964) 446.

the net tax-revenue per *iugum* in the Asia evidence.[31] In 440, a levy reported as being as much as 7 solidi per *millena* was taking place in Italy.[32]

If the Jones estimate of the *iugum* is accepted, the implied revenue-figure of 1 solidus for 61 *iugera* in Asia is hardly comparable with the tax-rate at Antaeopolis of 1 solidus for 3.44 *iugera*. They differ by a factor of 18 (60.75/3.44).[33] If the present estimate of the *iugum* is substituted, the factor of difference falls to 3 (10.5/3.44). Since the smaller discontinuity must represent the lesser hypothesis, this result is also likely to support the present interpretation of the *iugum* in Asiana.

5 Consequences for manpower

These comparisons suggest amongst other things that the manpower figures seen in Asiana at the start of the fourth century conform to those from the Italian agricultural writers. In his important studies of the later Empire, Jones was led to an opposite view. This was because the much larger size which he deduced for the *iugum* meant that related to area, the manpower levels in these same inscriptions dwindled to very small proportions. Since his *iugum* contained 100 *iugera* of arable, or 24 of vineyard, Jones's assessments of area were several times greater than those implied in the present estimates.[34]

Jones's immediate conclusion was that 'the registered agricultural population was very thin on the ground . . . average density being . . . well under half the minimum for efficient cultivation as reckoned by (ancient) agricultural experts'.[35] In his later survey, he commented on the same figures that 'landlords no doubt employed both tenants and casual labour not registered on their estates, but even allowing for this, the shortage of agricultural manpower is striking'.[36] This deduction may also have influenced Jones's more generalised discussions of the shortage of agricultural labour in the later Empire.[37] Other arguments for shortage, based for example on lack of *coloni*, and on evidence for land going out of cultivation, still require careful examination. But the present findings (section 4) mean that Jones's numerical illustration of shortage of agricultural labour from the census inscriptions cannot be accepted in itself.

6 Consequences for land-taxation

Most important for assessing the effectiveness of Diocletian's system of land-taxation is the extent to which it was standardised. If tax-rates were allowed to

---

[31] *NMaj* 7.16.

[32] *NVal* 5. In assessing such high figures it should be remembered that substantial land-areas seem to have been either exempt, or liable to tax at a reduced rate (Cyrrhus n.13, Asia n.26).

[33] The levy of 20 siliquae per *centuria* in Numidia in 451 which Jones takes as a valid source of comparison is far below the examples quoted (about one solidus from 240 *iugera*; Jones (1964) 464; *NVal* 34.2).

[34] (1974) 230.   [35] (1974) 244.   [36] (1964) 818.

[37] (1974) 87-8; 299–300; (1964) 63; cf. 1042: 'The labour shortage is most manifest on the land.'

vary dramatically from province to province for reasons of custom or tradition, then the system, though introduced or formalised at a time of recognised crisis, cannot be seen as one which made efficient use of resources. Diversity certainly continued in the naming of tax-units, with 'iugum' or 'zugon' in most of the East, 'millena' in Italy, 'centuria' in Africa and 'iulia' in Illyricum.[38]

We can, however, see that a largely standardised system was assumed in the East in the constitution of 377 setting the rate of clothing-tax. It assigned a levy of 1 'vestis' or military uniform to every 30 *terrena iuga* in Egypt and in Oriens, to every 30 *iuga* or *capita* in Asiana, Pontica, Scythia and Moesia, and to every 20 *iuga* or *capita* in Thrace (subject to the proviso that Oriens, excluding Osrhoene and Isauria, could commute the levy for money).[39]

Copious local evidence implies that Egypt was not actually taxed in *iuga*; the reference to 'terrena iuga' from which 'capita' are omitted, seems to imply that the tax-schedules available there only allowed a conversion in terms of area (in other words 'iugatio' but not 'capitatio').[40]

This difference apart, the one direct tax-anomaly in a list which explicitly applies to all the dioceses in the East, is the payment by Thrace at a rate per *iugum* 50% higher than all the other provinces. That may argue that a heavier burden was deliberately being assigned to one of the provinces closest to the northern frontier; or it may reflect a tax-unit which was actually 50% larger in Thrace. But in general, the list is consistent with the view that the *iugum* was treated as a standard measure from province to province in the East.

Looking outside the provinces in which *iugatio* was current, we find the *millena* in Italy and the *centuria* in Africa. As already seen, the *millena* appears to have been a twin of the *iugum* first-class known to Epiphanius, with an area of 12½ *iugera*. Identity between the two measures appears to be directly implied by a constitution of the mid-fifth century, in which a charge of specified amount (2½ solidi) is made 'per iuga singula sive singulas millenas'.[41]

The *centuria* in Africa is known to have had 200 *iugera*, going back to the large survey-units of the Republic and Principate used in 'centuriation' in Italy as well as in Africa.[42] The 'centuria' and 'iugum' are referred to together in one passage.[43] But there is no evidence which shows the two units being taxed at the same rate. Consequently the unreal orthodoxy passed down by Seeck, which sees

---

[38] Déléage (1945) 220.
[39] *CTh* 7.6.3. See in general Jones (1974) 280–92.
[40] (1974) 289–90, contesting the existence of an actual *iugum*-measure in tax-practice in Egypt. Déléage (1945) 115 nevertheless made a suggestion about its size, but only by combining the generic reference in *CTh* 7.6.3 of AD 377, with tax-rates from a papyrus (*POxy* 1905) which may be as much as 60 years earlier.   [41] *NMaj* 7.16, AD 458.
[42] The size is indicated by *CTh* 11.28.3. For the *centuria* as a survey unit, see Duncan-Jones (1980c) 127.   [43] *NIust* 128.1.3.

the 'centuria' in Africa as directly equalling the 'iugum' in the tax-burdens that it received, seems to lack any substantive foundation.[44]

One result of Seeck's view would be that a given area of prime arable land would pay 15 times less in direct taxation if it lay in Africa than it would if it lay in a province in which Epiphanius's *iugum* was in force, despite Africa's size, wealth and renowned fertility. An anomaly on this gigantic scale is hardly consistent with the view that the tax-system of the late Empire had any rational basis. And it stands in obvious contrast to the fact that direct equivalence is seen between the tax-units in use in different parts of the empire, in the case of the *millena* and the *iugum* first-class. In practice the 'centuria' could have been incorporated in the rest of the system by simple calculation, since it was an exact multiple of the 'iugum–millena' module.[45]

7 Conclusions

Diocletian's system of land-tax was less original but also less inconsistent than has been assumed. Examined in detail, the Cibyra evidence leaves little doubt that something close to the later system of land-tax based on *iugatio* already existed in Roman Phrygia, two and a half centuries before the reign of Diocletian. The *iugum* as a customary and official measure existed in Spain during the Republic. And further back, an equivalent called the *zugon* can already be seen in Greece in the late classical period. In Trajan's time, tax proportioned to land-quality receives a categorical description from a source referring to Pannonia, without any suggestion that it was a recent innovation. And quantification of land by sowing quantity, assessing productivity rather than area, is used by Columella in the Julio-Claudian period.

The systems apparently based on crude area that are found in Egypt and Africa imply that consistency was not enforced beyond a certain point.[46] Nevertheless, such direct evidence for tax-measures as there is suggests relative consistency. Epiphanius, who seems to know little of western measures, but more than most about measures in Cyprus and the south-east Mediterranean, was probably describing tax-units in Oriens, the diocese in which Cyprus lay.[47] His units

---

[44] Summarised by Déléage (1945) 15 and 20–1; Seeck's view is still followed by Jones (1974) 292; cf. also Faure (1961) 109, n.277 (read *CTh* 11.1.10).

[45] An incidental detail suggests that within the African provinces themselves tax-practice was relatively homogeneous. The 'horse-tax' was commuted at 18 solidi per mount in Proconsularis and Numidia, and 15 in Byzacena and Tripolitania (*CTh* 11.1.29, AD 401).

[46] For area measures in Egypt, cf. Déléage (1945) 115 (unconvincing, see n.40 above); for Africa see n.42.

[47] Dean's summary of Epiphanius's measures (Dean 142–4) shows 6 mentions of Cyprus and its towns, 9 of places in the south-east corner of the Mediterranean (in Egypt and Palestine), 5 references to Pontus and Bithynia, 2 to Italy and 1 to Sicily. Even more striking than the very limited representation of the West is the omission of Syria and the nearer parts of Asia. The pattern suggests that Epiphanius, who was born in Palestine, and lived in Egypt and Cyprus, mainly

broadly agree with those shown in Asiana by the census inscriptions. And his first-class *iugum* is the same as the *millena* in Italy. The position in Syria is indistinct, as the evidence from Cyrrhus does not seem to support the explicit tariff in the Syro-Roman Lawbook. Taken by itself, the Cyrrhus evidence would nevertheless be broadly consistent with the Epiphanius *iugum*, which is likely to refer to Oriens.

Apart from large-scale census activities, Diocletian's achievement in the taxation of land consisted of stitching together ingredients most of which already existed, and possibly applying them to a wider area than before. The extent of his innovation remains difficult to define without more explicit knowledge of what he inherited. The further schematic contrast sometimes suggested, between a Principate taxed in money and a Dominate taxed in kind, is clearly unconvincing.[48]

depended for regional information on what he could pick up at first hand. The fact that he nevertheless identifies local measures where he can shows Epiphanius as a relatively conscientious source.

[48] For the mixture of taxation in money and taxation in kind under the Principate see chapter 12. For the Dominate, note for example the fact that 'vestis' might be paid in money in large parts of the East in 377 (*CTh* 7.6.3), the money charges in n.31 above, and the combined taxation in wheat and money in n.29. Tax-payments in kind called 'annonae' were already apparently being levied in the late Principate (*CJ* 10.16.2, AD 260).

ADDENDUM

A much older manuscript, dating from *c.* 1210, may show that the land-area defined in the Syro-Roman Lawbook is smaller than supposed (English translation of the Syriac in A. Vööbus, *The Synodicon in the West Syrian tradition*, Louvain (1976) 2.155–6). Here 5 *yugre* (*iugera*) = 10 *peltare* (*plethra*) = 1,000 *qenin*; and the *qanya* (singular of *qenin*) = 1/500 of a mile. If the mile is the Roman mile of 5,000 feet, the *qanya* is 10 Roman feet (the Roman *pertica*, *MSR* 2.248). That would make the square *plethron* 100 × 100 feet, as in Greek texts (*MSR* 2.210; Epiphanius's 'plethron' of 120 × 120 feet in Appendix 6 is evidently the Roman *actus*, *MSR* 2.229). And the present *iugerum* would contain 20,000 square feet. The *iugum* of first-class arable, with 20 of these *iugera*, would have 400,000 square feet, or 13.88 standard *iugera*, close to the figure for vineland at Thera (p.204 above) and comparable to Epiphanius's 12 1/2 *iugera* first-class (Appendix 6).

This text also makes the *qanya* = 8 *amin* or cubits. Starting from that co-ordinate instead, if the cubit is the 1 1/2 foot version (*MSR* 2.209), the present *iugerum* would equal the standard Roman *iugerum* ((1 1/2 × 8)² × 200 = 28,800). But the mile would be one-fifth longer than the standard Roman mile (12 × 500 = 6,000), and the 1,000 paces which define it, though the same number as in the Roman mile, would be correspondingly longer than average.

APPENDICES

APPENDIX I

COIN-HOARD STATISTICS
(see chapter 2, section 3.2)

A. *Denarii of Sabina and denarii of Hadrian*

First assemblage

Hoard	Hadrian	Sabina
1. Lawrence Weston	138	10
2. Falkirk	235	19
3. Londonthorpe	98	7
4. E. Anglia	122	6
5. Bristol	128	10
6. Stockstadt	267	13
7. Cologne	105	7
8. Viuz-Faverges	93	5
9. Via Braccianese (Rome)	969	52
10. Verona	381	29
11. La Magura	528	34
12. Salasuri	372	18
13. Mocsolad	197	14
14. Tolna Megye	165	13
15. Osiek	295	12
16. Szombathely	191	14
17. Vyskovce	245	10
18. Drzewicz Nowy	187	13
19. Cyprus	100	6
20. Tell Kalak	327	21

Second assemblage

Hoard	Hadrian	Sabina
21. Reka-Devnia	5908	623
22. Adamklissi	142	25
23. Sascut	128	22

B. *Denarii of Trajan, Marciana and Matidia*

Hoard	Trajan	Marciana	Matidia
2. Falkirk	215	—	—
4. E. Anglia	102	—	—
5. Bristol	102	—	—
6. Stockstadt`	244	—	—
9. Via Braccianese (Rome)	1052	—	—
10. Verona	435	—	—
24. Castagnaro	410	—	1
11. La Magura	622	—	—

12. Salasuri	581	—	—
13. Mocsolad	210	—	—
14. Tolna Megye	163	1	1
17. Vyskovce	321	—	—
18. Drzewicz Nowy	101	1	—
21. Reka-Devnia	5217	4	3
22. Adamklissi	146	1	—
20. Tell Kalak	320	1	1
25. Egypt	132	—	1

C. *Denarii of Commodus and 'Divus Marcus'*

Hoard	Commodus	'Divus Marcus'
4 E. Anglia	239	1
8 Viuz-Faverges	89	1
18 Drzewicz Nowy	93	8
21 Reka-Devnia	2823	301
22 Adamklissi	145	13
26 Rustschuk	122	10
27 Nietulisko Male	252	30
28 Golub	120	9
29 Wroclaw	88	10

References

R. Bartoccini, *AIIN* 3 (1956) 217 (no.9)
BMCRE VI, 35–8 (nos.2, 4, 7, 21, 26)
Bolin (1958) (nos.10, 13–15, 17, 24, 25)
A.M. Burnett *Coin-hoards from Roman Britain* 8 (1988) (no.1)
A.M. Burnett, R.A.G. Carson *British Museum Occasional Papers* 6 (1979) 9–24 (no.3)
FMRD 1.6, pp.67–95 (no.6)
B.S. Katalin *Folia Arch.* 12 (1960) 75 (no.16)
Kunisz (1973) (nos.18, 27–9)
H. Mattingly *NC* (1939) 86 (no.5)
W.E. Metcalf *ANSMN* 20 (1975) 35–108 (no.20)
W.E. Metcalf *NC* (1979) 35 (no.19)
V. Mihailescu-Birliba, I. Mitrea *Tezaurul de La Magura* (1977) (no.11)
B. Mitrea *Dacia* 24 (1980) 374ff. (n.22)
I. Molnar, I. Winkler *Acta Mus. Nap.* 2 (1965) 269ff. (no.12)
H-G. Pflaum, H. Huvelin *TM* 3 (1981) 33 (no.8)
Dr Severeanu *Bucurestii* (1935) 219ff. (no.23)

APPENDIX 2

DATED BUILDING EVIDENCE
(see chapter 4, section 1)

	Spain (1)	Syria (1)	Italy (2) (non-imperial)	Italy (2) (emperors)
Tiberius	15	3	16	3
Caligula	2	3	—	
Claudius	11	—	9	1
Nero	3	1	3	—
Vespasian	15	1	6	4
Titus	—	—	1	—
Domitian	2	2	4	—
Nerva	2	—	—	—
Trajan	15	5	4	4
Hadrian	14	10	11	10
A. Pius	21	11	15	7
M. Aurelius	18	9	5	—
Commodus	4	5	2	—
S. Severus	16	10	1	3
Caracalla	5	—	4	1

	Lepcis Magna (1)	Sabratha (1)	Thugga (2)
Tiberius	10	—	4
Caligula	—	—	1
Claudius	5	—	2
Nero	1	—	—
Vespasian	4	1	—
Titus	—	—	—
Domitian	5	—	—
Nerva	—	—	—
Trajan	7	1	—
Hadrian	14	—	3
A. Pius	17	5	2
M. Aurelius	3	7	3
Commodus	5	4	4
S. Severus	57	4	2
Caracalla	7	1	1
Elagabalus	—	—	—
S. Alexander	3	4	5

Notes:

(1) All dedications, buildings and statues (milestones excluded).
(2) Building dedications only.

APPENDIX 3

TOTALS OF DATED PAPYRI BY REGNAL YEAR
(see chapter 4, n.32)

	Hadrian	A. Pius	M. Aurelius
1.	5	14	33
2.	84	101	63
3.	62	82	47
4.	55	76	41
5.	47	90	32
6.	36	59	33
7.	66	72	43
8.	56	84	34
9.	50	95	23
10.	51	81	14
11.	62	68	34
12.	63	76	18
13.	91	71	27
14.	55	65	42
15.	79	53	21
16.	112	40	24
17.	74	55	33
18.	75	56	33
19.	73	51	32
20.	70	42	14
21.	54	53	—
22.	53	103	—
23.	—	97	—
24.	—	28	—

APPENDIX 4

SMALL ARMY UNITS AND GARRISONS UNDER THE LATE EMPIRE

A tendency towards smaller army units has been recognised in the fourth century.[1] Vegetius (2.3) writes that it is no longer possible to keep the legions up to strength, and indicates that service in the auxiliaries was now preferred because of the less rigorous conditions. Figures in Ammianus for the siege of Amida in 359 have been taken to suggest legionary strengths of the order of 1,000.[2] The creation of the 'small' legion is laid at the door of Diocletian's successors.[3]

But terminology had also changed. The *Notitia Dignitatum* compiled about the end of the fourth century, but containing Diocletianic material (chapter 7, n.19) refers indifferently to a unit as a legion whether it was a whole legion or only part of one. Thus the *legio III Diocletiana* is listed five times, four times in Egypt and once in Thrace. The only indication in any of these listings that the whole legion was not there is the fact that it recurs

---

[1] See e.g. van Berchem (1952) 110; Jones (1964) 680–2; Várady (1962) 367.
[2] Ammianus 19.2.15. Grosse (1920) 30ff.; Jones (1964) 681–2.   [3] Cf. e.g. Várady (1962).

elsewhere.[4] The same usage emerges from literary sources. Multiple listings in the *Notitia* show that two Theban legions in Thrace (one of them *III Diocletiana*) were only parts of legions, since they recur in Egypt. Yet Ammianus, discussing affairs in Thrace in 354, calls them 'Thebaeas legiones in vicinis oppidis hiemantes', giving no hint that they were less than complete legions.[5] If Ammianus and his contemporaries did not distinguish a legion from a legionary detachment, what Ammianus says about the siege of Amida need not prove anything about legionary establishment.[6] But the loosening of terminology is significant, and Grosse's observation that legions were now commanded by a tribune, the officer who had commanded one-sixth of a legion under the Principate, has obvious interest.[7]

Jones saw Diocletian as working in terms of full-strength army units of the Principate, and his interpretation of the Panopolis papyri seemed to bear this out.[8] The present analysis offers different conclusions, pointing to an *ala* and a unit of *equites sagittarii* with only about 120 men each, and an auxiliary cohort with only 160 or so (Table 41, ll. 7, 8, 10). The legionary strengths in the Panopolis papyri refer to vexillations and other subsidiary units. Though they imply 500 as the nominal strength for a vexillation, they leave the position about overall legionary numbers uncertain. Vegetius (1.17) states that the two legions of Mattiobarbuli in Illyricum founded before Diocletian each had 6,000 men. The fact that the totals for a full legion of the Principate were now worth spelling out may mean that they had become exceptional.

There is also more clear-cut evidence about small-size units. The *centenaria* were small forts, apparently commanded by a centurion, himself called a *centenarius* by Vegetius' day (2.8).[9] These were presumably garrisoned by a force equivalent to a *centuria* of 100 men, though a *centuria* might be as few as 80 or 60 in some contexts.[10] The forts varied considerably in size.[11] Their existence before Diocletian's time is beyond doubt. A *novum centenarium* was built at Tentheos on the *limes Tripolitanus* in AD 244/6. A *centenarium* at Aqua Frigida in Mauretania Caesariensis was restored under Diocletian.[12] Other *centenaria* are recorded during the fourth century.[13]

Other references to miniature units occur in the *Notitia*. Though the date of its compilation is not earlier than 395, in some cases where its evidence can be corroborated the garrisoning appears to go back to Diocletian.[14] The *Notitia* lists a *cohors [c]entenaria* at Tarba in Palaestina. At Bethallaha in Mesopotamia it lists a *cohors quinquagenaria Arabum*. In a third case we find a *tribunus cohortis* stationed at a *burgus Centenarius* in Valeria.[15]

The forts called *centenaria* and the *cohors centenaria* point to units whose strength, nominal or actual, was about 100 men. The *cohors quinquagenaria* (if the text is sound) was

4 *ND* ed. Seeck, 310 s.v. *III Diocletiana*.   5 Or. 8.36, 37; Ammianus 14.11.15.
6 Cf. van Berchem (1952) 110 'Le titre de legion . . . ne doit pas faire allusion sur leur effectif réel.'
7 Grosse (1920) 34.
8 Jones (1964) 1.56; 680; 3.187–8. But the same view, advanced by Nisscher, was soon contested by Parker (1933) 187.
9 Leschi (1957) 47–57; Goodchild (1976) esp. 28–30; Matthews (1976) 171.
10 Cf. Birley (1966) 54.
11 Tentheos (Gasr Duib) 2 storeys, 0.02 hectares, Goodchild (1976) 24ff. Tibubuci, probably 2 storeys, 0.09 hectares, Gauckler (1902) 327–30. Aqua Viva, 0.76 hectares, Goodchild (1976) 40. For the size of other African forts, see Romanelli (1970) 40ff.   12 *IRT* 880; *ILS* 6886.
13 See e.g. *CIL* VIII 8713; 910.   14 Cf. above at n.4 and Bowman (1978).
15 *ND* Or. 34.40: a 'cohors prima agentenaria'; 'centenaria' Gelenius (1552) Or. 36.35. Oc. 33.62.

apparently a unit of 50.[16] Both figures occur in a military context in the *Anonymus de rebus bellicis* (5.5), whose author suggests that gaps in the standing army should be filled by the recruitment of 'centeni aut quinquageni iuniores, extra hos qui in matriculis continentur'. The coincidence with the *Notitia* evidence may suggest that the writer was thinking of unit-sizes current in his own day.

The size of forts provides some circumstantial evidence for small units. A small fort in Raetia of 0.16 hectares has been identified as the fort at Pinianis, listed in the *Notitia* as headquarters of a *tribunus cohortis*, though far too small to hold a conventional cohort of 500 men.[17] And the fort at Rutupiae (Richborough) at which the *Notitia* locates the prefect of *legio II Augusta* is 2.4 hectares in overall area, enough only for 1,000 legionaries by conventional British standards.[18]

Other examples of late Roman forts whose units are known from the *Notitia* are shown in Table 50.[19] Auxiliary forts of the Principate in Germany show the following median average sizes: cohorts 2.2 hectares (N = 14); cavalry cohorts 2.7 (N = 12); *alae* 3.5 (N = 2).[20] The median area of the three late cohort forts (Table 50, lines 4–6) is 0.25 hectares. The three late *ala* forts (lines 1–3) show a median size of 0.22. The area of the fort at Betthoro (no. 7) available for the *legio III Martia* is about 25% of the average for full-size legionary fortresses in Britain.[21]

Even after allowing for any variations in the assessment of occupied area underlying these statistics, the comparisons show drastic reductions in fort area per unit in the later period which must reflect reduction in numbers. Thus the archaeological evidence likewise points to some much lower unit-strengths in the late Empire.

---

[16] This numeral might be a corrupt version of the cohort serial number. The units adjacent in the list are numbered *ala secunda, ala octava, ala quintadecima* and *cohors quartadecima* (Or. 34.32–4, 36).

[17] Bersu (1964), plan p.44. Richmond (1965) 493 comments that 'the accommodation . . . suits a centuria and its centenarius, with his under-officers'. No comprehensive discussion of barrack space per man is available, but see e.g. Breeze–Dobson (1976) 17; Breeze (1977). Some other garrison and size data are in Nash-Williams (1969) 163; Baatz (1975) 79ff.; Hanson–Maxwell (1983).   [18] Frere (1978) 268; *ND* Oc. 28.19.

[19] For abbreviated titles, see sources for Table.

[20] Baatz (1975) 79–282 (data extracted from his list). The subject of changing fort sizes in the different parts of the empire and their implications for army manpower is one which calls for synthesis by a military archaeologist.   [21] Frere (1978) 253.

Table 50. *Some units in the* Notitia *and their fort sizes*

Unit	Fort name	Fort area (hectares)	Modern name	Province	Source
1. *ala I Francorum*	Cunna	0.17	Han al-Qattar	Foenice	*ND* Or. 32.35; Poidebard 48–9
2. *ala nona Diocletiana*	Veriaraca	0.22	Han al-Hallabat	Foenice	*ND* Or. 32.34; Poidebard 48–9
3. *ala V Praelectorum*	Dionysias	0.76	Qasr Qarun	Aegyptus	*ND* Or. 28.34; Schwartz–Wild 63
4. *cohors II Aegyptiorum*	Vallis Diocletiana	0.25	Han as-Sawat	Foenice	*ND* Or. 32.43; Poidebard 43, 54
5. *cohors V Pacata Alamannorum*	Onevatha (Anab[atha]?)	0.19	Han Aneybé	Foenice	*ND* Or. 32.41; Poidebard 47, 50; *RE* s. v. Syria 1703
6. *cohors I Iulia lectorum*	Vallis Alba	0.81	Han al-Manquoura	Foenice	*ND* Or. 32.42; Poidebard 45–6
7. *legio IIII Martia*	Betthoro	4.6	El Leggun	Arabia	*ND* Or. 37.22; Brünnow–Domaszewski 11 25; Brünnow 71
8. *equites sagittarii*	Acadama	0.77	Qdeym	Syria	*ND* Or. 33.21; Poidebard–Mouterde 109–10

Note: An alternative identification makes Han al-Qattar (line 1) the site of Neia (Carneia); Honigmann, *RE* s.v. Syria 1679, 1703. But if so it was still the fort of an *ala*, the *ala I Alamannorum* (*ND* Or. 32.36).

Sources: A. Poidebard *La trace de Rome dans le désert de Syrie: le limes de Trajan à la conquête arabe* (1934); J. Schwartz, A. Badawy, R.W. Smith, H. Wild *Fouilles franco-Suisses. Rapports II: Qasr-Qarun/Dionysias 1950* (1969); R. Brünnow, A. von Domaszewski *Die Provincia Arabia* (1904–9); R. Brünnow 'Die Kastella des arabischen Limes', *Florilegium M. De Vogüé* (1909) 65–77; A. Poidebard, R. Mouterde *Le limes de Chalcis* (1945).

Table 51. *A.H.M. Jones's interpretation of the Beatty payments (Jones (1964) 3.187–8)*

	Lines	Unit	Nature of payment date	Amount of payment	Number of recipients [conjectured]	Rate of payment [conjectured]
A	36ff.	*ala I Iberorum*	*stipendium,* 1 Jan. 300	73,500 den.	367½	× 200 [4 months]
B	36ff.		*annona,* 1 Sept.–31 Dec. 299	23,600 den.	354	× 66⅔ [4 months]
C	57ff.	*legio III Diocletiana*	*stipendium,* 1 Jan. 300	343,300 den.	1,716½	× 200 [4 months]
D	161ff.	*equites sagittarii*	*donativum,* 20 Nov. 299	302,500 den.	242	× 1,250
E	161ff.		*donativum,* 22 Dec. 299	302,500 den.	242	× 1,250
F	168ff.	*ala II Herculia dromedariorum*	*donativum,* 20 Nov. 299	53,750 den.	215	× 250
G	168ff.		*donativum,* 22 Dec. 299	53,750 den.	215	× 250
H	180ff.	*vexillatio of legio II Traiana*	*donativum,* 22 Dec. 299	1,386,250 den.	1,109	× 1,250
I	186ff.	*vexillatio of various Eastern legions*	*donativum,* 20 Nov. 299	2,496,250 den.	1,997	× 1,250
J	192ff.		*donativum,* 22 Dec. 299	2,496,250 den.	1,997	× 1,250

Table 51 (Cont.)

Lines	Unit	Nature of payment date	Amount of payment	Number of recipients [conjectured]	Rate of payment [conjectured]
K 197ff.	*praepositus of equites promoti of legio II Traiana*	*stipendium,* 1 Jan. 300	18,000 den.	1	× 18,000 [4 months]
L 197ff.		*donativum,* 20 Nov. 299	2,500 den.	1	× 2,500
M 197ff.		*donativum,* 22 Dec. 299	2,500 den.	1	× 2,500
N 204ff.	*equites promoti of legio II Traiana*	*donativum,* 1 Jan. 300	93,12[5] den.	149	× 625
O 245ff.	*vexillatio of legio III Diocletiana*	*salgamum,* 1 Sept.–31 Dec. 299	8,280 lb. oil and sext. salt	1,035	× 2 per month
P 259ff.	*lanciarii of legio II Traiana*	*donativum,* 20 Nov. 299	1,097,500 den.	878	× 1,250
Q 259ff.		*donativum,* 22 Dec. 299	1,097,500 den.	878	× 1,250
R 266ff.		*donativum,* 1 Jan. 300	526,875 den.	843	× 625
S 285ff.		*salgamum,* 1 Nov. and 31 Dec.	3,596 lb. oil and sext. salt	899	× 2 per month
T 291ff.	*cohors XI Chamavorum*	*stipendium,* 1 Jan. 300	65,500 den.	524	× 125 [4 months]
U 291ff.		*annona,* 1 Sept.–31 Dec. 299	32,866 den.	493	× 66⅔ [4 months]

Note: The few arithmetical mistakes in Jones's Table have been corrected and italicised here.

APPENDIX 5

EXISTING INTERPRETATIONS OF THE BEATTY FIGURES

The main figures have been interpreted by both Jones and Skeat. Skeat's interpretation owes something to interim suggestions by Jones, but appears to have been overtaken by Jones's later conclusions.[1] For Jones's results see Table 51 below.

I. J. first noted that an officer explicitly received 2,500 denarii for the birthday or accession day of an Augustus (22 December and 20 November in the present evidence) (L–M). He then observed that the highest common factor in the sums given to four of the units in respect of the same donative was 1,250 denarii. From this he deduced that the rank and file received half the rate of officers (D–E, H–J, P–Q), 1,250 denarii in these cases.

II. Comparing the donative given to the *lanciarii* of the *legio 11 Traiana* on the consulship of the Caesars (1 January), 526,875 denarii instead of 1,097,500 (P–R), J. deduced that the rate was half as much as in the other donatives, namely 625 denarii. In support of this he pointed to the total 93,12[5][2] denarii given to the *equites promoti* of *legio II Traiana* for the same occasion (line N). Divided by 625, 93,12[5] equals 149, a prime number.

III. J. then argued that the 53,750 denarii given to the *ala II Herculia dromedariorum* (F–G) for the first and second donatives implied a much lower rate of benefit, 250 denarii being the only plausible figure (presumably because a higher rate would have made the unit too small). The total strength arrived at is 215 (not 211 as in Jones's summary).

IV. J. argued that the *annona* total of 32,866 denarii for 4 months in line U can hardly represent anything but 493 men at $66\frac{2}{3}$ denarii for the four-monthly period, i.e. 200 denarii a year. He found the same rate plausible in B ($23,600/66\frac{2}{3} = 354$).

V. The ratio of T:U argues that *stipendium* for *alares* was three times their rate of *annona*, and the ratio of A:B argues that the *stipendium* of *cohortales* was twice the (same) rate of *annona*. This approximately suggests annual salaries of 600 denarii for *alares* and 375 for *cohortales* which yield plausible strengths (lines A–B, T–U).

VI. 'For the *stipendium* of legionaries C appears decisive (343,300 for soldiers of the *legio III Diocletiana*): any higher rate than 200 (600 a year) involves fractions less than a half, and so far as we know the half *stipendium* (for a *sesquiplicarius*) was the lowest fraction used.'

In most cases the observations show scrupulous regard for the numerical co-ordinates. But some of the results nevertheless contain clear inconsistencies. And Jones did not look closely at payments in kind, ignoring entirely those in the first Beatty papyrus.

Under II, J. concluded that successive donatives paid to the *lanciarii* of *legio II Traiana* in a ratio of 1,097,500:526,875 argued that the smaller was made at half the rate of the larger. However the ratio is not 2:1, but 25:12.[3] Therefore, if the higher donative was 1,250 denarii as J. thought, the smaller would be 600, not 625. This correction would mean that there was no change in the number of recipients between the two donatives. If the lower rate was 12/25 and not half the higher rate, J.'s conjecture in line N also needs to be emended.

---

[1] Cf. PBeatty Panop. xxvi–xxx.

[2] The 5 in 93,125 has been restored by the editor, following Jones's view that 625 was the common factor in all the donatives (PBeatty Panop. p.147, cf. xxvii–xxviii).

[3] In the smaller total, 75 denarii or 0.01% are apparently superfluous. For inexact totals see below and chapter 7, n.18 above.

Under IV and V, J. deduced that *cohortales* received annually salary (*stipendium*) of 375 and ration-payment (*annona*) of 200 denarii. That led to another significant discrepancy, this time between totals for the *cohors XI Chamavorum* (T-U). *Stipendium* made them 524, but *annona*, paid on the same day, 493. But again the ratio has not been read correctly. It is effectively 2:1 (65,500:32,866 = 1.99:1). That would make annual *stipendium* 400 if *annona* were 200, as J. argued. This reduces the discrepancy from 6.3% to 0.4%.[4]

These are not the only cases in which J.'s interpretations are unconvincing. A third is the oil payments to the *lanciarii* (see chapter 7, 1.4 above). The present alternatives suggest that argument from whole-number factors and highest common denominators by themselves cannot always establish the implications of this evidence. The approach assumes that the products of simple multiplication sums accurately executed were always forwarded intact to the units concerned. If instead there were small calculating errors, or if some paymasters took a commission, as conjectured from earlier pay records, the figures as they stand will not always exactly reflect troop strength.[5] There is a strong possibility of deductions (see chapter 7, n.18). Besides the indirect evidence of Egyptian army records, we know that triple commission was deducted from payments for grain requisition in Sicily under Verres.[6] The levying of commission by officials is indicated in the supplementary payments imposed on taxpayers in Egypt and elsewhere, and by the fifth century the practice had become so regular that it was acknowledged and consolidated by imperial ruling.[7]

Other tools with which to interpret the Beatty figures are therefore needed. As has been seen, those supplied by the payments in kind lead to quite different results.

[4] At the higher rate argued above, this discrepancy becomes less than 1 man (Table 41, line 10).
[5] For deductions in Egyptian army pay records, see Speidel (1973) 144.
[6] This may not have been uncommon (*Verr.* 2.3.181–4; compare 2.3.214–5, where Verres is blamed for doing what two of his predecessors had done).
[7] For supplementary charges in Egypt, Wallace (1938) 38–41. For the fees of tax-collectors in the later Empire, see Jones (1964) 3.131 n.137, and Johnson–West (1949) 289ff.

APPENDIX 6

THE *IUGUM* IN EPIPHANIUS
(chapter 13)

The definitions of the *iugum* in Epiphanius's treatise on Weights and Measures written in AD 392 have not been fully utilised in discussions of late Roman taxation, although briefly referred to by Segré (1945) and Cérati (1975) 192 n.4.

Epiphanius presents a matrix of broadly coherent equivalences between units whose exact relationships he does not always seem to have understood. Much the fullest version of his treatise survives in a Syriac translation (Dean (1935), who also gives an English text). The unascribed fragment in *MSR* 1.56–7 (cf. 2.153) is a version of part of the Greek text, more of which, though sometimes corrupt, is given in Lagarde (1877–80) 1.218–19, with 2.200–1. The conclusions for the size of the *iugum* by Viedebantt (1911) 70–3 and Schilbach (1970) 77–9 are not consistent with the co-ordinates of the full Syriac version. The Old Georgian translation published in 1984 lacks the section dealing with the *iugum*.

The *iugum* first-class

Epiphanius (Dean 67–8) states that the *iugum* of first-class land:

1. Contains 13 *iugera* (or 12 in one version (Lagarde (1877–80) 2.201).
2. Or 5 'fields' (glossed as 'arourae' in the Syriac text (Dean 67, n.473)).
3. A field of first-class land contains 5 *plethra*.
4. It is also a square of 133⅓ cubits (20 *akaina*).
5. The *iugum* first-class also equals 30 *sataia* (seed-measures).
6. The *sataion* contains 1 'overfull' modius, which is 1⅓ of Epiphanius's normal modii.
7. The *plethron* is a square with a side of 20 cubits and is equal to the *sataion*.

Proposition 7, making the *plethron* very small, is out of line, but the other statements generally cohere. The most important is the first, indicating the size of the *iugum* first-class as 12–13 *iugera*. Propositions 2 and 3 between them give the *iugum* 25 *plethra*, suggesting that the *plethron* in question equalled a half-*iugerum*, and thus implying the *iugum*'s exact size as 12½ *iugera*.

The cubit in 4 is evidently Heron's cubit measuring 2 Roman feet (*MSR* 1.188.15, 194.21; 1.42–4), since 2.5 *iugera* have a side of 268.3 Roman feet, and 268.3/133.33 = 2.01.

Propositions 5 and 6 point to a sowing quantity per *iugum* of 36 of Epiphanius's basic modii, which he defines elsewhere as 22 *xestai* (Dean 41). Depending on whether these *xestai* are Italic or Alexandrian (cf. Dean 13), the modius thus contains 1.375 or 1.5 Italic modii. The total sowing area is therefore 49.5/54 Italic modii per *iugum*, and 3.96/4.5 modii per *iugerum*. Both figures are close to the range of sowing quantities per *iugerum* in standard authors (5 modii in Varro; 4–5 in Columella; 5 in Pliny; *ERE*[2] 49 n.).

The *iugum* second-class

Epiphanius gives its size as:

1. 6 fields.
2. 6 × 6 = 36 *plethra*.
3. 60 *sataia*.

These definitions are mutually contradictory, since 1 gives the second-class *iugum* an excess of 20% over the *iugum* first-class, 2 gives it 44%, and 3 gives it 100%. Definitions 2 and 3 seem to be confused elaborations of the first. Proposition 1, which is the most definite, would make the second-class *iugum* equal to 15 *iugera*.

BIBLIOGRAPHY

Citations of primary evidence and of encyclopedias and other standard works are not reproduced. Journals are generally abbreviated as in the *Année philologique* (for other abbreviations see p.xv above). Books and monographs are listed by author, title and place of publication.

Abulafia, D. (1987) *Italy, Sicily and the Mediterranean, 1100–1400* (London)

Albertini, E. (1920) 'Table de measures de Djemila', *CRAI*, 315–19

Alföldi, G (1966) 'Zur Inschrift des Collegium centonariorum von Solva', *Historia* 15, 433–44

Ashburner, W. (1909) *The Rhodian sea-law* (London)

Ashtor, E. (1969) *Histoire des prix et des salaires dans l'Orient médiéval* (Paris)

Atti (1974) *Atti del Convegno internazionale sul tema: I diritti locali nelle province romane con particolare riguardo alle condizioni giuridiche del suolo, 1971* (1974) (Problemi attuali di scienza e di cultura n.194)

Audollent, A. (1901) *Carthage romaine* (Paris)

Aymard, M., Bresc, H. (1975) 'Nourritures et consommation en Sicile entre xive et xviiie siècles', *Annales ESC* 30, 592–9

Baatz, D. (1975) *Der römische Limes: archäologische Ausflüge zwischen Rhein und Donau* (Berlin)

Bagnall, R.S. (1985) 'Agricultural productivity and taxation in late Roman Egypt', *TAPhA* 115, 289–308

Bailey, D.M. (1980) *A catalogue of lamps in the British Museum, London II: Roman lamps made in Italy* (London)

(1987) 'The Roman terracotta lamp-industry: another view about exports', in Th. Oziol, R. Rebuffat (edd.) *Les lampes de terre cuite en Méditerranée, Lyon 1981* (Paris) 59–63

(1988) *A catalogue of lamps in the British Museum, London III: Roman provincial lamps* (London)

Baladié, R. (1980) *Le Péloponnèse de Strabon* (Paris)

Beloch, K.J. (1937) *Bevölkerungsgeschichte Italiens* 1 (Berlin)

Berchem, D. van (1939) *Les distributions de blé et d'argent à la plèbe romaine* (Geneva)

(1952) *L'armée de Dioclétien et la réforme constantinienne* (Paris)

Berger, A. (1953) *Encyclopedic dictionary of Roman law* (Philadelphia)

Bersu, D. (1964) *Die spätrömische Befestigung 'Burgle' bei Gundremmingen* (Munich)

Bingen, J. (1951) 'Les comptes dans les archives d'Héroninos', *CE* 26, 378–85

Birley, A.R. (1967) 'The Augustan History', in T.A. Dorey (ed.) *Latin Historians* (London) 113–38

(1971) *Septimius Severus, the African Emperor* (London)

Birley, E.R. (1966) 'Alae and cohortes milliariae', *Corolla E. Swoboda* (Graz) 54–67

Boak, A.E.R. (1955) *Manpower shortage and the fall of the Roman Empire in the West* (Ann Arbor)

Boeswillwald, E., Cagnat, R., Ballu, A. (1905) *Timgad, une cité africaine sous l'empire romain* (Paris)

Bolin, S. (1958) *State and currency in the Roman Empire up to* AD *300* (Stockholm)

Bonneau, D. (1964) *La Crue du Nil* (Paris)

Bossu, C. (1982) 'M' Megonius Leo from Petelia (regio III): a private benefactor from the local aristocracy', *ZPE* 45, 155–65

Bove, L. (1960) *Ricerche sugli 'agri vectigales'* (Naples)

Bowersock, G.W. (1969) *Greek sophists in the Roman Empire* (Oxford)

Bowman, A.K. (1971) *The town-councils of Roman Egypt* (Toronto)

   (1978) 'The military occupation of Upper Egypt in the reign of Diocletian', *BASP* 15, 25–38

   (1985) 'Landholding in the Hermopolite Nome in the Fourth Century AD', *JRS* 75, 137–63

Boyaval, B. (1976) 'Remarques sur les indications d'ages dans l'épigraphie funéraire grecque d'Egypte', *ZPE* 21, 217–43

Braudel, F. (1972) *The Mediterranean and the Mediterranean world in the age of Philip II* (London)

Breeze, D.J., Dobson, B.W. (1976) *Hadrian's Wall* (London)

Breeze, D.J. (1977) 'The garrisoning of Roman fortlets', *Studien zu den Militargrenzen Roms* II (*BJ* Beih. 38), 1–6

Breglia, L. (1950) 'Circolazione monetale ed aspetti di vita economica a Pompei', in [A. Maiuri (ed.)] *Pompeiana: Raccolta di studi per il secondo centenario degli scavi di Pompei* (Naples) 41–59

Brothwell, D. (1981) *Digging up bones* (London)

Broughton, T.R.S. (1929) *The Romanization of Africa Proconsularis* (Baltimore)

   (1951) 'New evidence on temple-estates in Asia Minor', *Studies A.C. Johnson* (Princeton) 236–50

   (1969) 'The territory of Carthage', *REL*, 47.2, 265–75

Brunt, P.A. (1950) 'Pay and superannuation in the Roman army', *PBSR* 18, 50–71

   (1971) *Italian manpower, 225* BC–AD *14* (Oxford)

   (1974) 'Conscription and Volunteering in the Roman Imperial Army', *Scripta Classica Israelica* 1, 90–115

   (1980) 'Free labour and public works in Rome', *JRS* 70, 81–100

   (1981) 'The Revenues of Rome', *JRS* 61, 161–72

Bureth, P. (1964) *Les titulatures impériales dans les papyrus, les ostraca, et les inscriptions d'Egypte (30 a.C–284 p.C.)* (Brussels)

Burnett, A.M. (1987) *Coinage in the Roman world* (London)

Calderini, R. (1950) 'Gli *agrammatoi* nell' Egitto greco-romano', *Aegyptus* 30, 14–41

Callu, J-P. (1969) *La politique monétaire des Empereurs romains de 238 à 311* (Paris)

Campbell, J.B. (1984) *The emperor and the Roman army, 31* BC–AD *235* (Oxford)

Carandini, A. (1983) 'Pottery and the African economy', *TAE*, 145–62

Carcopino, J. (1922) 'Fermier général ou Sociétés publicaines?', *REA*, 12–36

Carter, J.M. (1967) 'Eighteen years old?', *BICS* 14, 51–7

Casson, L. (1971) *Ships and seamanship in the ancient world* (Princeton)

   (1980) 'The role of the state in Rome's grain trade', in D'Arms–Kopff (1980) 21–33

Castrén, P. (1976) *Ordo populusque Pompeianus* (Rome)

Cérati, A. (1975) *Caractère annonaire et assiette de l'impôt foncier au Bas-Empire* (Paris)

Châlon, G. (1964) *L'Edit de Tiberius Julius Alexander* (Lausanne)

Chastagnol, A. (1978) *L'Album municipal de Timgad* (Bonn)

  (1981) 'Une firme de commerce entre l'ile de Bretagne et le continent gaulois à l'époque des Sévères', *ZPE* 43, 63–6

Cheesman, G.L. (1914) *The auxilia of the Roman imperial army* (Oxford)

Chilver, G.E.F. (1941) *Cisalpine Gaul* (Oxford)

Christiansen, E. (1988) *The Roman coins of Alexandria: quantitative studies* (Aarhus)

Cimma, E. (1981) *Ricerche sulle società di publicani* (Milan)

Cipolla, C.M. (1969) *Literacy and development in the West* (Harmondsworth)

Clauss, M. (1973) 'Probleme der Lebensalterstatistik aufgrund römischer Grabin-schriften', *Chiron* 3, 395–417

Coale, A.J., Demeny, P. (1983) *Regional model life-tables²* (Princeton)

Corbier, M. (1977) 'Le discours du prince d'après une inscription de Banasa', *Ktema* 2, 211–32

Crawford, D.J. (1976) 'Imperial estates', in M.I. Finley (ed.) *Studies in Roman property* (Cambridge) 35–70, 173–80

Crawford, M.H. (1977) 'Republican denarii in Romania: the suppression of piracy and the slave-trade', *JRS* 67, 117–24

Crawford, M.H., Reynolds, J.M. (1979) 'The Aezani copy of Diocletian's Price Edict', *ZPE* 34, 163–210

Crook, J.A. (1967) *Law and life of Rome* (London)

D'Arms, J.H. (1981) *Commerce and social standing in ancient Rome* (Cambridge, Mass.)

D'Arms, J.H., Kopff, E.C. (edd.) (1980) *The seaborne commerce of ancient Rome* (Rome)

Day, J. (1956) *Tax-documents from Theadelphia* (New York)

Dean, J.E. (1935) *Epiphanius' treatise on weights and measures: the Syriac version* (Chicago)

Déléage, A. (1945) *La capitation du Bas-Empire* (Nancy)

Develin, R. (1971) 'The army pay-rises under Severus and Caracalla, and the question of annona militaris', *Latomus* 30, 687–95

Duncan-Jones, R.P. (1963) 'Wealth and munificence in Roman Africa', *PBSR* 31, 159–77

  (1964A) 'The purpose and organisation of the alimenta', *PBSR* 32, 123–46

  (1964B) 'Human numbers in towns and town-organisations of the Roman Empire: the evidence of gifts', *Historia* 13, 199–208

  (1967) 'Equestrian rank in the cities of the African provinces: an epigraphic survey', *PBSR* 35, 147–88

  (1972) 'Patronage and city-privileges: the case of Giufi', *Epig. Stud.* 9, 12–16

  (1974) 'The procurator as civic benefactor', *JRS* 64, 79–85

  (1976A) 'Some configurations of landholding in the Roman Empire', in M.I. Finley (ed.) *Studies in Roman property* (Cambridge) 7–33, 163–73

  (1976B) 'The price of wheat in Roman Egypt under the Principate', *Chiron* 6, 241–62

  (1976C) 'The choenix, the artaba and the modius', *ZPE* 21, 43–52

  (1976D) 'The size of the modius castrensis', *ZPE* 21, 43–52

  (1977) 'Age-rounding, illiteracy and social differentiation in the Roman Empire', *Chiron* 7, 333–53

  (1978) 'Pay and numbers in Diocletian's army', *Chiron* 8, 541–60

  (1979A) 'Age-rounding in Graeco-Roman Egypt', *ZPE* 33, 169–78

  (1979B) 'Variation in Egyptian grain-measure', *Chiron* 9, 347–75

  (1980A) 'Age-rounding in Roman Carthage', *University of Michigan Excavations at*

Carthage 5, 1–6 (New Delhi)

(1980B) 'Demographic change and economic progress in the Roman Empire', in *Tecnologia, economia e società nel mondo Romano, Como 1979* (Como) 67–80

(1980C) 'Length-units in Roman town-planning: the pes monetalis and the pes Drusianus', *Britannia* 11, 127–33

(1984) 'Problems of the Delphic manumission–payments 200–1 BC', *ZPE* 57, 203–9

(1985) 'Who paid for public building in Roman towns?', in F. Grew, B. Hobley (edd.) *Roman urban topography in Britain and the western Empire* (London) 28–33

(1989A) 'Weight-loss as an index of coin-wear in currency of the Roman Principate', in G. Depeyrot, T. Hackens (edd.) *Rhythmes de la production monétaire, de l'antiquité à nos jours* (Louvain, in the press) 235–54

(1989B) 'Mobility and immobility of coin in the Roman Empire', *AIIN* 36, 121–37

Dupâquier, J. (1973) 'Sur une table (prétendument) florentine d'espérance de vie', *Annales ESC* 28, 1066–70

Duthoy, R. (1978) 'Les Augustales', *ANRW* 2.16.2, 1254–309

Eck, W. (1979) *Die staatliche Organisation Italiens in der hohen Kaiserzeit* (Munich)

(1980) 'Die präsenz senatorischer Familien in den Städten des Imperium Romanum bis zum späten 3 Jahrhundert', in *Festschrift F. Vittinghoff* (Cologne) 283–322

(1981) 'Altersangaben in senatorischen Grabinschriften: Standeserwartungen und ihre Kompensation', *ZPE* 43, 127–34

Ery, K.K. (1969) 'Investigations on the demographic source-value of tombstones originating from the Roman period', *Alba Regia* 10, 51–67

Etienne, R., Fabre, G. (1970) 'Démographie et classe sociale: l'exemple du cimetière des officiales de Carthage', in C. Nicolet (ed.) *Recherches sur les structures sociales dans l'antiquité classique* (Paris) 81–97

Evans, J.A.S. (1961) 'A social and economic history of an Egyptian temple in the Greco-Roman period', *YClS* 17, 149–283

Fanfani. A. (1940) *Indagini sulla 'rivoluzione dei prezzi'* (Milan)

Faure, G. (1961) *Etude de la capitation de Dioclétien d'après le Panegyrique VIII* (Paris)

Forni, G. (1953) *Il reclutamento della legioni da Augusto a Diocleziano* (Milan)

(1974) 'Estrazione etnica e sociale dei soldati delle legioni nei primi tre secoli dell'impero', *ANRW* 2.1, 339–91

Fossey, J.M. (1982) 'The city archive at Koroneia, Boiotia', *Euphrosyne* 11, 44–59

de Franciscis, A. (1966) 'Note sui "Praedia Dianae Tifatinae"', *RAAN* 41, 241–6

Frank, T. (1933–40) (ed.) *An Economic Survey of Ancient Rome* (Baltimore)

Fraser, P.M. (1972) *Ptolemaic Alexandria* (Oxford)

Frederiksen, M. (1973) 'The contribution of archaeology to the agrarian problem in the Gracchan period', *DArch* 4–5, 330–67

French, A. (1964) *The growth of the Athenian economy* (London)

Frere, S.S. (1978) *Britannia²* (London)

Friedlaender, L. and others (1921–2) *Darstellungen aus der Sittengeschichte Roms¹⁰* (Leipzig)

Frier, B.W. (1982) 'Roman life-expectancy: Ulpian's evidence', *HSPh* 86, 212–51

(1983) 'Roman life-expectancy: the Pannonian evidence', *Phoenix* 37, 329–44

Fulford, M. (1980) 'Carthage: overseas trade and the political economy, c. AD 400–700', *Reading medieval studies* 6, 68–80

(1984) 'The long distance trade and communications of Carthage c. AD 400 to c. AD 650', *Excavations at Carthage: the British mission* 1.2, 256–62

(1987) 'Economic interdependence among urban communities of the Roman Mediterranean', *World Archaeology* 19, 58–75

Gabba, E. (1962) 'Progetti di riforme economiche e fiscale in uno storico dell'età dei Severi', *Studi A. Fanfani* 1 (Milan), 39–68

Gagé, J. (1969) 'Italica adlectio', *REA* 71, 65–84

Le Gall, J. (1974) 'Les investissements privés sous le Haut-Empire romain', *RHES* 52, 37–50

Galsterer, H. (1971) *Untersuchungen zum römischen Städtewesen auf der Iberischen Halbinsel* (Berlin)

Galsterer-Kröll B. (1972) 'Untersuchungen zu den Beinamen der Städte des Imperium Romanums', *Epigr. Stud.* 9, 44–145

Garnsey, P. (1974) 'Aspects of the decline of the urban aristocracy in the Empire', *ANRW* 2.1, 229–52

(1975) 'Descendants of freedmen in local politics: some criteria', in B. Levick (ed.) *The Historian and his materials: Essays C.E. Stevens* (London) 167–80

(1988) *Famine and food-supply in the Graeco-Roman world: responses to risk and crisis* (Cambridge)

Gascou, J. (1972) *La politique municipale de l'empire romain en Afrique proconsulaire, de Trajan à Septime Sévère* (Rome)

Gauckler, P. (1902) 'Le centenarius di Tibubuci (Ksar-Tarine)', *CRAI*, 321–40

Ghinatti, F., Uguzzoni, A. (1968) *Le tavole greche di Eraclea* (Rome)

Gill, D. (1987) 'An Attic lamp in Reggio: the largest batch notation outside Athens?', *OJA* 6, 121–5

(1988) 'Silver anchors and cargoes of oil: some observations on Phoenician trade in the western Mediterranean', *PBSR* 56, 1–12

Gilliam, J.F. (1961) 'The plague under Marcus Aurelius', *AJPh* 82, 225–51

Goffart, W. (1974) *From caput to colonate* (Toronto)

Goitein, S.D. (1967) *A Mediterranean society: the Jewish communities of the Arab world as portrayed in the Cairo Geniza* 1 (Berkeley)

Gonzalez, J. (1986) 'The lex Irnitana: a new copy of the Flavian municipal law', *JRS* 76, 147–243

Goodchild, R.G. (1976) *Libyan studies: select papers* (London)

Goody, J. (1977) *The domestication of the savage mind* (Cambridge)

Grosse, H. (1920) *Römische Militargeschichte von Gallienus bis zum Beginn der byzantinischen Themenverfassung* (Berlin)

Gsell, S. (1913–30) *Histoire ancienne de l'Afrique du Nord* (Paris)

Gualandi, G. (1963) *Legislazione imperiale e giurisprudenza* (Milan)

Guéry, R. (1979) 'Les marques de potiers sur terra sigillata découvertes en Algérie I: sigillées provinciales (hispanique et gallo-romaine)', *AntAfr* 13, 23–97

Guiraud, P. (1893) *La propriété foncière en Grèce jusqu'à la conquête romaine* (Paris)

Hansen, H., Schiöler Th. (1965) 'Distribution of land based on Greek-Egyptian papyri', *Janus* 52, 181–92

Hanson, W.S., Maxwell, G.S. (1983) *Rome's northwest frontier* (Edinburgh)

Harkness, A.G. (1896) 'Age at marriage and at death in the Roman Empire', *TAPhA* 27, 35–72

Harris, W.V. (1980A) 'Roman terracotta lamps: the organisation of an industry', *JRS* 70, 126–45

(1980B) 'Towards a study of the Roman slave-trade', in D'Arms–Kopff (1980) 117–40

(1983) 'Literacy and epigraphy I', *ZPE* 52, 87–111

Hassall, M. (1978) 'Britain and the Rhine provinces: epigraphic evidence for Roman trade', in Taylor (1978) 41–8

Henry, L. (1959) 'L'age au decès d'après les inscriptions funéraires', *Population* 14, 327–9

Herlihy, D. (1967) *Medieval and Renaissance Pistoia* (New Haven)

Herlihy, D., Klapisch, C. (1978) *Les Toscans et leurs familles* (Paris)

Hoffmann, D. (1969) *Das spätrömische Bewegungsheer und die Notitia Dignitatum* (Düsseldorf)

Hohlwein, N. (1938) 'Le blé d'Egypte' *EPap* 4, 33–120

Hombert, M., Préaux, C. (1952) *Recherches sur le recensement dans l'Egypte romaine* (Leyden)

Honoré, T. (1981) *Emperors and lawyers* (London)

Hopkins, M.K. (1966) 'On the probable age-structure of the Roman population', *Population Studies* 20, 245–64

(1980) 'Taxes and trade in the Roman Empire, 200 BC–AD 400', *JRS* 70, 101–25

(1982) 'The transport of staples in the Roman Empire', *Eighth International Economic History Congress, Budapest 1982* (Budapest) B 12, 80–7

Horstkotte, H.J. (1984) 'Magistratur und Dekurionat im Lichte des Albums von Canusium,' *ZPE* 57, 211–24

Jacques, F. (1977) 'Les cens en Gaule au IIe siècle et dans la première moitié du IIIe siècle', *Ktema* 2, 285–328

(1984) *Le privilège de liberté: politique impériale et autonomie municipale dans les cités de l'Occident romain (161–244)* (Paris)

Jahn, J. (1980) 'Zum Rauminhalt von Artabe und modius castrensis', *ZPE* 38, 223–8

(1983) 'Der Sold römischer Soldaten im 3 Jh. n.Chr.: Bemerkungen zu ChLA 446, 473 und 495', *ZPE* 53, 217–27

(1984) 'Zur Entwicklung römischer Soldzahlungen von Augustus bis auf Diocletian', in M.R. Alföldi (ed.) *Studien zu Fundmünzen, II Aufsatze* (Berlin) 53–74

Jarrett, M.G. (1972) 'Decurions and priests', *AJPh* 92, 513–38

Johnson, A.C. (1936): see Frank (1933–40) vol. 2

Johnson, A.C., West, L.C. (1949) *Byzantine Egypt: economic studies* (Princeton)

Jones, A.H.M. (1940) *The Greek city* (Oxford)

(1960) *Studies in Roman government and law* (Oxford)

(1964) *The later Roman Empire* (Oxford)

(1971A) 'Rome and the provincial cities', *RHD* 39, 513–51

(1971B) *Cities of the eastern Roman provinces*[2] (Oxford)

(1974) ed. P.A. Brunt, *The Roman economy* (Oxford)

Jones, C.P. (1978) *The Roman world of Dio Chrysostom* (Cambridge, Mass.)

Jouffroy, H. (1986) *La construction publique en Italie et dans l'Afrique romaine* (Strasbourg)

Kajanto, I (1968) *On the problem of the average duration of life in the Roman Empire* (Helsinki)

Kehoe, D.P. (1987) *The economics of agriculture on Roman imperial estates in North Africa* (Göttingen)

Kent, J.H. (1948) 'The temple-estates of Rheneia and Mykonos', *Hesperia* 17, 243–338

Kolendo, J. (1980) 'L'arrêt de l'afflux des monnaies romaines dans le "Barbaricum" sous Septime-Sévère', *Les Dévaluations à Rome* 2 (Rome) 169–72

Kreutz, B. (1976) 'Ships, shipping and the implications of change in the early medieval Mediterranean', *Viator* 7, 79–110

Kunisz, A. (1973) *Katalog skarbow monet rzymskich odkrytych na ziemiach polskich* (Warsaw)

Laet, S.J. de (1949) *Portorium* (Bruges)

Lagarde, P. de (1877–80) *Symmicta* (Göttingen)

Lane, F.C. (1934) *Venetian ships and shipbuilding of the Renaissance* (Baltimore)

(1964) 'Tonnages medieval and modern', *EcHR* 2.17, 213–33

(1966) *Venice and history* (Baltimore)

Langhammer, W. (1973) *Die rechtliche und soziale Stellung der magistratus municipales und der decuriones* (Wiesbaden)

Lasserre, F. (1982) 'Strabon devant l'empire romain', *ANRW* 2.30.1, 867–96

Lepelley, C. (1979–81) *Les cités de l'Afrique romaine au Bas-Empire* (Paris)

Leschi, L. (1957) *Etudes d'épigraphie, d'histoire et d'archéologie africaines* (Paris)

Levison, W. (1898) 'Die Beurkundung des Civilstandes im Altertum', *BJ* 102, 1–82

Liebenam, W. (1900) *Städteverwaltung im römischen Kaiserreiche* (Berlin)

Littmann, R.J., Littmann, M.L. (1973) 'Galen and the Antonine plague', *AJPh* 94, 243–55

Lo Cascio, E. (1986) 'La struttura fiscale dell'Impero romano', in M.H. Crawford (ed.) *L'Impero romano e le strutture economiche e sociale delle province* (Como) 29–59

Mackie, N. (1983) *Local administration in Roman Spain AD 14–212* (Oxford)

MacMullen, R. (1974) *Roman social relations, 50 BC to AD 284* (Cambridge, Mass.)

(1986) 'Frequency of inscriptions in Roman Lydia', *ZPE* 65, 237–8

MacVe, R. (1985) 'Some glosses on Ste. Croix's "Greek and Roman Accounting"', in P. Cartledge, F.D. Harvey (edd.) *Crux: Essays G.E.M. de Sainte Croix* (London) 233–64

Magie, D. (1950) *Roman rule in Asia Minor* (Princeton)

(1951) 'A reform in the exaction of grain at Cibyra under Claudius', *Studies A.C. Johnson* (Princeton) 152–4

Mallett, M.E. (1967) *Florentine galleys in the fifteenth century* (Oxford)

Marquardt, J. (1881–5) *Römische Staatsverwaltung*² (Berlin)

Marrou, H-I. (1965) *Histoire de l'éducation dans l'antiquité* (Paris)

Martin, T. (1977) 'Fouilles de Montana: note préliminaire sur les résultats de la campagne 1975', *Figlina* 2, 51–78

Matthews, J.T. (1976) 'Mauretania in Ammianus and the Notitia', in R. Goodburn, P. Bartholomew, (edd.) *Aspects of the Notitia Dignitatum* (Oxford) 157–88

(1984) 'The tax-law of Palmyra', *JRS* 74, 157–80

Mattingly, D.J. (1988) 'The olive-boom. Oil surpluses, wealth and power in Roman Tripolitania', *Libyan Studies* 19, 21–42

Millar, F.G.B. (1963) *A Study of Cassius Dio* (Oxford)

(1977) *The emperor in the Roman world* (London)

(1984) 'Condemnation to hard labour in the Roman Empire', *PBSR* 52, 124–47

Milne, J.G. (1933) *A catalogue of Alexandrian coins in the Ashmolean Museum* (Oxford)

Mols, R. (1956) *Introduction à la démographie historique des villes d'Europe du XIVᵉ au XVIIIᵉ siècle* vol. 3 (Louvain)

Montevecchi, O. (1973) *La papirologia* (Turin)

Morris, J.A. (1964) 'Leges annales under the Principate', *LF* 12, 316–37

Mouchmov, L.A. (1934) *Le Trésor de Réka-Devnia (Marcianopolis)* (Sofia)

Nash-Williams, V.E. (1969) *The Roman frontier in Wales*² (Cardiff)

Neesen, L. (1980) *Untersuchungen zu den direkten Staatsabgaben der römischen Kaiserzeit*

(27 v.Chr.–284 n.Chr.) (Bonn)

(1981) 'Die Entwicklung der Leistungen und Ämter (munera et honores) im römischen Kaiserreich des zweiten bis vierten Jahrhunderts', *Historia* 30, 203–35

Neeve, P.W. de (1985) 'The price of agricultural land in Roman Italy and the problem of economic rationalism', *Opus* 4, 77–109

Nollé F. (1982) 'Epigraphica varia', *ZPE* 48, 267–82

Nutton, V. (1971) 'Two notes on immunities: Digest 27.1.6.10 and 11', *JRS* 61, 52–63

Oliver, J.H., Palmer, R.E. (1955) 'Minutes of a meeting of the Roman Senate', *Hesperia* 24, 320–49

Pachtère, F.G. de (1908) 'Le règlement d'irrigation à Lamasba', *MEFR* 28, 373–400

(1920) *La table hypothécaire de Veleia* (Paris)

Panella, C. (1981) 'Le merci: produzione, itinerari e destini', in A. Giardina, A. Schiavone (edd.) *Società romana e produzione schiavistica* (Bari) 431–59, 843–5

(1984) 'I commerci di Roma e di Ostia in età imperiale: le derrate alimentari', in *Misurare la terra: centuriazione e coloni nel mondo romano* (Rome) 180–9

Parker, A.J. (1984) 'Shipwrecks and ancient trade in the Mediterranean', *Arch. Review from Cambridge* 3.2, 99–112

Parker, H.M.D. (1933) 'The legions of Diocletian and Constantine', *JRS* 23, 175–89

Paterson, J. (1982) 'Salvation from the sea: amphorae and trade in the Roman West', *JRS* 72, 146–57

Pavolini, C. (1975/6) 'Una produzione italica di lucerne: le *Vogelkopflampen* ad ansa traversale', *BCAR* 85, 45–134

(1981) 'Le lucerne nell'Italia romana', in A. Giardina, A. Schiavone (edd.,) *Società romana e produzione schiavistica* (Bari) 139–86

Peacock, D.P.S. (1978) 'The Rhine and the problem of Gaulish wine in Roman Britain', in Taylor (1978) 49–51

Peacock, D.P.S., Williams D.F. (1986) *Amphorae and the Roman economy* (London)

Pékary, T. (1980) 'Les limites de l'économie monétaire à l'époque romaine', *Les dévaluations à Rome* (Rome) 2, 103–20

Perler, O. with J.L. Maier (1969) *Les voyages de Saint Augustin* (Paris)

Pflaum, H-G (1960) *Les carrières procuratoriennes équestres* (Paris)

(1978) *Opuscula Romana* I (Paris)

Piganiol, A. (1962) *Les documents cadastraux de la colonie romaine d'Orange* (Paris)

Pippidi, D.M. (1945) *Autour de Tibère* (1945) (Bucharest)

Pleket, H.W. (1983) 'Urban elites and business in the Greek part of the Roman empire', *TAE*, 131–44

Poinssot, C. (1958) *Les ruines de Dougga* (Tunis)

(1962) 'Immunitas perticae Carthaginiensium', *CRAI*, 55–76

(1966) 'Aqua Commodiana civitatis Aureliae Thuggae', *Mélanges J. Carcopino* (Paris) 771–86

(1969) 'M. Licinius Rufus, patronus pagi et civitatis Thuggensis', *BCTH* n.s. 5, 215–58

Préaux, C. (1952) 'Le règne de Vitellius en Egypte', *Mélanges G. Smets* (Brussels) 571–8

Price, R.M. (1976) 'The limes of Lower Egypt', in R. Goodburn, P. Bartholomew (edd.) *Aspects of the Notitia Dignitatum* (Oxford) 143–55

Procaccini, P. (1981) 'Ancora a proposito dell' "industria" delle lucerne nell' Impero romano', *Studi F. Grosso* (Rome) 507–21

Pryor, J.H. (1988) *Geography, technology and war: studies in the maritime history of the Mediterranean 649–1571* (Cambridge)

Pucci, G. (1983) 'Pottery and trade in the Roman economy', *TAE*, 105–17

Rathbone, D. (1982) 'The grain-trade in the Hellenistic East', *Eighth International Economic History Congress, Budapest 1982* (Budapest) B 12, 44–51

(1983) 'Italian wines in Roman Egypt', *Opus* 2, 81–98

(1986) 'The dates of recognition in Egypt of the emperors from Caracalla to Diocletianus', *ZPE* 62, 101–29

Reddé, M. (1986) *Mare Nostrum: les infrastructures, le dispositif, et l'histoire de la marine militaire sous l'Empire romain* (Paris)

Richmond, I.A. (1965) Review of Bersu (1964) *BJ* 165, 493

Rickman, G. (1980) *The corn-supply of ancient Rome* (Oxford)

Riepl, W. (1913) *Das Nachrichtenwesen des Altertums* (Leipzig)

Ritterling, E. (1903) 'Zum römischen Heerwesen des ausgehenden dritten Jahrhunderts', *Festschrift O. Hirschfeld* (Berlin) 345–9

Röhricht, R., Meisner, F. (1880) *Deutsche Pilgerreisen²* (Berlin)

Romanelli, P. (1959) *Storia delle province romane dell'Africa* (Rome)

(1970) *Topografia e archeologia dell'Africa romana* (*Enciclopedia classica* 3.10.7, Turin)

Rostovtzeff, M.I. (1918) 'Synteleia tirōnōn', *JRS* 8, 26–33

(1957) *Social and economic history of the Roman Empire²* (Oxford)

Rougé, J. (1952) 'La navigation hivernale dans l'Empire romain', *REA* 54, 316–25

(1966) *Recherches sur l'organisation du commerce maritime en Méditerranée sous l'Empire romain* (Paris)

Le Roux, P. (1983) *L' armée romaine et l'organisation des provinces ibériques d'Auguste á l'invasion de 409* (Paris)

Sacerdoti, A. (1962) 'Note sulle galere da mercato veneziane nel XV secolo', *Boll. Ist. Stor. Ven.* 4, 80–105

Salmon, E.T. (1969) *Roman colonization under the Republic* (London)

Samuel, A.E., Hastings, W.K., Bowman, A.K., Bagnall, R.S. (1971) *Death and taxes: ostraka in the Royal Ontario Museum* (Toronto)

Sardella, P. (1948) *Nouvelles et spéculations à Venise au début du XVIᵉ siècle* (Paris)

Sartori, F. (1967) 'Eraclea di Lucania', *MDAIR* Erg.-heft 11, 16–48

Schilbach, E. (1970) *Byzantinische Metrologie* (Düsseldorf)

Schuman, V.B. (1952) 'The seven-obol drachma of Roman Egypt', *CPh* 47, 214–18

Segré, A. (1945) 'Studies in Byzantine economy: iugatio and capitatio', *Traditio* 3, 101–27

Shaw, B.D. (1982) 'Lamasba: an ancient irrigation community', *AntAfr* 18, 61–103

Shelton, J.C. (1981) 'Two notes on the artab', *ZPE* 42, 99–106

Sijpestein, P.J. (1964) *Penthemeros-certificates in Roman Egypt* (Leyden)

(1986) 'Princeton II 50 and the number of soldiers in Egypt', *ZPE* 65, 168

Sijpestein, P.J., Worp, K.A. (1976) 'Documents on transportation by ship', *ZPE* 20, 157–65

Smallwood, E.M. (1966) *Documents of the reigns of Nerva, Trajan and Hadrian* (Cambridge)

Solin, H. (1971) *Beiträge zur Kenntnis der griechischen Personennamen in Rom* (Helsinki)

Spalinger A. (1987) 'The grain system of Dynasty 18', *Stud. altagypt. Kultur* 14, 283–311

Speidel, M. (1973) 'The pay of the auxilia', *JRS* 61, 141–7

Straus, J.A. (1973) 'Le prix des esclaves dans les papyrus d'époque romaine trouvés dans l'Egypte', *ZPE* 11, 289–95

Swiderek, A. (1960) *La propriété foncière privée dans l'Egypte de Vespasien* (Wroclaw)

Syme, R. (1988A) *Collected papers* 4–5 (Oxford)

(1988B) 'Journeys of Hadrian', *ZPE* 73, 159–70

Szilagyi, J. (1961) 'Beiträge zur Statistik der Sterblichkeit in den westeuropäischen Provinzen des Römischen Imperiums', *AArchHung* 13, 125–55

(1962) 'Beiträge zur Statistik der Sterblichkeit in der illyrischen Provinzgruppen und in Nord Italien', *AArchHung* 14, 297–396

(1963) 'Die Sterblichkeit in den Städten Mittel- und Sud-Italiens sowie in Hispanien', *AArchHung* 15, 129–224

(1965) 'Die Sterblichkeit in den nordafrikanischen Provinzen I', *AArchHung* 17, 309–34

(1966) 'Die Sterblichkeit in den nordafrikanischen Provinzen II', *AArchHung* 18, 235–77

(1967) 'Die Sterblichkeit in den nordafrikanischen Provinzen III', *AArchHung* 19, 25–59

Taylor, J. du P., H. Cleere (1978) (edd.) *Roman shipping and trade: Britain and the Rhine provinces* (London)

Taylor, L.R. (1961) 'Freedmen and freeborn in the epitaphs of Imperial Rome', *AJPh* 82, 113–32

Tchernia, A. (1986) *Le vin dans l'Italie romaine* (Paris)

Temporini, H. (1978) *Die Frauern am Hofe Trajans* (Berlin)

Thomas, H.S. (1974) *Horses: their breeding, care and training* (South Brunswick)

Thomas, J.D., Davies, R.W. (1977) 'A new military strength-report on papyrus', *JRS* 67, 50–61

Thulin, C. (1913) (ed.) *Corpus agrimensorum Romanorum* 1 (Leipzig)

Udovitch, A.L. (1978) 'Time, the sea and society: duration of commercial voyages on the southern shores of the Mediterranean during the High Middle Ages', *Settimane di studi del Centro italiano di Studi sull' Alto Medioevo* 25, 503–46

Unger, J.J. (1887) 'De censibus provinciarum Romanarum', *Leipz. Stud.* 10, 1–75

Unger, R.W. (1980) *The ship in the medieval economy* (London)

Van't Dack, E. (1974) 'Le papyrologie et l'histoire du Haut-Empire: les formulae des empereurs', *ANRW* 2.1, 857–88

Várady, L. (1962) 'Contributions to the late Roman military economy and agrarian taxation', *AArchHung* 14, 403–38

Vedel, J. (1975) 'La consommation alimentaire dans le Haut Languedoc au xviie et xviiie siècles', *Annales ESC* 30, 478–90

Viedebantt, O. (1911) *Quaestiones Epiphanianae* (Leipzig)

Vittinghoff, F. (1971) 'Die rechtliche Stellung der canabae legionis und die Herkunftsangabe castris', *Chiron* 1, 299–318

Wallace, P.W. (1979) *Strabo's description of Boiotia: a commentary* (Heidelberg)

Wallace, S.L. (1938) *Taxation in Roman Egypt* (Princeton)

Ward-Perkins, J.B. (1980) 'The marble trade and its organisation: evidence from Nicomedia', in D'Arms–Kopff (1980) 325–38

Watson, G.R. (1969) *The Roman soldier* (London)

Weaver, P.R.C. (1972) *Familia Caesaris* (Cambridge)

Weber, E. (1968) 'Zur Centonarieninschrift von Solva', *Historia* 17, 106–14

Weber, M. (1891) 'Agrarverhältnisse im Altertum', in *Ges. Aufsatze zur Sozial- und Wirtschaftsgeschichte* (Tübingen 1924) 1–288

Westermann, W.L. (1920) 'The "uninundated lands" in Ptolemaic and Roman Egypt', *CPh* 15, 120–37

(1922) 'The "dry" land in Ptolemaic and Roman Egypt', *CPh* 17, 21–36

Whittaker, C.R. (1964) 'The revolt of Papyrius Dionysius, AD 190', *Historia* 13, 348–69

(1985) 'Trade and the aristocracy in the Roman Empire', *Opus* 4, 49–75

Wielowiejski, J. (1980) 'Der Einfluss der Devaluation des Denars auf die Annahme römischer Münzen durch die hinter der Donau ansässigen Völker', *Les Dévaluations à Rome 2* (Rome) 155–67

Willems, P. (1887) *Les élections municipales à Pompei* (Paris)

Wright, R.P. (1942) 'New readings of a Severan inscription from Nicopolis near Alexandria', *JRS* 32, 33–8

Youtie, H.C. (1971A) '*Agrammatos*: an aspect of Greek society in Egypt', *HSPh* 75, 161–76

(1971B) '*Bradeōs graphōn*: between literacy and illiteracy', *GRBS* 12, 239–61

INDEX